DATE DUE

NEW PERSPECTIVES ON THE EDUCATION OF ADULTS
IN THE UNITED STATES

NEW PERSPECTIVES ON THE EDUCATION OF ADULTS IN THE UNITED STATES

HUEY LONG

CROOM HELM
London & Sydney

NICHOLS PUBLISHING COMPANY
New York

© 1987 Huey Long
Croom Helm Ltd, Provident_____
Beckenham, Kent, BR3 1AT

Croom Helm Australia, 44-50 Waterloo Road,
North Ryde, 2113, New South Wales

British Library Cataloguing in Publication Data

The education of adults in the United States.
— (Croom Helm series in international adult
education)
1. Adult education — United States
I. Title
374'.973 LC5251

ISBN 0-7099-1693-0

First published in the United States of America in 1987
by Nichols Publishing Company, Post Office Box 96,
New York, NY 10024

Library of Congress Cataloging-in-Publication Data

Long, Huey B.
New perspectives on the education of adults in the
United States.

Bibliography: p.
Includes index.
1. Adult education — United States. 2. Aged —
Education — United States. I. Title.
LC5251.L67 1987   374'.973   86-21738
ISBN 0-89397-263-0

Printed and bound in Great Britain by Mackays of Chatham Ltd, Kent

EDITOR'S NOTE

The Croom Helm Series in International Adult Education brings to an English-speaking readership a wide overview of developments in the education of adults throughout the world. Books in this series are of four different types:

(a) about adult and continuing education in a single country
(b) having a comparative perspective of two or more countries
(c) studies having an international perspective
(d) symposia from different countries having a single theme

This book is of the first type, a perspective upon adult and continuing education in the United States of America, written by Huey B. Long who is himself well qualified to produce such an overview. However, as he himself has written, this is a personal perspective, since there is such a wide variety of adult and continuing education in the United States. It is hoped that this study will provide the reader with some insight into this vast field of study.

Huey Long is a former President of the Adult Education Association of the United States of America. Currently, he is Professor of Adult Education at the University of Georgia and he is the author of numerous books and articles about adult education.

Peter Jarvis.
Series Editor.

CONTENTS

List of Tables and Figures
Preface
Acknowledgements

Part One - INTRODUCTION 1

1 - PARTICIPATION AND ADULT EDUCATION AGENCIES   3

               Participation.   4
               Variables. 11
               Providers. 13
               Summary. 14

2 - PHILOSOPHIES, PURPOSES & CONCEPTUALIZATIONS
    OF EDUCATION OF ADULTS. 17

               Philosophies 19
               Purposes 30
               Conceptualizations 37
               Summary. 47

Part Two - CLIENTELE OF EDUCATION OF ADULTS   51

3 - EDUCATION OF ADULTS IN THE CORPORATE IMAGE 53

               Corporate Trends 59
               Justification. 61
               Cooperation and Competition. . . . 64
               Corporate Approach 69
               Corporate Cooptation 75
               General Discussion 77
               Summary. 80

4 - NEW PERSPECTIVES ON THE EDUCATION OF THE
    ELDERLY IN THE UNITED STATES   83

        Importance of the Elderly as
            Clientele   85

        Participation Characteristics. .   87
        Scope of Programs for Older
            Adults.   94
        Responding to Heterogeneity . .   99
        Perspectives on the Future . . .   103
        Summary.   105

5 - NEW PERSPECTIVES ON LITERACY EDUCATION
    IN THE UNITED STATES   107

        Overview   108
        Definitions.   110
        Scope of Adult Illiteracy in the
            United States   113
        Critiques of the Educational
            Establishment   118
        Speculations on a New Approach .   121
        Summary.   125

Part Three - RESEARCH AND THEORY   127

6 - NEW PERSPECTIVES ON THE STUDY OF ADULTS   129

        Some New Perspectives.   130
        Status of Adult Education Re-
            search.   140
        Research Approaches.   143
        Needed Research.   149
        Research Needs   151
        Observations and Speculations. .   158
        Summary.   161

7 - THEORETICAL PERSPECTIVES   163

        Selected Developments.   165
        Participation Theory   169
        Andragogy.   174
        Learning vs. Education   177
        Perspective Transformation . . .   182
        Program Planning and Development   185
        General Models   186
        Evaluation   188
        Continuing Professional Educa-
            tion.   191

                Other Theoretical Ideas. 194
                Observations 196
                Summary. 199

Part Four - THE FUTURE 201

8 - PERSPECTIVES ON THE FUTURE 203

                Governmental Roles 204
                A New Initiative 206
                Selected Major Changes 208
                Certification. 214
                Technology 218
                Some Issues. 219
                Some Predictions 221
                Summary. 222

BIBLIOGRAPHY. 225

INDEX. 255

LIST OF TABLES & FIGURES

Figure 3:1 - Four Inter-related Systems in
             the Education of Adults in the
             United States 55
Figure 6:1 - Individual Differences. 138
Figure 7:1 - Framework Linking CPE and
             Behavioral Change 190

Table 4:1 - Categories of Institutions
             Providing Educational Experiences
             for Older Adults. 93

PREFACE

The education of adults is the most rapidly growing
sector of American education, increasing by 17
percent between 1978 and 1981 (Cross, 1984). The
rate of growth in education for and of adults
provides a foundation for much of this book.
Expansion of educational opportunities and
participation by adults parallels other significant
social, demographic and economic developments.
Furthermore, the expansion of education
opportunities and involvement are believed to be
structurally related with many if not most of the
changes occuring in modern American society. As a
consequence, a variety of issues are generated by
these developments (Cross, 1984). Issues such as
who are to be the providers? under what
circumstances or conditions will education services
be provided? who will, can or should participate?
what kind of quality assurance can or should be
provided? by whom? and how? and what kind of
relationship does and should exist between
education of adults and economic revitalization?,
are just a few of the issues that are of interest
to practitioners, researchers, policy makers and
others.
     Given the rapid and significant growth of
education of and for adults it is not surprising to
observe that the education of adults in the United
States is changing. Some of these changes are
subtle and cumulative, as a result, they may not be
readily apparent without some benchmark
observations. Changes in the education of adults
encourage us to look once again at adult education
as an area of graduate studies and field of
practice in order to revise our perspectives and
expectations. Without continuing re-examination and

criticism we are apt to become trapped by old definitions, program concepts and ideas of earlier generations outmoded by contemporary developments. Analysis and reflection should enable us to discover the strengths of older ideas while discovering new applications and extensions. As a consequence, new perspectives emerge. Therefore, one of the purposes of New Perspectives on the Education of Adults is to provide an opportunity where both the author and reader may engage in some occasional perspective transformations, to experience some differences of opinion and to consider some different conceptualizations. Of course, new perspectives must be constrained by reality in reporting and interpreting current events and programs in education of adults to be useful.

More is said later about the content, but one or two observations are appropriate here. Given the scope and scale of education of and for adults in the United States some parameters concerning the thrust and content of a book on new perspectives are required. Therefore, it was necessary to select what appears to be among the most significant issues and subject matter. The topics discussed meet this basic criterion. For example, participation questions are among the more important questions addressed in adult education literature. It is desirable to know who participates, why, where, when and how. Understanding of these questions contribute to program development and the provision of education services consistent with a variety of need schemes. These schemes may range from those that focus on the individual to those that emphasize the larger society. Thus, three program areas that demonstrate this in some way are addressed. Finally, there is a need for knowledge and comprehension of the research and theory bases of education of and for adults. These topics, plus some final observations and speculations provide the framework for the discussion of new perspectives.

New Perspectives on the Education of Adults in the United States is designed to navigate the middle way between reporting "old perspectives" and creating a fantasy perspective. This Preface contains important information on how this was done. Definitions, a brief description of the structure of the book and chapter summaries are provided. Definitions are reluctantly included because so often the process of defining concepts appear to become ends within themselves. The

definitions provided in the following pages are
given only because they seem to be necessary to
understanding the objectives and content of the
book. Descriptive information concerning the
content is also kept to the barest essential
minimum as brief introductions are provided at the
beginning of each of the four major divisions of
the book..

DEFINITIONS

New
Prior to any meaningful dialogue on new
perspectives on the education of adults in the
United States, agreement on the use of terms is
desirable, if not necessary. The topic contains
several terms that may be used with different
meanings. The word new, for example, has a variety
of connotations. To observe that a neighbor has a
"new" automobile may communicate different images;
one person may assume that the automobile has not
been owned previously by anyone other than the
dealer and manufacturer; another person may accept
the statement to mean the neighbor has an
automobile of the latest model (the question of
prior ownership is not important); yet another
person may understand that the neighbor has simply
purchased a different automobile, it may be one or
twenty years of age, but it is new to the neighbor.
   The American Heritage Dictionary (Morris,
1969) contains a rather lengthy list of definitions
for new. Eight different uses of the term are
given:

1. Of recent origin, having existed only a
   short time . . .
2. (a) Not yet old; fresh; recent; (b) used
   for the first time...
3. Recognized or experienced lately for the
   first time, although existing before;
   recently become known;...
4. Freshly introduced;unfamiliar; unaccus-
   tomed...
5. Begun afresh; . . .
6. (a) Newly entered into a state, position
   or experience. (b) changed for the better;
   refreshed; rejuvenated; ...
7. Different and distinct from what was
   before; . . .

8. (a) Modern; current; fashionable ... (b)
In the most recent form, period, or
development of something...
(Morris, 1969, pp. 883-84)

New as used in this work emphasizes current
perspectives in the education of adults. It is a
desire that the work is, in some respects,
different and will provide a new experience for the
reader, but it is not necessarily designed to be
novel. Nevertheless, some obervations are provided
that are believed to be fresh in the sense that
they have not been frequently published or given
attention as provided here. The distinctiveness of
the work will be found in interpretation, synthesis
and criticism of what has existed before, plus some
speculation about future directions. Hence, the
first, third, fourth and eighth uses of the term
new, as noted above, have served as a guide in this
book.

Perspective

Perspective is not as difficult to define as the
word new. The story of the blind men who described
an elephant as a tree, as a snake and as a wall
according to the different parts of the animal's
body they touched, communicates the nature of
perspective. A perspective is generally derived
from one's relative position, physical, cognitive
or emotional. Perspective, thus, connotes a point
of view.

Taken together, the words new and perspective,
suggest that the individual who has a new
perspective has a point of view that differs in
some way from other points of view. This need not
be original, it may not be completely different
from a perspective of another person, i.e., it need
not be unique, but it must differ in some manner.
One individual may have a new perspective that is
similar to that of a majority of his or her peers,
but it is new to the individual. Therefore, the
use of the term new perspective in this book does
not necessarily connote originality, novelty, or
uniqueness. The emphasis is upon a degree of
distinctivenes as suggested by the selected
connotations of new as discussed in the previous
paragraph.

Education

Education, as the two previously discussed terms, has a variety of meanings. The American Heritage Dictionary (Morris,1969) defines education in terms of a systematic process of imparting or obtaining knowledge or skill and as a field of study. Scholars and philosophers frequently place additional limits to the definition. Paterson (1979) for example observes that education is clearly the concept of some kind of purposive activity. It is an activity because it is perceived to be the kind of things that does not just happen to a person. It represents some degree of deliberate contrivance by the educator and the individual who is the object of the activity. It is purposive in the sense that it sets out to attain specific or general essential objectives. Furthermore, according to Paterson it is these objectives that provide the main grounds by which we pick out the "educational" activities from the many other activities that may be similar to them. There is no single empirical activity or group of activities that are in themselves educational. Citing R. S. Peters (1967), Paterson (1979, pp. 14-15) says education "refers to no particular process; rather it encapsulates criteria to which any one of a family of processes must conform."

Essential objectives that contribute to an activity's designation as education are best stated according to Paterson (1979, p. 15) "in relation to our nature as persons, as conscious selves, moving centres of action and awareness whose being is the radically finite being of individuals conscious of the shifting but ever-present limits placed upon their being by time, space, and matter, but conscious also that these limits exists to be surpassed." Hence, an educational activity is one that is intended to foster, and in fact does foster, the highest development of individuals as persons. Later he adds "a recipient of education, then, is someone whose potentialities of becoming a full person are being developed and who is therefore being treated, by those responsible for his education, as immanently a being whose existence is worthwhile in his own right" (p. 17).

The communication of knowledge is at the center of Paterson's concept of education. It is through the communication of knowledge and the initiation of the individual into rationally organized and objectively validated systems of publicly shared belief that an individual engages in any truly educational undertaking. Such a thought is critical to Paterson's idea of education as a body of knowledge, as he believes that body of knowledge enshrines our most sustained and thorough attempts to grasp and penetrate some meaningful reality and of which we seek enlarged awareness (p. 21). Furthermore, to be truly educated, a man must care profoundly about the bodies of knowledge in which he has been initiated - about the manner in which they have been arrived at and the manner in which they will be preserved and transmitted. Education in enlarging man's awareness, should enlarge his awareness of the value of his awareness, according to Paterson.

Eventually Paterson equates educational activity with liberal education and the goal of developing those desirable intrinsic qualities and capacities that constitute personhood. From this position it is only a short step to critical comment on the appropriateness of labelling vocational courses as "educational" on the grounds that they do not address those central processes of being that are critical to the definition of education.

Paterson's position is logical and attractive. It fails, however, to reflect the reality of the definition of education as used in the United States. Increasingly the boundaries between education and training in the United States are becoming blurred and indistinct. The terms are often used interchangeably without any effort to distinguish between them, more is said on this point in the main body of the book. It is also possible that it will fail to represent the reality of the education of adults in most of the western industrialized nations within a few years.

When the term education is used in this work, the emphasis is upon the cumulative process of obtaining knowledge or skill (including the cognitive affective and psychomotor adjustments that follow) and the social provisions for facilitating the process. No effort is made to discriminate between different kinds of knowledge or skills or institutional providers. Thus, education of adults includes skill development in business and industry as well as more cognitive based learning. It also includes a similar range of aims of higher education.

Adults

As other terms defined in the preceding paragraphs, the word "adult" is used in various senses. Morris

(1969) provides four definitions, two for adult as a noun, and two for adult as an adjective. All four definitions emphasize maturity. When adult is defined as a noun, maturity is linked with age or what is described as a fully grown, mature organism. Criteria to determine adult status have changed over the centuries. Anania (1969) provides a useful discussion of the social, legal and economic characteristics associated with the meaning of the word. His explication of adult as a concept reveals that adulthood was once believed to contain a number of preliminary stages that eventually led to full adulthood. Certain rights and privileges were associated with each of the preliminary stages. For example, the right of marriage was associated with a younger age than the right of inheritance. Full adulthood was marked by the age at which a male qualified for ordination as a Priest.

Educators of adults in the United States have not developed such an hierarchy of biological, economic and legal stages and associated social scales and privileges to distinguish among adults. Neither have they always agreed on the criteria to be used in defining an adult for data collection and theory building purposes. These definitions have included several legal age definitions from the normal compulsory school age of 16 to legal voting age 18-21 to the so-called traditional college student age of 22. A review of the various individual books that constitute the 1980 Handbook Series in Adult Education suggests the contributors preferred to not become involved in the struggle to define either adults or adult education. Long (1980) discusses definitions along lines similar to the following observations.

Since Bryson (1936) defined an adult for adult education purposes as one "...engaged in the ordinary business of life" (p.3) some others such as Jensen (1964) and Houle (cited by Schroeder, 1970) have also favored that limitation. Other characteristics, such as being responsible for self or others, have sometimes been added (Verner,1964). These characteristics were added to get away from legal age restrictions while providing for maturity and independence from parents. Despite all the mental gymnastics that have been used to arrive at a definition of an adult, the most workable one seems to be aged based. Therefore, for the purpose of this book, an adult is defined as any person beyond compulsory school age (16) who is not regularly enrolled in a secondary school (grades 9-12) and or who meets one or more social, civic and legal definitions of adulthood. No effort will be made to distinguish between the 17 year old who has dropped out of school and the one who has graduated or the 24 year old who is living independently and the 26 year old graduate student who receives regular maintenance support from parents or others.

Education of Adults

Two different phrases are often used interchangeably, "Education of adults" and "adult education." In its broadest sense, education of adults can be used to include all systematic efforts of adults to obtain knowledge or skill. Adult education is frequently a much more narrow term. It is usually used to refer to people (adults) who meet specific age, legal or social characteristics who are involved in a specific educational activity such as adult basic education, hobby and craft activities, religious education and so forth. As a result, the term adult education often connotes a program of instruction for a target group and is a noun, in contrast education of adults connotes action and may be thought of as a verb phrase. Adult education by definition frequently excludes college and university students despite an increasing trend toward a combination of work and educational careers. For the objectives of this book, adult education is broadly defined, and includes all systematic and purposive efforts by the adult to become an educated person (obtain knowledge and skill).

Grattan (1955, p. 3) defines adult education as education that occurs after formal education, or what is called "schooling." Nevertheless, he notes that the two are related in many ways. For example, opportunities for adults to continue their education are often offered by schools, from the public school through higher education. But, it would be incorrect to assume that adult education is inextricably connected with the schooling system at any level. Grattan correctly observes adult education is free to address adults as adults and that this uniqueness is the real field of adult education (p. 4).

Consequently, in keeping with the title of this book, a new perspective that encompasses a broader view of adult education and which more closely equates with the education of adults influences the observations and conclusions shared in the following pages. Education of adults and

adult education both include a variety of
postcompulsory educational opportunities and
independently conceived, designed and pursued
learning activities. Graduate education,
baccalaureate degree work, non-credit activity,
staff development programs in business and
industry, and self-directed (autonomous) learning
activities qualify for inclusion in the discussion.
        The terms adults, adult education and
education of adults as used in this book are
inclusive rather than exclusive in nature. Hence,
adults are defined to include those individuals who
by virtue of one or more of social, civic and legal
definitions have assumed the status of adults in
American society. Included is the 16 year old
mother, the 17 year old secondary school dropout
and the 22 year old college student.
Institutionally, education of adults begins upon
completion or termination of secondary school. The
18 or even 19 year old who is a regular high school
student is not included in the definition of adult,
but the 16 year old college freshman is. As most
definitions of adult status, the one used here is
controversial, and is not generally used in adult
education literature in the United States.
        Equally controversial is the interchangeable
use of the term adult education and education of
adults. However, once one accepts the idea that
adult education is broader than schooling, it is
much easier to move to the position of
interchanging the terms. Using the term
interchangeably has a practical benefit; the author
is not limited to the continuous use of the rather
awkward term, education of adults. Adult education
is easier to write and to read.

New, Perspectives, Education of Adults
Collectively, the selected definitions of the
above terms imply that New Perspectives on the
Education of Adults in the United States is
designed to achieve the following objectives:
(a) to provide descriptive, interpretative and
critical comment on selected important aspects of
education of adults in the United States of
America; (b) to challenge some of the older
positions that either may no longer be appropriate
or which may have never been valid; and (c) to
provide some speculations concerning future
directions in the education of adults in the United
States. Three general criteria were used in the
selection of content and trends: (a) the topics

selected and discussed are sufficiently related to lend coherence to the commentary; (b) discussion of the selected topics provides a new point of view (as established in the section on definitions) of education of adults in the U.S.; and (c) the variety of sources selected for inclusion such as popular trends, latent trends (trends that always have not been duly noted, but which are apparent upon examination), recently reported positions and views in the practice and study of adults contribute to a subsequent new point of view on the education of adults in the United States.

Based on the definitions discussed in the preceding pages, the following chapters are designed to provide a personal point of view on the current developments and trends in the ways and means by which adults obtain knowledge and skills in the United States. Novelty is not a goal, neither is originality in its strictest and narrowest sense. Yet, it is hoped that a creative use of what is known, believed and espoused or frequently debated will provide a fresh, accurate and rational view of the education of adults in the United States. To accomplish this objective, New Perspectives...is divided into four sections: (a) introductory concepts; (b) clientele for education; (c) theory and practice; and (d) conclusions.

Part one has two chapters, chapter one and chapter two. The first chapter is designed to present a brief overview of the status of adult participation in education as reported by the National Center for Educational Statistics. Other selected related works on participation are also examined and discussed.

Chapter two, focuses on philosophies, purposes and conceptualizations in the education of adults in the United States. The introduction to Part One provides additional information.

Part two contains three chapters concerning perspectives on the clientele of education for adults. It was difficult to determine which program areas to include in this section. Finally, corporate education, education of the elderly and literacy education were selected. Separately and collectively these three kinds of education services appear to be part and parcel of the post industrial American society. Corporate education is perhaps one of the most significant developments in education of adults in the last quarter of the century. Education of the elderly is a yet relatively uncharted area despite its increasing prominence in educational gerontolgy, but because

of the increasing significance of the elderly in
American society it is one of the program areas of
the future. Literacy education is far from new in
the United States. But, the involvement of the
Federal government in the program is relatively
recent, beginning in 1964. The contradiction
inherent in the existence of millions of illiterate
adults in a high tech society emphasizes the
importance of literacy education.

Two of the three chapters in part two are
co-authored. Bradley Courtenay, a well known
educational gerontologist, is the senior author of
chapter four. Curtis Ulmer, an experienced
specialist in literacy education, is senior author
of chapter five.

Part three, theory and practice is comprised
of two chapters. Chapter six provides new points
of view in the study of adults; chapter seven
discusses theoretical developments. Additional
comment on the content of these two chapters is
found in the introduction to Part three.

Part four contains one chapter which, among a
variety of topics, offers some speculations about
future directions in adult education in the United
States.

Huey B. Long
Athens, Georgia

ACKNOWLEDGEMENTS

Developing and writing a book is seldom a solitary task. Many actors were involved in the process of writing this one. They include the scholars whose work is reviewed, analyzed and criticized. Without their previous scholarship and hard work this book would not have been possible. Also included are the faculty, students and secretaries whose assistance and encouragement was invaluable. Without them the job would have been more difficult. Important intangible support and stimulation was also frequently provided by the author's family and friends. The understanding and gentle yet strong support for this kind of endeavor provided by my wife Marie was critical to completion of the project. Specifically, I wish to express my appreciation and recognize my obligations to Marie, to my friend and colleague Peter Jarvis, and to secretaries Pauline Heuberger and Beverly Massey. The list of other colleagues whose work and support has been a source of stimulation is too long to identify individually here. Their names are to be found in the index and in the body of this work.

PART ONE

INTRODUCTION

Two important topics important in the education of American adults are discussed in this section. Chapter one is primarily a report on the related topics of participation, variables in particiaption and adult education agencies. Chapter two, in contrast, challenges some of the traditional views concerning philosophies, purposes and conceptualizations of education of adults in the United States.

As set forth in chapter one, the education of adults in the United States is far from a simple monolithic phenomenon. Even the number of adults who annually engage in some kind of educational activity is debatable. A range of estimates exists, however, none of the estimates including those provided by the National Center for Educational Statistics are perceived to accurately define adult participation in the nation. Limited discussion of the relationship between participation and diverse variables is provided. It is also suggested that new and different research methodologies, including statistical procedures, are desired.

The picture of adult participation is further obfuscated by the complexity of the provider scene. Efforts to conceptually organize the purveyors of education of adults are noted.

Chapter two follows upon the topical heels of the first chapter. The purpose of this chapter is to provide a range of views concerning the philosophies, purposes and concepts in use today. Some of the more cherished concepts such as the idea of adult education as a social movement and as

1

Introduction

a province of the voluntary learner are challenged. The philosophical positions of educators of adults such as Apps (1973, 1979), Cotton (1968), Elias and Merriam (1980) and Kallen (1962) are reported. In addition, two conceptual schemes of adult education purposes separated by approximately fifty years are noted.

Chapter One

PARTICIPATION AND ADULT EDUCATION AGENCIES

Participation of adults in all kinds of instruction
increased considerably over the past decades and is
expected to continue to increase into the 1990's
(USDE 1983). Educational participation of adults
in the United States is a multi-faceted phenomenon
that defies accurate description. From the 17th
century to the present American adults have
participated in diverse educational activities provided by all kinds of providers (Long, 1976).
Nevertheless, it has never been accorded the same
status as childhood education. As a result the
provisions for education of adults have been
uncoordinated, unregulated and almost invisible in
the history of education.

Changing conditions associated with increasing
technological advances and social complexity over
the past century have contributed to the steady and
continuous emergence of adult education. Numerous
institutions emerged in the 18th, 19th and 20th
centuries to address educational needs and
aspirations of American adults. These institutions
include the Mechanics Institutes, American Lyceum,
Chatauqua, University Extension, Cooperative
Extension Service and a variety of special purpose
programs such as Americanization, agricultural
education and literacy education.

The contemporary scene is even more complex.
Education of adults is provided by all kinds of
community, volunteer, professional organizations as
well as educational institutions, business and
industry and governmental agencies. Education of
adults includes those services provided by the
department of defense, (civilian and military),

3

educational institutions such as the public schools and postsecondary education institutions, professional associations, and corporations. They include special purpose education activities such as religious education, corrections education and personal development activities from transcendental meditation to positive thinking and assertiveness training.

The number of adults annually engaged in education in the United States is unknown. Various estimates are available in the literature (Long, 1983b). Some estimates are as low as about 13% while others range up to 90%. Numbers vary from about 21 million to 60 million. Scholars who have carefully considered the various estimates of adult participation generally agree that despite the questionable validity of most estimates, education of adults is an important educational activity in the United States. The range of providers and purposes of programs preclude the possibility of providing any kind of comprehensive description of education of adults in the United States in one brief book. The only way to accomplish such an undertaking would be to limit the book to a gazetteer.

Therefore, instead of attempting to be overly comprehensive this chapter, like the book, tends to be concerned with specific and selective topics while addressing particular current themes and developments. It is not offered as a balanced representation of the entire range of education services and activities for adults in the United States in the 1980's. Particular concerns that are discussed include (a) trends in educational participation as reflected by one authoritative source, (b) variables often identified in studies of participation and some contempory trends in participation, (c) the provider scene, which some believe is becoming increasingly complex (Cross, 1984), and (d) a summary.

PARTICIPATION

Participation of adults in education is one of the most popular topics in the literature of the field. Educators of American adults have been interested in ascertaining motives and justifications for participation in education for more than half a century. Love's (1953) work may be one of the better known early example of modern inquiry into the topic. Certainly Houle's (1961) work is

4

perceived as an important contribution that stimulated research and conceptualization concerning participation.

Estimates of participation have been reported by Aslanian and Brickell (1980), Carp, Peterson and Roelfs (1974), Cartright (1935), Cross, (1981), Holden (1958), Johnstone and Rivera (1965), Knowles (1955, 1977), Long (1983b) and Tough (1978) to cite a few. Studies of local and state participation rates have also been reported (Long, 1983b). One thing the various studies of participation have in common is their uniqueness. Most of the investigations of participation have used their own definitions of adult education and of adults. For example, the age criterion ranges from age 14 (Holden, 1958; Knowles, 1955) to 25 years of age (Aslanian and Brickell, 1980). Similar variations are discovered in definitions of participation. Therefore, the range of estimates from approximately 21 million by the NCES to about 50 million by Peterson (1979) is understandable. But, while it is easy to understand the discrepancies among estimates, the problem of determining a reasonably accurate appraisal of total participation or the percentage of participation is not resolved. For example, recent estimates of participants in employer sponsored education, as cited in chapter three, is over 12 million or approximately 57 percent of the total estimate for 1981.

The available information contributes to some paradoxical conditions. For example, possibly most students of the topic would agree that between one of three and one of five adults annually engage in some educational activity (variously defined). Yet, standard national statistics published by the National Center for Educational Statistics (U.S. Department of Education, 1983 p. 158) reports a participation rate of approximately 13 percent. This more conservative estimate seriously fails to portray what is believed to be an accurate and realistic picture of the scope and size of adult education. One of the more serious problems with the 13 percent figure is associated with the definition used by the Census Bureau.

Adult education as defined by NCES is as follows: The term adult education is used to describe all part-time instruction, including nonacademic as well as degree-credit activities engaged in by adults. Specifically as defined in the 1981 Adult Education Participation Survey it refers to all courses and organized educational activities, excluding those taken by full-time students in programs leading to a high school diploma or an academic degree. It also excludes courses taken as part of occupational training programs of 6 months or more duration. For the purposes of the most recent NCES survey, adults were defined as persons 17 years of age and older. Full-time students also engaged in part-time adult education activities were included as participants (U.S. Department of Education, 1983, p. 158).

Note the NCES excludes (a) educational courses and activities taken by full-time students in programs leading to a high school diploma or academic degree, (b) courses taken as part of occupational training programs of 6 months or more duration. It is difficult to accurately determine the effects of the above exclusions. For the purposes of this book it is noted that the 13 percent rate of participation fails to represent the true rate of participation of adults in education as discussed in the Preface. Despite the obvious limitations of the NCES data they are preferred for some purposes for several reasons. First, they provide a national data base. Second, the data are perceived to be more reliable than other estimates (based on the definition employed). Third, they are widely available for use. Fourth, within reason, they can be used for noting trends and possible changes in participation over a number of years. Fifth, they have been obtained regularly and reported every three years since 1969. Therefore, comments made in this chapter, unless noted otherwise, are based on NCES data.

For the year ending in May 1981, more than 21 million people participated in adult education programs in the United States. This is an increase of over 3 million since 1978, or almost 17 percent. Part of this increase can be explained simply by increases in the adult population; in 1978, 72 percent of the population was 17 years old and over, compared to 74 percent in 1981. However, even accounting for the effects of population growth, the rate of participation in adult education also increased, by over 8 percent (U.S. Department of Education, 1983). In 1981, almost 13 percent of all adults chose to further their education through participation in part-time instruction (U.S. Department of Education, 1983).

Participation rates varied substantially by age; the most active participants in adult education were 25 to 34-year-olds. For example, almost one of every five adults between the ages of

6

25 and 34 participated in some form of adult education program, and over 15 percent of persons aged 35 to 54 were participants. The lowest participation rates were registered by older persons; less than 8 percent of those between the ages of 55 and 64, and only 3 percent of persons 65 and over participated in education. While the 55 and over age group comprised 28 percent of the total adult population, this group represented only slightly more than 11 percent of all adult education participants.

Even though the older age groups reported lower rates than 25- to 34-year-olds in 1981, it was the older groups that showed real growth in the rate of participation over the 1978 figures. Any growth in the number of 25- to 34-year-old participants was attributable solely to the increasing pool of persons in this age group (U.S. Department of Education, 1983). Among the population 35 years old and over, however, increases were due to both growing size and higher rates of participation. For example, the participation rate rose by 15 percent among the 35- to 64-year-old group between 1978 and 1981 and by about 29 percent among the 65-year-old-and-over group. Given that the total adult population is projected to increase during the 1980's, and that rates remain at the same high level among younger adults and increase among older adults, participation in adult education should continue to grow.

Higher participation rates among 25- to 34-year-olds held across racial/ethnic groups and the sexes. Whites in this age group participated at a rate of almost 22 percent. The highest participation for any subgroup was among white females (24 percent). The second highest participation was by white males with 20 percent participating (U.S. Department of Education, 1983). It was only among the 25- to 34-year-old group that blacks and Hispanics approached the average participation rate for all age groups. Over 12 percent of blacks in this age group participated, slightly under the participation rate for the entire population. Hispanics in this age range also participated at a relatively high rate among their racial/ethnic group, almost 12 percent (U.S. Department of Education, 1983).

These figures, however, reveal a marked disparity in participation by various racial/ethnic groups. As documented in past surveys, whites continued in 1981 to participate in adult education

7

programs at a much higher rate than blacks and
Hispanics. However, the participation rate of
blacks increased in 1981, rising from under 6
percent in 1978 to almost 8 percent in 1981, an
increase of almost 400,000 black participants in
adult education. Despite the increase, blacks
still represented only 6 percent of all adult
education participants, compared to 10 percent of
the total adult population. The participation rate
of Hispanics remained virtually constant at
slightly over 8 percent. And, even though the
proportion of white adult education participants
decreased somewhat from 1978, they made up almost
88 percent of all participants in adult education.

Females accounted for 56 percent of
participants in adult education in 1981, about the
same proportion as in 1978. Their participation
rates were about 2 percentage points higher than
male rates overall and in each of the younger age
groups. Among the older adults, participation
rates for females were only slightly higher than
those for males, but because there were more women
in the older population, they represented a
disproportionate share of participants.

One of the most stable and most significant
factors influencing participation in adult
education activities is a person's level of
education attainment. For both 1978 and 1981,
there was a direct positive relationship between
the number of years of schooling and the rate of
participation in adult education. Persons with an
eighth grade education or less participated in
adult education at a rate of only 2 percent in
1981. On the other hand, 31 percent of persons
with more than 4 years of college had taken part in
an adult education activity during the year. A
little over 11 percent of high school graduates
with no college experience participated in adult
education, while over 26 percent of those with 4
years of college participated (U.S. Department of
Education, 1983).

The correspondence between higher educational
attainment and greater participation in adult
education was evident across all racial/ethnic
groups and was most notable among females. Within
each racial/ethnic group, the more well-educated an
individual was, the more likely he or she would
participate in adult education activities. The
relationship between greater attainment and
participation was even more pronounced among
females than among males. Male participation rates
ranged from 2 percent for those with less than 9

8

years of formal schooling to over 28 percent for those with 5 or more years of college. While women with an eighth grade education or less also participated at a rate of only 2 percent, those with 5 or more years of college participated at a rate of almost 36 percent, 8 percentage points higher than men with the same level of schooling.

Another factor associated with participation in adult education is the level of family income. As with educational levels, the higher the level of family income, the greater the rate of participation in education programs. In 1981, only 6 percent of the total population with family incomes less than $7,500 participated in adult education. At the same time, persons with family incomes of at least $50,000 participated in adult education programs at a rate of nearly 19 percent. While it is generally true that persons from lower economic levels participated less frequently in adult education programs, women in the lower income groups participated at a higher rate than men in the same income groups. For example, of the 1.7 million adult education participants in the income category under $7,500, 69 percent were women. This relationship also held true for women in the other lower income categories, below $15,000, where the proportion of female participants was 64 percent. In income categories at or above $25,000, the proportions of male and female participants in adult education were nearly the same.

As is true for the general population, the majority of participants in adult education resided in metropolitan areas -- over 72 percent, compared with 68 percent of the total population, for a participation rate of almost 14 percent. However, some conspicuous differences are apparent among regions. For example, the Western States, representing 19 percent of the population, had 27 percent of the adult education participants, or a participation rate of nearly 18 percent. The North Central States had a participation rate of almost 14 percent; in contrast, the Northeast and the South had less-than-average rates of 10 and 11 percent, respectively.

Participants in adult education were more likely than the general population to be in the labor force. Workers accounted for 83 percent of participants compared with 65 percent of the overall population. Of those in the labor force, employed persons were much more likely to participate than the unemployed: almost 17 percent of the former participated compared to 11 percent

9

of the latter. By comparison, only 8 percent of persons keeping house were adult education participants (U.S. Department of Education, 1983).

Of the 17 million employed persons who took adult education courses, 70 percent were in white-collar jobs compared with 53 percent of the general population in these jobs. Professional, technical, and kindred workers accounted for the large percent difference between the participants and the total population. As discussed later in this book, professional and technical workers, such as teachers, physicians, and other health workers, are in occupations that require frequent refresher or upgrading courses, and about a third of all workers in these fields took an adult education course in 1981. Among individual occupations, 43 percent of health workers, 39 percent of physicians and dentists, and 37 percent of teachers (except college teachers) took at least one course (U.S. Department of Education, 1983).

Participants in adult education took over 37 million courses during the year ending May 1981 -- an average of almost 2 courses per participant. The types of courses taken by adults ranged from hobby and recreational activities to highly technical training. Nearly half of the courses taken by adults were in three fields; business (23 percent), health (14 percent, including health care and health education), and engineering (10 percent). Over 54 percent of the courses taken by males and 41 percent of those taken by females were in these fields. Courses in business were the most popular for both men and women. By contrast, 81 percent of the engineering courses were taken by men and the majority of the health courses were taken by women. Among the rest of the courses, the number taken by women exceeded those taken by men in almost every field except agriculture, social sciences, and "other" courses. Very few courses in home economics were taken by men, and three times as many courses in physical education were taken by women than by men (U.S. Department of Education, 1983).

Differences among the educational interests of men and women were also noted in Botsman's (1975) study of blue color workers in New York. According to Botsman male workers reported two reasons for participating more frequently than female workers. They were to work toward certification or licensing and to take courses to help advance in their present job. In comparison, female workers cited three different reasons more often than did the

male workers. The preferences of women workers
were as follows: to meet new people, to learn more
about their background and culture and to improve
their spiritual well-being.

The relationship between work and adult
education is demonstrated by the 1981 data. For
example, job-related reasons were most often cited
as the purpose for taking an adult education
course. Sixty percent of the courses were taken to
advance in a job, to get a new job, or for some
other job-related reason. Both males and females
each took about 11 million job-related courses, but
this figure represents a higher proportion for men
than for women, 69 percent compared with 54
percent. Most non-job-related courses were taken
for personal or social reasons rather than for
school credit or other scholastic recognition.
Only about 6 percent of the courses were taken for
credit leading to an elementary or secondary school
diploma or vocational certificate, while 18 percent
were applied to a college degree at any level.

It is interesting, but not surprising, that
while only 24 percent of the courses applied to
school credit, nearly 54 percent of the courses
were provided by schools. The rest was given by
business or industry, community organizations,
government agencies, and other non-schools. Over
58 percent of the courses provided by schools and
62 percent of those given by other providers were
for job-related reasons. Nearly a fourth of all
courses were provided by the employer of the
respondent (U.S. Department of Education, 1983).

VARIABLES

Ten variables are often investigated in studies of
participation in adult education (Long, 1983b).
They are age, education, ethnic and racial factors,
family and youthful characteristics, income,
learning locations, marital status, place of
residence, sex and other socioeconomic variables.
Of these, age and educational achievement level are
presented as being the most highly correlated with
educational participation. Yet, even age and
educational level have very low correlations with
participation. The correlation between age and
participation according to the 1975 NCES data was
.18 (Darkenwald, 1979). Hence only .03 of the
variance was explained by age.

Education, as noted previously, has the
highest correlation with participation. Anderson

and Darkenwald (1979) report a correlation coefficient of .25 between education and participation compared with .12 for income, .04 for race, and .01 for sex. Collectively, all of the variables studied by Anderson and Darkenwald account for only 10 percent of the variance in participation. Thus, 90 percent remains to be explained.

Anderson and Darkenwald's (1979) analysis of the 1975 NCES data appears to be quite discouraging. However, alternate positions may be considered. First, the traditional position, based on the use of multiple and simple Pearsonian correlation statistics implies that the variables are not very important ones, i.e., there are others that are more important that have yet to be identified, or that participation is a highly complex phenomenon that includes an extensive array of dynamic variables. The second, and heretofore unexplored, possibility is that the above variables are important ones that are not sensitive to the Pearsonian statistical procedures, but which might prove to be more sensitive to other statistical analyses.

Trends

While specific figures from surveys before 1978 are not strictly comparable to more recent data, gross measures suggest a steady rate of growth in adult education. In part, the aging of the U.S. population contributes to this growth, directly, by expanding the pool of participants, and indirectly, by encouraging schools and colleges to seek new markets beyond that of traditional college age. Also contributing to its growth are the demands of the workplace to upgrade and update the occupational skills of American workers, as evidenced in the abundance of educational activities offered by employers. In addition, the expansion and heightened importance of leisure time also may have encouraged the growth of educational activities. Since these features are expected to characterize American life into the 1990's, people may continue to seek adult education for learning, training, and enjoyment in the future.

PROVIDERS

As suggested by the discussion of adult participation presented in the previous sections the providers of adult education are numerous. It is almost as difficult to accurately describe them as it is to enumerate the individual adults they serve. Numerous schemes have been devised to provide some kind of classification concept. Some of these are discussed below.

Knowles (1962) provides an abstract classification scheme for organizing the diverse multitude of agencies, institutions and organizations whose business includes education of adults in some way. He suggests that all the entities providing education to adults fall into one of the four categories listed below:

1. Agencies that were initially concerned with education of young people but have assumed the additional task of educating adults.
2. Agencies that were created primarily to serve adults.
3. Agencies that were created to serve the entire community.
4. Agencies that are primarily concerned with other goals but which need adult education in order to achieve them.

Peterson, et al (1979) provide a lengthy table that classifies sources of education and learning in the United States according to two general sets: (a) deliberate education and learning and (b) unintentional learning. Set "a" contains three major divisions, schools, nonschool organizations and individually used sources. These three divisions are further divided into 25 subdivisions. Unintentional learning contains five categories, according to Peterson's scheme. Much of what is most often referred to as adult education is included Peterson's Nonschool Organizations category. He lists 12 kinds of agencies and organizations in that classification. They include private industry, professional associations, trade unions, government service, federal manpower programs, military services, agricultural extension, city recreation departments, community organizations, churches and synagogues, free universities and parks and forests.

Other efforts to identify providers of adult education services include the various handbooks on

13

adult education. Knowles (1960) lists 32 sources
for adult education. Smith, Aker and Kidd's (1970)
work contains chapters on 21 different program
areas and agencies. The variety of programs for
adults did not necessarily decline between 1960 and
1970, however. The decrease in numbers of program
and agency chapters merely reflects other editorial
interests and objectives.

SUMMARY

This chapter presents a general overview of
participants and providers of adult education in
the United States. The scope and range of adult
involvement in education is difficult to accurately
describe because of its very nature. It is a
complex, pluralistic, diverse and dynamic
enterprise (Long, 1980d). As a result description
of adult education is usually general and
approximate rather than specific and accurate.
Emphases such as mandatory continuing education
requirements in professional areas may temporarily
alter the outlines of the subject only to change
themselves within a short time. Social changes
that effect sub-elements of the population may also
change the profile of adult education participation
and nature of educational activities. For example,
some studies of participation (Botsman, 1975)
indicate that the purposes of education for women
may have been (be?) different from the educational
objectives of men at one time. However, as the
percentage of women entering and staying in the
work force continues to increase it is possible
that the work related objectives reflected by men
may also become increasingly popular among women's
motives to engage in educational activities. Thus,
even the best description of 1986 may be only an
approximation by 1990.

The data reviewed for this chapter, however,
suggest some long term trends that are not likely
to change significantly in the short term. They
include (a) rising rates of adult participation,
(b) increasing participation by minorities and (c)
deepening trends toward occupational justifications
for adult education. These three trends are
interrelated and interact with broader social,
technological and economic developments. For
example, increasing dependence upon an educated
workforce in a high tech society has implications
for education in the workplace, education of older
people and literacy education. Additional

implications are also posed for philosophies, purposes and conceptualization of adult education and theory and inquiry in the field. These topics are discussed in the following chapter.

Chapter Two

PHILOSOPHIES, PURPOSES AND CONCEPTUALIZATIONS OF EDUCATION OF ADULTS

Education of adults in the United States is neither structurally nor programmatically monolithic. It is not limited to a single purpose activity such as literacy or national culture, provided by or even coordinated by, one agency. Education of adults in the United States is multi-purpose, provided by numerous agencies, based on several philosophies and is variously conceptualized. Unlike the 1920s when much of the literature on education of adults focused on social change (Kallen, 1962; Lindeman, 1961), the literature of the last past two decades has been characterized by varied justifications and philosophies (Kreitlow and Associates, 1981; Rauch, 1972).

This chapter discusses education of adults in the United States as a multi-dimensional activity that finds support among various individuals and diverse groups of philosophies. Adherents include pragmatic individuals as well as visionary utopians. It is a way to prepare adults to improve their wages as well as a way to foment radical social change; it is a way to improve the minds of men and women as well as a way to improve their personal relations.

Attempts to describe the broad parameters of education of adults in the United States have been made before. Many of these attempts, such as the various handbooks of adult education (Smith, Aker and Kidd, 1970; Knowles, 1960) have been partially successful. One explanation for their limited success has been in the neglect of abstract foundations such as philosophy and

17

conceptualizations of purpose and structure. In the final analysis, this current work may also fall short of its goal, but it will not do so for the reasons noted above. In keeping with the overall objectives of the book a new direction is taken within these pages to explain some aspects of education of adults in the United States. The emphasis is occasionally upon the abstract rather than upon the concrete. At the barest minimum such a different treatment of the topic should complement the existing works in the field; it is unlikely that it can completely replace them.

This chapter contributes to a new perspective on the education of adults in the United States in several ways. First, it provides a systematic discussion of three related significant critical abstractions in education of adults: philosophy, purpose and conceptualization. Second, some favored themes in the field of adult education are subjected to critical analyses. Third, an important newly vitalized trend that may ultimately alter the structure and appearance of education in America is identified.

The structure of the chapter itself is quite simple. It contains three major topical divisions, plus a summary. The topical divisions contain varying numbers of subdivisions; for example, the philosophical section is based on a review and analysis of the contribution of selected authors whose works were published between 1962 and 1980. The works and authors chosen for discussion here were selected for several reasons. First, they were perceived to be among the most widely read philosophers in adult education. Second, their views, with some minor exceptions, appear to reflect general thinking among practicioners. Third, publications cited are available for further analysis and reflection.

In contrast to the first chapter division, the chapter section on purposes explicates the views of two individuals whose views are separated by almost fifty years. Finally, the topic of conceptualizations is developed through observations on six different concepts offered by an equal number of individuals.

Adult education in the United States is widely spread throughout the nation's social institutions. There is no one agreed upon philosophy, purpose or conceptualization of education of adults. As indicated in chapter one, even definitions of adults vary greatly among practitioners and academics. It is easy to see how disagreements about how to define adults could also be paralleled by differences over philosophy and purpose of education for those people. The array of ideas and pronouncements concerning the reasons for adult education, the purpose of it and ways of thinking about it provide the basis for dialogue, however.

PHILOSOPHIES

The philosophical basis of education for adults seems to vary according to the providers of programs. Throughout the history of the United States it has been common for at least two or more philosophical justifications to coexist. Perhaps the most simple period, when agreement on the philosophy of education for adults was highest, was during the late seventeenth century and early eighteenth century when the philosophical thrust was in terms of the religious imperative for self-improvement. Even that position was not as simple as it sounds, as different existing religious views concerning the nature of God and man as held by the Diests, Quakers and Puritans interacted with views of education. Over the years philosophical views have become more complex with several philosophical positions coexisting simultaneously.

Educators of adults in the United States have been described as having a limited interest in philosophical dimensions of the field (Long, 1983b). Truly, most practitioners and academicians, and perhaps a large proportion of adult learners, do not have a coherent unified formal philosophy of education for adults. Nevertheless, it is quite likely that most have some kind of ill defined and vague philosophy. The distinction here is between the disciplined scholarly philosophy and one's everyday set of guiding principles.

Five books by educators of adults published since 1962 have contributed to current ideas about philosophy of adult education. The authors of the books are Apps (1973, 1979), Elias and Merriam (1980), Cotton (1968) and Kallen (1962). Apps and Elias and Merriam have greater current visibility in adult education literature than Cotton and Kallen. Thus the works of the first two seem to constitute the important current philosophical works among adult educators while the views of Cotton and Kallen, though dated, are also

important. A brief overview of the main ideas of
Apps, Elias and Merriam, Cotton and Kallen follows:
Apps

Apps (1979) emphasizes the nature of the human
being in his philosophical approach. According to
his work human beings may be conceptualized in two
distinctive ways. One of these is described as
organismic or mechanistic. The organismic concept
of humanity is based on the belief that human
beings are essentially related to other life forms.
The other position is based on the opinion that
humans are basically different from other life
forms. The latter view is what is often referred
to as humanistic. Apps' dichotomy is not as broad
as the scheme used by some other scholars. Langer,
(1969), for example, uses a scheme popular with
psychologists, based upon a three cell
classification. One category, the mechanistic one,
is similar to App's first classification. Beliefs
that fall into this category emphasize the
environmental effects on human behavior.
Behavioral psychology is based on this view. The
name of the second category is similar to a term
Apps uses for his second type: organic.
Subscribers to this view believe humans develop by
their own actions; the idea is somewhat related to
the humanistic view.   The third category is
labelled psychoanalytic and is derived from the
work of Freud.   In contrast with the organismic
view, according to the psychoanalytic perspective,
humans are perceived to be conflicted beings driven
to action and growth both by their passions or
instincts and by external demands. The rational
element present in the humanistic philosophy is
either absent or limited in the psychoanalytic
belief!

        Both of the above constructs appear to ignore
philosophical concepts based on religious views
that are present in the Judeo-Christian precepts
and doctrine. Vitalism as a concept used to
account for a spiritual force as an element in
human nature is not considered by either of the
above views. Thomism, derived from St. Thomas
Aquinas, is one of the major philosophies based
upon mystical or spiritual concepts (Maritain,
1970). Even though none of the philosophies of
adult education presented in this chapter discuss
this view, there are adult educators who find the
views of Apps and Langer too limited and who
prefer to think of the human in additional ways
(Stokes, 1970).

chronology they are as follows: (a) perennialism, (b) essentialism, (c) progressivism, (d) reconstructionism and (c) existentialism. Some of the basic elements of the five educational philosophies identified by Apps are provided below.

Perennialism. Individuals who subscribe to this philosophy have the view that basic beliefs and knowledge of the past are currently as applicable as they were centuries earlier. Perennialists focus on activities that are believed to discipline the mind, and the important content to be mastered. It is of a disciplinary and spiritual nature; it is found in mathematics, languages, logic, and great books. Immediate use and application are not important concepts.

As perennialism is believed to be a philosophical ancestor of essentialism there are some expected similarities between them. Both philosophies advocate teaching techniques that emphasize memorization, reading, writing, drill and recitation. These techniques are consistent with the stress on disciplining the mind, and with the belief that learning requires a properly exercised mind. Perennialism has also been identified as an elist philosophy of education for the intellectually gifted while the less able obtain vocational training.

Essentialism. According to Apps, essentialism is one of the popular educational philosophies practiced in the U.S. schools. The essentialists believe the essential elements of education are to be derived from historical and contemporary knowledge. The philosophy is drawn from both idealism and realism. From idealism the content of education is obtained from history, foreign language and the classics. The realists believe the content of education is derived from the physical world and such disciplines as mathematics and the natural sciences.

Based on the view that the purpose of education is one of preserving and transmitting the culture to future generations, essentialism emphasizes subject matter and a traditional approach to education.

Progressivism. In contrast to the more authoritarian nature of essentialism, progressivism is opposed to authoritarianism and prefers human experience as a basis of knowledge. Adherents to this philosophy do not believe in absolute knowledge. All things are in transition and relative. Progressivism is rooted in the pragmatism of Charles S. Pierce and William James and the educational aspects were developed by John Dewey (Long, in Press a).

Rather than emphasizing mastery of content, progressivism is designed to help students learn problem solving or how to think. Experimentalism is a foundation for progressivism, hence, the scientific method is stressed as a way of discovering knowledge and solving problems. Process is emphasized rather than content. According to progressivism, the purpose of education is to improve human life in society (Apps, 1973).

Progressive education ideas have been highly visible in adult education literature since the 1920s. Horace Kallen, Eduard Lindeman and others associated with the New School of Social Research in New York, along with other individuals such as the historian Charles A. Beard and the educator William Heard Kilpatrick, contributed to these ideas. More recently, Malcolm Knowles' efforts on behalf of the andragogy concept have continued to link adult educators with the progressive education philosophy.

Reconstructionism. Reconstructionism is sometimes viewed as a part of progressivism. As there are smilarities between perennialism and essentialism, there are also similarities between progressivism and reconstructionist views, for example, see Kilpatrick (1951; 1933). Both of the latter suggests values are relative to culture, time and place and are generated by human experience (Apps, 1973). In contrast to progressivism, reconstructionism focuses more on ends (truths) than means (process). In this respect, reconstructionists are similar to perennialists and essentialists. Differences are noted between how the ends are determined, however. To the perennialists and essentialists ends are absolute and eternal, and are determined through nonempirical approaches. Reconstructionists, as the progressivists, rely on the scientific method to discover truth and believe that truth or ends are relative, not absolute.

Existentialism. Existentialism emphasizes the purpose of education. Accordingly, the objective of education is individual self-fulfilment. It is directly opposed to essentialism and perenialism in three specific ways: (a) education is not primarily an agency of society to perpetuate a cultural heritage; (b) education is not a pipeline of perenial truths; (c) education is not a means for social life adjustment in a democratic community. Instead, education exists for the individual. Thus, it is an instrument for encouraging maximum individual choice and autonomy.

Apps thus illustrates the major philosophies of education. These philosophies are directed from broader schools of philosophy and applied directly to educational issues such as the aims of education. They are also more frequently identified with education in general. Elias and Merriam (1980), discussed below, relate educational philosophies directly to adult education.

Elias and Merriam
Elias and Merriam (1980) suggest six philosophies can be found in adult education in the United States: analytical, behavioristic, humanistic, progressive, liberal, progressive, and radical. The six philosophies noted by Elias and Merriam are not as easily classified and defined as the basic two noted by Apps (1979) or the three attributed to Langer (1969). Like the five philosophical perspectives identified by Apps (1973) they are not exactly parallel and occasionally overlap, as noted below.

Analytical philosophy, sometimes referred to as conceptual analysis (Wilson, 1966), is more closely allied with a procedure to analyze the meaning of terms or to clarify philosophical concepts. The techniques of such analysis are used when the meaning of a concept is ambiguous. Katchadourian (1967, p. 4) says: "the overall aim of philosophical inquiry, negatively speaking is the elimination of perplexity, confusion, or error in regard to phenomena generally regarded as objects of philosophical inquiry."

23

Thus, in contrast with the other five philosophies identified by Elias and Merriam, analytical philosophy is more a procedure of inquiry that focuses on language as the unit of study. The impact on education is indirect as analytical philosophy helps to clarify terms and concepts, and to address considerations of fact and/or value (Wilson, 1966).

Behaviorism and humanism as philosophical concepts appear to be established upon concepts of the human being. They reflect the dichotomy addressed by Apps. As such, they both suggest objectives of education and ways of designing and conducting education. Concepts concerning motives of individuals and society can also be implied by these two contrasting philosophical positions concerning the nature of humans and the learning process. For example, humanistic views are more frequently associated with discovery learning, self-direction in learning and techniques that encourage freedom and independence. In contrast, behavioristic views are reflected in atomistic, highly structured and controlled learning activities.

Liberal, progressive and radical philosophies of education for adults are different in many respects, but they agree in a major way. They all seem to be based on a humane view of people as opposed to a behavioristic concept. Some major differences are as follows: Liberal education is perceived to relate more directly to content of learning and its impact on the rational logical behavior of humans. Progressive education is perceived to emphasize the procedures or process of learning. Radical education focuses on the use of knowledge for reform purposes.

Liberal education is based on a view of the human being as an optimizing creature that is capable of logical analysis, rational behavior and transfer of broad and general principles. Education in the liberal tradition is usually based heavily upon the great works of literature. It is assumed that problems of morality, political expediency, interpersonal relations, diplomacy and strategies for operating in business can be addressed by the educated mind as long as the mind is educated in the liberal tradition. The liberal

24

view contrasts with the training orientation that emphasizes specific learning in a narrow specialized applied area. The conflict between these two philosophies is becoming increasingly apparent in education of adults in the United States. It is quite safe to suggest that Americans generally have favored applied education to liberal education. However, it appears that the stress on applied or instrumental education recently has become even more emphatic in education at all levels. More is said on this important development later in this chapter.

Progressive education reflects an approach to learning and teaching attributed to the philosopher John Dewey. Dewey was also an avowed humanist. Progressive education has been variously described, praised and criticised in the education literature. It has many elements. Some of the important ones include an emphasis upon learning through discovery or personal inquiry. Closely allied with the discovery is learner goal setting, independence and evaluation. Progressive education emphasizes learning in contrast to teaching. Education of adults in the United States has drawn from the progressive education tradition; as noted previously, andragogy as espoused by Knowles (1980) is derived from progressive philosophy.

Radical education places its emphasis upon the uses to which education are put. Specifically, radical education is for the purpose of social, political and economic change. The utopian world view is contrasted with reality for the purpose of generating change. Hence, literacy, occupational skills, and other learning objectives are perceived as instruments for reforming society in some way. The radical education philosophy continues to have adherents in adult education in the United States (Kreitlow and Associates, 1981; Long, Anderson and Blubaugh, 1973). They lack the prominence enjoyed by their philosophical ancestors of the 1920s and 1930s, however. The relative declining significance of radical education in the recent thirty years is suggested by the limited attention given to community development in adult education over the period. Community development, which might have at times qualified for the label of radical education was last discussed in the 1960 handbook of adult education edited by Knowles (1960). Since 1970 community development has declined in visibility in adult education literature. More is said about the reformist philosophy in the following paragraphs.

Assuming that the above interpretation and assessment of the six major philosophies of adult education in the United States, as identified by Elias and Merriam, is correct, it is quite likely that individuals subscribe to a mixture of positions and concepts derived from several of the philosophies. For example, one may eclectly use analytical philosophical procedures for clarifying concepts of education such as satisfaction (McDougald,1983) and adopt a humanistic (Kidd, 1973) or behavioristic approach in liberal education based on progressive education methods for radical applications (Friere,1973).

Cotton

Eclectism is also noted by Cotton (1968) who identified three general philosophical orientations in the literature of adult education published between 1919 and 1968. He identified them as social reformist, professional and eclectic orientations.

Social Reform, according to Cotton, is the oldest of the traditions which dominated the field through the mid-thirties. Subscribers to the social reformist view are critical of the status quo, special interests of those other than the oppressed, traditional education and the prevailing cultural environment. Educators of adults who hold these views generally believe that individual and social intelligence have to be mobilized, on a large scale, to solve critical social, economic, and political problems. Representatives of this group include Joseph K. Hart, W. H. Kilpatrick, Harold Laski and Eduard C. Lindeman (Cotton,1968).

The professional tradition is more recent. It seems to have emerged as a reaction against the social reformist philosophy and is temporarily associated with the development and expansion of graduate programs in adult education. Subscribers to the professional philosophy, as used by Cotton, perceive the function of adult education more in terms of educational ends than in social goals. The emphasis has been on the establishment of adult education on an additudinal parity with other levels of the traditional educational structure. Consequently, individuals identified by Cotton with the professional tradition have been most concerned with professionalization, establishment of the discipline of adult education, and institutionalization of adult education. They include Lyman Bryson (1936), and Wilbur Hallenbeck (Cotton, 1968).

Eclectic philosophical positions are identified with adult educators whose views tend to fall somewhere between the positions of the social reformists and professionals as discussed above. Robert J. Blakely, Dorothy Canfield Fisher, Alvin Johnson, and Harry Overstreet are examples (Cotton, 1968).

The increasing study of adult education in the United States through graduate programs seems to have had two related results. First, systematic study of education of adults in the country produced information on the extensive character of the activity. Studies in various geographic regions, urban communities and rural villages and historical inquiry has done much to dispel any ideas that adult education, in practice, was limited to one ideology or the servant of one social organization. Second, graduate curricula were designed to prepare graduates of adult education, to function in a variety of institutional settings. Hence, the professional philosophy was neutral on the issue of radical reformation education. According to the professional view, the practitioner could function equally well as a functionary of a social agency designed to maintain the status quo or as an agent in another organization dedicated to change. Individual philosophy, not educational preparation per se, is the critical element.

Even though the work of Apps, Elias and Merriam and Cotton are based on different strategies and sources, they reflect considerable agreement as well as expected differences. Apps' emphasis on the nature of the human being overlaps with Elias and Merriams' philosophical orientations. In turn, their classifications are not wholly inconsistent with Cotton's system. It is significant that philosophical thought regarding the aims and objectives of adult education in the United States is distributed along a continuum from a scholastic approach to the "liberation of the mind" (existential and liberal) to various applied forms of political/economic and social liberation (radical). Related positions taken by other authors address what Miller (1967) has described as the issue of individual growth versus social

27

concern. While Miller favors the former, Lindeman (1961) and Bergevin (1967) discuss the aims of adult education in terms of social improvement. Bergevin encourages adult education because it promotes the democratic way of life, while Lindeman thinks of adult education as a way to democratic life. Knowles with his emphasis on individual development (humanistic, progressive) apart from external concerns, is represented by Elias and Merriam as having a position similar to Miller's. From Knowles' perspective, the aim and mission of adult education is to help adults become mentally or cognitively liberated, with the individual determining what he or she will be when free.

The tension in the education of adults in the United States concerning goals and objectives is believed to be more severe than the literature suggests. The sources of philosophical conflict are not different than those identified by Cotton, and they may be no deeper than they were in the 1920s and 1930s. Unfortunately, it is difficult to know, as philosophy of adult education is not well developed, these positions are not often discussed in contemporary literature. Some of the anxiety concerning professionalization and social reform, for instance, has been revealed in the Forum section of Adult Education (now Adult Education Quarterly) and in discussions at professional conferences. But the attention the issue has been given in the literature does not reflect the potential breadth, depth and scope of the conflict.

Kallen

The complexity of the philosophy of adult education is discussed in a most scholarly manner by Kallen (1962). His treatment of the topic "Philosphical Issues in Adult Education" is profound and difficult to summarize adequately. A major point developed in the essay is development of an ultimate ideology through the use of a combination of philosophic ideas to approach issues in adult education. Kallen was well aware of criticism of such an idea. Nevertheless, he summarized his philosophy of adult education as "the American Idea" (p. 51).

In turn, he associates the American Idea with James Truslow Adams' American Dream as set forth in his historical work (1944). Adams represented the American dream as a dream of a land in which life is better and richer and fuller for every man, with opportunity for each according to his ability of achievement. The opportunity available to each person must transcend economics, and it must extend culture. The American dream, according to Kallen, must be nurtured by the American Idea as expressed by Theodore Parker in 1850 (Kallen, 1962).

Kallen's general writings suggest he might be classified as eclectic in philosophical orientation, following Cotton's scheme. He reveals a reformist belief and a progressive position concerning the teacher-learner relationship. Much of adult learning is represented by Kallen as unlearning and of personal liberation. This theme is currently evident in the writing of Mezirow (1981) which is discussed in some detail in chapter seven. Self-directed, independent, autonomous learning with limited interference by teachers is a theme in Kallen's work (1962).

A Changing Emphasis

None of the authors discussed above seem to address a philosophical position concerning education of adults that seems to be increasingly popular in the United States. The position does not have a title yet, but it may be referred to as the certification philosophy or the corporate philosophy. In the final analysis these two labels may designate two different philosophical structures, but for our purposes they shall be treated as elements of the same syndrome. They are possibly distantly related to James' pragmaticism and to different strains of utilitarianism or instrumentalism. Utilitarianism has been described as both a doctrine and ethical philosophy (Gove, 1961). But, the certification philosophy and corporate philosophy do not appear to have been systematically and directly related to these earlier philosophical origins. To suggest that the certification philosophy is directly concerned with issues of truth as was James, or that the corporate philosophy is established upon questions of ethical morality and the nature of happiness as discussed by utilitarian philosophers stretches a point (Barrow, 1975; Miller and Williams 1982) Perhaps a closer association exists between the certification/corporate philosophy and instrumentalism which is defined (Gove, 1961) as a conception that the significant factor of a thing is its value as an instrument. Hence, education of adults translated into a certificate or a skill (competency) in a work setting is valued because of its direct usefulness. The emphasis in what is labelled here as the certification or corporate philosophy is (a) an emphasis on a certificate, or some other means of certifying educational activity; (b) instrumental skills; and (c) a focus on skills useful in employment.

As the other philosophies of education of adults, this philosophical orientation has not been systematized by adult educators. It does, however, contain some common elements as noted above. Providers are also quite varied, but the major purveyors of education according to the certification or corporate philosophy are business and industry, consulting firms, higher education, government, the military and professional associations. Also, as in the other philosophies, a variety of planning mechanisms, curricula, and instructional strategies may be noted among the subscribers to this philosophy. They range from the humanistic methods identified with Knowles (1970) to highly sophisticated behaviorally based programmed instruction used in the military. The combination of an emphasis on certifying learning for adults and the increasing tendency to use education of adults as an instrument for addressing specific corporate and national economic, manpower and political policies represents one of the greatest challenges experienced by adult education in the United States. More is said on this topic in another section of this chapter.

Considering the range of philosophical views among educators of adults in the United States, one could predict a similar distribution of ideas concerning the purposes of education of adults. Moving from the philosophical positions noted above one could predict a range of comments concerning the purposes or objectives of adult education. Certain purposes are strongly implied by the philosophical views noted. For example, there should be some strong justification of education for adults as a means for improving society. There should also be support for education of adults as a means of self-improvement. The following discussion identifies the range of views expressed in the literature concerning this topic..

PURPOSES

What is the purpose of education of adults in the United States? Answers to this question are not difficult to come by, numerous politicians, practitioners and scholars have answers to the question. Agreement is less readily achieved. The problem with the identified purposes is, frequently, only one purpose is given by each spokesman, and those purposes differ among the sources, even in something as basic as adult literacy education. For some, the purpose of literacy education is to teach adults basic literacy skills. For others, literacy education is to accultrate and socialize the illiterate into the mainstream society. Yet, a third group believes literacy education should be central to reform activities. Darkenwald and Valentine (1984, p. 1) have noted that adult education is primarily concerned with "...applications or impact of education to functioning in everyday life". If disagreement on the purposes of literacy education divides the field, then it should come as no surprise that differences of opinion exist in other areas.

The philosophical perspectives discussed in the previous part of this chapter imply that the purposes of adult education should fall into one of three general categories: (a) education for self-improvement, and (b) education for social change, or (c) education for corporate or national goals. Unfortunately, none of these major types of purposes are simple. They are complex ideas that contain several subcategories. Each of the larger purposes is examined in some detail below.

Education for self-improvement seems to be quite straightforward. It should be simple and easy to understand. But alas, education for self-improvement includes the following:

1. self-improvement in the area of health
2. self-improvement in the area of personality and psychological adjustment
3. self-improvement in the area of civic competence
4. self-improvement for preoccupational purposes
5. self-improvement as a practicing professional
6. self-improvement in the area of arts, humanities and literature

Education for social change also addresses a variety of different purposes as follows:

1. social change based on learning activities in use of democratic procedures
2. social change based on non-violent resistance

3. social change based on power conflict
   models

Education designed to address corporate or
national goals may be the easiest to classify in
terms of general purposes, but specific educational
objectives of adult education within this
philosophical category are also quite variable.
The justification for education of adults according
to the corporate philosophy is examined in the next
major section of this chapter.

Two efforts to organize and systematize the
purposes of education of adults are instructive.
The first of these was provided in 1936 by Lyman
Bryson and the second is the result of my own
historical study of education of adults in the
United States.

Bryson's Typology
Bryson's (1936) typology of purposes is as follows:
remedial, occupational, relational, liberal and
political. The educational functions as discussed
by Bryson are elaborated upon in the following
paragraphs:

Remedial education, according to Bryson, is more or
less formal study that is undertaken to give an
adult whatever is needed to bring the individual up
to a desired educational minimum standard that is
believed to be necessary for life in America. It
includes the ability to read and to write, and for
immigrants it includes a knowledge of spoken
English and of American citizenship. Training in
homemaking and childcare on an elementary basis, in
all the simple rules of health and civilized
behavior, are also remedial, according to Bryson.

Occupational training may be for several objectives
such as, (a) for advancement on the job; (b) for
advancement on another job; (c) for the industrial
rehabilitation of the victim of machineless
employment; and (d) for guidance in choosing or
adjusting to an occupation.

Relational education includes parent advocates and
also the studies of emotions, attitudes and
psychological habits that are designed to help us

32

better to understand ourselves and our relations with other persons.

Liberal education is the best term available to describe activities that are undertaken chiefly for their own sake, for the pleasure that is in them. Although all adult studies should be liberal and "liberating" according to Bryson, the first two types listed above are instrumental, and to a lesser extent, the third also. They are expected to produce results beyond the satisfaction of achievement. In the pursuit of art, or philosophy, or science, one can find, no doubt, the motive of self-advancement, but these activities are not so directly applicable to one's daily life, or to one's daily human relations, according to Bryson. And the recreational element, the sheer enjoyment of pleasant effort, although also is, or should be, present in every form of educational activity, is stronger perhaps in this field than elsewhere.

Political education includes all those studies, practices, and experiences that men deliberately undertake to make themselves better members of the nation. This includes not only the study of "politics" as a subject, but also all forms of training for political action (p. 31).

Even though Bryson's typology was developed in the 1930s it continues to be useful. One of the major areas not directly addressed by Bryson is continuing professional education. The functions he identified are associated with educational institutions. In contrast, he believed continuing professional education would not be an important responsibility for these institutions. It would be provided primarily by professional associations and societies.

Historical Purposes

My conceptualization of the purposes of education in the United States emphasizes the uses to which education has been put. The typology was obtained through study of educational efforts over a three hundred year period. The categories that emerge are broader than the types of purposes identified by Bryson but are not totally inconsistent with his ideas. They are as follows:

1. Education for Americanization
2. Education for application

3. Education for enlightenment
   (personal liberation)
4. Education for social improvement (or
   social liberation)
5. Education for literacy (which may be
   subsumed under all of the above)

A close scrutiny of education for adults, in what is now the United States, since 1700 and earlier, reveals that adults have continuously engaged in learning related to each of the above purposes. Each of the five purposes has been addressed in a persistent and continuous manner to this date. There have been changes within each of the types of learning. For example, the first kinds of learning activity that could be characterized as learning for Americanization focused on learning about the new territory, its climate, vegetation, soil characteristics, animals and native people. Subsequently, the colonists changed and modified the old and familiar British institutions to meet the requirements of a new nation. By the twentieth century Americanization was frequently defined in terms of language education, cultural assimilation and citizenship education.

Over the centuries, then, the content required to achieve each of the five identified purposes of education for adults has varied. Not surprisingly, the sources of learning have also been modified as society has become more complex and modern. For example, in the seventeenth and eighteenth centuries, education for application or occupational education, often was provided through the apprentice system. Over the years different sources for occupational education have emerged. More is said on this point later.

Despite the changes in learning activities, content and sources of education for adults, the basic purposes as identified have been remarkably persistent. The relative permanence of the five purposes of education for adults in the United States, regardless of historical, social, economic and political changes, suggests that the five purposes emerge from some significant underlying social and personal phenomena. The fact that the relative importance of each of the purposes has fluctuated is important and reasons for the variations in popularity should be an interesting topic of study. It is more significant in the conceptualization of education of adults in the United States to note that despite irregular losses

34

and gains in popularity and prominence, elements of each purpose are consistently visible across the historical period.

Education for occupational purposes is now in an ascendant status. Therefore, a few comments based on historical information might be informative and support the argument in support of my conceptualization of five major purposes that coexist in education for adults.

Around 1900 occupational justifications for education of adults began to be a concern of the federal government. Up until that time American adults individually had addressed the need for occupational competence with a few exceptions. The Mechanics Institutes of the 1820s represented a major social intervention in the education of adults for vocational purposes. But, the institutional provisions such as the Mechanics Institutes were not governmentally supported. Federal action concerning vocational education has been inconsistent, but persistent, since the Presidential Commission on National Aid to Education in 1914. Support has been stimulated at regular intervals by national study panels; study commissions were formed in 1914, 1936 and 1961 (Long, in press b).

The 1961 committee made five recommendations concerning vocational education. The panel said vocational education must do the following: (a) offer training opportunities to the non-college graduates who would enter the labor force in the 1960s; (b) provide training or retraining for the millions of workers whose skills and technical knowledge must be updated, as well as whose jobs would be lost due to increasing efficiency, automation, or economic change; (c) meet the critical needs for highly skilled craftsmen and technicians through education offered during and beyond the high school years; (d) expand vocational and technical education training programs consistent with employment potential and national economic needs; and (e) make educational opportunities equally available to all persons regardless of race, sex, scholastic aptitude, or place of residence.

Current emphasis on worker education is evident in media treatment of education for adults. A national news magazine described adult education as "the newest tool for job hunters"(U.S. News and World Report, August 16, 1982, p. 69). The authors of the report had the following to say:

>Once dismissed by many academics as Mickey
>Mouse courses in underwater basketweaving;
>adult education has become the new focus of
>career development. Postsecondary schools
>facing a shrinking pool of people, ages 18 to
>22, are tailoring more and more programs to
>the working student over 25. (p. 69)

An official of Cuyahoga Community College described adult students as follows: "people who come here are not looking for ivy walls or college football games. They're looking for training that's going to lead to a job." (p. 69)

Education for occupational improvement is apparently the main purpose of organized and sponsored education for adults today (Long, 1983e; Fiske, 1985). Education for purposes of developing literacy and Americanization are less popular, but visible, social purposes of education. Education for personal enlightenment and for social liberation are less visible, but available. Sponsored educational activities for adults tend to reflect the social, economic and political climate of the nation.

The period between 1900 and 1920 is frequently referred to as the "Progressive Era". It is no accident, then, that education for Americanization and literacy prominently emerged then. It is also interesting to observe the rhetoric and activity of intellectuals on behalf of education for social change in the 1920's and 1930's in the aftermath of the "Progressive Era."

Contemporary Developments

Education at all levels is increasingly identified with the social, economic and political goals of the nation. Both national policies and social expectations reflect the above kinds of goals. As a consequence, education of adults is described as having one or more of the following missions:

1. To provide social and educational equity.
   Educational opportunities are to be made
   available to all, barriers are to be reduced to facilitate the education of
   everyone regardless of social class, race
   or ethnic background, sex, age and any
   other similar variable.
2. To provide needed manpower ln critical
   social and industrial occupations such as
   health care providers, teachers, govern-

> mental administrators, engineers and scientists.
3. To provide basic generalized occupational competence for American industry.
4. To socialize and Americanize the population to broadly acceptable social behaviors, languages and political awareness (citizenship).
5. To meet national defense needs.

A long-term perspective reveals subtle changes in the attention and public support given to the different missions of adult education. There is, however, a long-term trend in education of adults in the United States that is a source of concern. Adult education appears to have become subject to the same kinds of pressures exerted on the kindergarten through grade 12 (K-12) and postsecondary educational systems. Following World War II an alliance was developed between industry and the federal government (Spring, 1976). That alliance has been expanded to become a coalition of government, higher education and industry. The mission or purposes of education for all age groups increasingly emphasizes the needs of the coalition. The philosophy, the process and the product of education are in turn influenced by the coalition's goals.

The phenomenon of government/education/industry agreement on educational goals is a little discussed, but very important, contemporary event in adult education. Because of the importance of the topic and the limited attention it has received, this topic is extensively developed in the next chapter.

CONCEPTUALIZATIONS

Bryson's (1936) description of adult education in the United States, even though written approximately 50 years ago, continues to reflect the field accurately. He said in 1936,

> "American adult education has not been a single and systematic character. It has never been a folk movement for the refashioning of a national culture like that undertaken in Denmark under the leadership of Bishop Grundtvig. It has not been largely a movement for the intellectual improvement of the underprivileged, particularly the 'working class', as in Great

Britain. Nor has it even been a definite concern of the government, used to propagate a
political philosophy as in Italy and Russia,
and more recently, in Germany. It has always
been carried on by a wide variety of agencies,
for a variety of purposes, and with many different kinds of people. For this reason, some
critics have called it formless and without
direction. Actually, it has penetrated to
more phases of life in America than in any
other country. It has been thoroughly in
accord with our basic democratic idea that
education is a common right, that learning is
neither something reserved for aristocracy nor
something bequeathed by a superior class to
inferiors." (p. 13)

Despite clear cogent remarks about the
education of adults by individuals such as Bryson,
adult education consistently has proved to be
difficult to conceptualize. Its variety and
diversity, the range of agencies involved, the
extent of purposes, differences in immediate and
long objectives, and the effects of diverse
philosophies have had their impact on
conceptualization of the field.
Education of adults in the United States has
been the topic of several conceptualization
efforts. Six different concepts that fall into
four different kinds of categories are worth
considering here. Two of the conceptualizations
are ideological in nature, one is concerned with
the status of practitioners and three are structual
in content.
The two different, but related, ideological
conceptualizations of education of adults include
(a) adult education as a social movement and (b)
adult education as a voluntary activity. The
concept based upon the status of practitioners is
referred to as the "professional" concept. The
three remaining ideas reflect the structural
relationship of education of adults with other
educational activities and institutions.

Social Movement
The social movement concept is possibly the
dominant conceptualization of adult education among
graduates of graduate programs in adult education.
Even individuals who entertain some doubts as to
its validity are familiar with the label. The
social movement tag seems to have evolved with

limited critical evaluation. Knowles (1962) asks
the question "what is an adult education movement?"
In answer to his own question, he equates
"movement" with "field" and proceeds to describe
the idea as bringing together into a definable
social system all the individuals, institutions,
and associations concerned with the education of
adults and portrays them as working toward such
common goals as the improvement of the methods and
materials of adult learning, the extension of
opportunities for adults to learn, and the general
advancement of the general level of culture (1962,
p. vi).

If one accepts criteria for a social movement
as stated by Ash (1972), there is reason for
questioning the validity of referring to adult
education as a social movement. Turning to Ash, we
find the following definition of a social movement:
"A social movement is a set of attitudes and
self-conscious action on the part of a group of
people directed toward change in the social
structure and/or ideology of a society and carried
on outside of ideologically legitimated channels or
which uses these channels in innovative ways" (p.
1).

In the process of identifying a phenomenon as
a social movement, Ash warns that one's definition
should distinguish four related phenomena from the
social movement itself as follows:

1. The definition distinguishes movements
    from movement organizations.
2. The definition distinguishes movements
    from attitudinal change without action.
3. The definition distinguishes movements
    from premovement rebellious acts.
4. The definition distinguishes movement
    from changes initiated by a ruling
    class, an elite with political power, or
    an intelligentsia associated with such an
    elite (Ash, 1972, p.2).

At least two aspects of Ash's comments attract
our attention. First, item four should stimulate
additional historical inquiry into the emergence of
the 'adult education movement' of the 1920s as
envisioned by Knowles (1952). Cursory knowledge of
the individuals involved in the formation of the
American Association for Adult Education inspires a
belief that many of them were associated with the
ruling class, political power and/or intelligentsia
of the period. This possibility is suggested by

what Schlesinger (1957) calls the revolt of the intellectuals.

Secondy, the above definition seems to require the simultaneous presence of three of four distinctive elements. The first factor is a set of (a) attitudes and (b) self-conscious action. The second factor concerns the impact of the first one upon the (b) social structure and/or ideology. The third factor is action (c) outside of the ideologically legitimate channels (i.e., various boycotts, sit-ins, etc.) or (d) the use of the legitimate channels in innovative ways. It is assumed that the minimum criteria for a social movement includes a, b, and c or d. Thus, a social movement might be defined as a set of attitudes and self-conscious action on the part of a group of people directed toward either a change in the social structure or ideology and carried on outside of ideologically legitimated channels or which makes uses innovative use of them.

Comparing the above minimum criteria of a social movement with Knowles' definition of the adult education movement, some discrepancies seem to emerge. Knowles does not indicate that a change in the social structure is a goal of the adult education movement. However, as suggestd earlier in this chapter, there are some educators of adults who subscribe to a reform ideology. For them, the main purpose of education for adults is to bring about a change in society. (See the earlier discussion of philosophy for individuals identified with this idea.) The current purposes of education of adults are not limited to the goals of the reformers even though it is possible that such an ideology motivated some of the original leaders in the American Adult Education Association.

Ash's definition of a social movement also contains a provision for a change in ideology, but it does not appear that Knowles' comments on the adult education movement addresses this element any more than it applies to the issue of changes in the social structure. It cannot be argued successfully that a single ideology of adult education emerged in the United States during the 1920's with the establishment of the American Association of Adult Education. There is evidence that belief in the efficacy of education for adults existed for decades prior to the formation of the American Association of Adult Education, an event sometimes identified with the birth of the "movement." The ideology of education of adults during the nineteenth century was nearly as inclusive as it currently is.

Finally, the adult education movement as described (Knowles, 1952) does not reflect evidence of being carried on outside the ideologically legitimate channels of society in innovative ways. Thus, two possible conflicting conclusions may be drawn from this analysis: (a) Ash's criteria are too restrictive and hence unacceptable; and (b) Knowles' definition of adult education as a social movement is overly generous, and incorrect.

The acceptance of the 'social movement' label also seems to ignore the historical views on the issue. Despite the well-known position of Lindeman and the lesser known views of Hart (1927) that have been used to justify the designation of adult education as a social movement, there were equally verbal scholars whose positions have been neglected. Kepple (1926) and Coleman (1928) represent the views of those who emphasized individual rather than social goals of adult education. Lorimer (1931), following his study of adult education in Brooklyn suggested that adult education was neither a social movement, as it might have been in England and Denmark, nor was it a far reaching force in American communities as desired by Lindeman and others. The decision among practitioners concerning the social value versus individual goals of adult education during the 1930s is best illustrated by its treatment in the association's journal during those years.

The concepts of adult education that emerged in the second decade of the twentieth century and as subscribed to by that zealous group forming the New School of Social Research in 1919, (Kallen, 1962) appear to come close to meeting Ash's criteria. Yet it seems that these individuals were a part of a larger movement of human-liberation that turned to adult education as an ideologically legitimate channel for changing the social structure and ideology. Thus, it is more appropriate to suggest adult education is one of the ideologically legitimate channels by which organizations such as the New School of Social Research and labor education sought to change social structure and ideology. In turn, to the degree that they reflected the ideology, the American Association of Adult Education and subsequent organizations were movement organizations, not a social movement within themselves. Thus, to refer to the adult education movement as a social movement in the United States

41

seems to attribute an ideological cohesiveness to adult education that does not exist today, if it ever did.

Voluntary

The education of adults in the United States is frequently conceptualized and described as a voluntary activity. It is commonplace to read or hear the trite expression that adult learners "vote with their feet" to indicate that adults are free to participate or not participate in learning activities. As late as the early twentieth century, education in the United States was described as spontaneous in contrast with more rigid systems of older nations (Bryson, 1936). An earlier discussion of major historical characteristics of adult education in America identifies the voluntary dimension of one of its major continuing characteristics. (Long, 1980).

The voluntary dimension of adult education as described by Kallen (1962) is increasingly suspect, or is in danger of becoming extinct. He described adult learners as ". . . a voluntary team going out upon an intellectual exploring expedition." (p. 18) While hard data has not been cited, the voluntary nature of education of adults in the United States seems to be declining in importance. The trend toward certificated learning, mandatory continuing education and occupationally focused learning is removing much of the voluntary nature from sponsored group learning activity. The voluntary characteristic seem to prevail in self-directed learning and the other forms of informal learning. But, based on current trends noted earlier in this chapter and concepts discussed in the following chapter "voluntary" may, in the future, be used as a description of adult education only when carefully defining the kind of adult education to which reference is made.

Professional

Houle (1960) is credited with devising the leadership pyramid to describe the field of adult education. His concept graphically represents the population of practitioners in adult education with professional leaders limited to the apex and amateurs at the base of the pyramid. In other words, education of adults is mostly an amateur field with numerous positions occupied by volunteers or others who are not formally trained, according to this concept.

Some observations concerning the current validity of this concept are appropriate. Due to the nature of the field it is difficult to determine the number of professionals actually employed in the education of adults. There is also difficulty in defining the professional adult educator. If the term is narrowly restricted to individuals with doctoral degrees with a major in adult education that number of approximately 3,000 validates the leadership pyramid concept. If one includes the approximate 750,000 trainers in business and industry (Eurich, 1985) and the thousands of faculty in community colleges, and other postsecondary education institutions, we are probably talking about a million individuals with some kind of professional preparation related to the education of adults.

The issue of professional preparation is a complex one. It has stimulated numerous discussions at meetings of the Commission of Professors of Adult Education for a number of years. Criteria for membership in the Commission has also been discussed, debated and occasionally modified. But, it has been difficult to agree upon an acceptable definition of a professor of adult education and a graduate program of adult education. Therefore, it should be no surprise to discover absence of agreement upon what constitutes professional preparation. If the minimum requirement is a baccalaureate degree or even a master's degree in adult education, a related social science, agriculture or business school program, then the professional cadre is a large one.

There is no question that many voluntary organizations will continue to make use of the lay person as a trainer. But, as will be noted later, it appears that the adult education field may be becoming further bifurcated. The two main divisions will be composed of groups of agencies, organizations and other providers who generally use professional leaders and whose focus is on some kind of certificate or similar product. The second group will be composed of those providers who generally use lay people as trainers and whose focus is on learning that aids a voluntary organization achieve its goals and/or primarily is for the personal satisfaction of the learners. Houle's leadership pyramid will continue to be useful to describe the second kind of education mentioned above. It may not be appropriate to use the pyramid to describe the kind of education for adults referred to above.

Structural

Three different concepts have been used to represent the "structural" characteristics of adult education. The oldest of these concepts was devised by Clark (1958) to describe public school adult education in California. The second concept was offered by Moses (1971) who studied higher education. Finally, the latest concept emerged from an effort to compare the various institutions, agencies and organizations engaged in education of adults with other educational systems (Long 1983b).

Marginal is how Clark (1958) described adult education. In his description of adult education in the California public school system, Clark claimed it was marginal because of (1) its position in the legal structure of the educational system which prevented it from having independent status; (2) its dependence upon part-time personnel who regard it as secondary to their primary occupation; (3) its lack of any separate capital facilities and its subsequent need to borrow regular elementaryland secondary school facilities; and (4) its identification as the first target of attack at times of budget cuts and economy drives.

As noted elsewhere (Long, 1983b), it is possible adult educators have been inclined to use marginality incorrectly in their blanket application of the term. Some of the four justifications for describing adult education as marginal, as given by Clark, do not equally apply to all adult education programs. Some agencies have their own capital facilities; they have specialized full-time career personnel and are no more nor no less susceptible to budget reductions in hard times than other organizational units. Finally, as far as most adult education organizations are concerned, the issue of legal status as determined by compulsory attendance laws is not a real issue. These observations challenging the universal validity of Clark's description do not negate the importance of the four factors in public school adult education. They do seriously question the appropriateness of generalizing the marginal characteristics to the entire field of adult education and all agencies currently involved in the education of adults.

44

The idea of marginality among adult educators unfortunately is not a new one. It has been discussed by adult educators even before they reached the "professional" status discussed previously in this chapter. Alvin S. Johnson, director of New York's New School for Social Research warned that adult education was not comparable in importance to primary, secondary or professional education. He implied that adult educators were characterized by "a sense of inferiority" while feeling themselves to be in "a class with repairmen" (Johnson, 1930, p.237). Thus, the inferiority mentality or the syndrome of marginality among American adult educators has a long and distinguished history. It is perhaps no accident that Clark picked up the term and Moses used a similar one.

Peripheral is the term Moses (1971) used to provide another popular conceptual description. In his study of U. S. education he referred to adult education as the "periphery" of the learning force, in contrast to the core represented by the traditional school system, including postsecondary education. Moses' thesis emphasized the existence of a learning force that includes the two educational systems in the United States. The first and most readily recognized "core" comprises the "educational system" composed of the institutions that are allied directly with the state and/or federal education establishment, including private schools and colleges; the second, and most difficult to define and describe is the periphery, composed of the thousands of agencies, institutions, organizations and services that contribute to the education of adults. The periphery includes manpower development schemes, proprietary and correspondence schools, and programs of organized instruction through educational television, for example.

It is interesting to observe the similarity between the descriptions chosen by Moses and Shils (1970). Edward Shils uses similar terms to describe the structure of society. Either purposely, or intentionally Moses' selection of core and periphery to label the two "systems" that contribute to the education of adults is instructive. It conveys the parallel between education and the broader social structures. Shils defines the center of a society as a realm of both symbols and action, identifiable by authority of elites and institutions shaped by the authority of the elites. The periphery of a society by exclusion is perceived to be those symbols and actions that lie outside the authority boundary of the elites.

The focus of educational planning in the United States, at least since the establishment of the U. S. Office of Education in 1867, has been dominated by the "core." The major tasks assigned to the core include the certifying processes for the larger society, selecting and sorting individuals for industrial and national goals (Moses, 1971). In contrast to the relative agreement on major purposes of the core, there is less agreement on the major educational purposes of the "periphery." Some idea of the task and objectives of the periphery is provided by the earlier discussion of philosophies and purposes in this chapter.

Moses' (1971) discussion of the learning force continues to be useful in observing contemporary issues and trends. His essay provides an appropriate foundation for noting the emergence of what may become an alternative system in the education of adults. Current developments in the corporate world suggest the possibility of the eventual development of three divisions in the learning force. They are (1) the core, composed of traditional educational institutions (including those with non-traditional approaches), (2) corporate educational agencies, and (3) the other agencies and providers Moses described as the periphery.

Diffuse
Long, Lester and Flowers (1979) metaphorically described the structure of adult education as a vine in contrast to the other systems of education, which might be thought of as individual trees. The system of higher education can be represented as trees with main trunks that represent the central ideas, philosophies, curricula, finance and curriculum. Oddities and innovative arrangements are represented by the limbs and leaves. Yet, all are ultimately related to the main trunk.

There is no main trunk of adult education. The various programs, agencies, organizations, and institutions involved in the education of adults often have limited areas of agreement or convergence. Ultimately, they emerge from the "soil" of humanity. But even the roots differ as different philosophies encourage the growth and provision of educational programs. There is little that binds these diffuse and diverse modes of learning except abstract and sometimes poorly conceived labels such as adult education, continuing education, education permanente, lifelong education, lifelong learning, and recurrent education. The idea of self-directed learning where the consumer more or less independently devises learning programs further complicates the picture.

SUMMARY

This chapter has identified and discussed some of the major philosophies and purposes of education of adults in the United States. Five specific scholarly sources concerning philosophy were examined. The views of Apps (1973, 1979), Elias and Merriam (1980), Cotton (1968) and Kallen (1962) are both different and similar. They are different in their typologies. Apps' latest work divides philosophies concerning the human beings into two categories. The human as learner influences one's views of education. Elias and Merriam (1980) provide a larger classification system. Considerable overlap exists among these categories, but for purposes of structure, they could be ranged along a continuum from a philosophy of liberal education to a philosophy of education for radical change.

Cotton's analysis of the writing of adult eduators led him to propose a typology consisting of three types of philosophical thought: social reformists, professional and eclectic.

In contrast, Kallen (1962) shares an "ultimate ideology" based on an eclectic configuration of various philosophical schools. His ultimate ideology is subsumed under the of the "American Idea" which among other things stresses a concept of human intellectual liberation.

The five works reviewed reflect some similarities. Each of the authors identify the social reformists or social change philosophy as one of the important philosophical orientations in the education of adults. Apps and Elias and Merriam also recognize the existence of a humanistic philosophy. The list of various philosophical schools identified by Apps (1973) is not greatly dissimilar from those identified by Elias and Merriam.

Cotton's "professional" type is not readily discerned in the lists of philosophical orientations provided by either Apps or Elias and Merriam. The debate concerning professionalism of adult education in the United States has occasionally flared into heated controversy since 1970. As Cotton's work was completed prior to that time, his identification of the professional philosophical orientation is noteworthy.

Elias and Merriam (1980) identify specific programs for the education of adults that are perceived to flow from selected philosophies. To observe that purposes of education emerge from philosophical sources is commonplace, but sometimes desirable. It is also useful in a discussion of philosophies of education to note the purposes to which education is, has been, or might be put. Purposes of education of adults as identified by Bryson and myself have been noted.

Bryson's enduring conceptualization, it is now about 50 years old, remains a valid general description of purposes. In contrast, my list of five purposes focus on other kinds of program descriptions based on historical analysis. The two descriptive lists are neither parallel nor identical, but neither are they contradictory.

The purposes identified serve as useful evidence that education for adults has many diverse purposes, just as it may be based on different philosophies. Logically, it follows that economic, political and social changes will interact with philosophies and purposes across time. Subsequently, it is rational to expect variations in the relative prominence and significance accorded to different purposes of education of adults.

In this discussion it was suggested that education for application, or for occupational reasons, is currently the ascendant purpose of education for adults in the United States. This is not to say that liberal education or education of adults for social change is dead. However, it is an observation that economic, social and political conditions are such that the occupational and applied emphases in the institutionally sponsored programs, and governmentally stimulated and encouraged education of adults, are now, or will be in the near future, the most important purposes of education. Importance is defined in terms of visibility level of support and numbers of participants.

The deepening relationship among government, higher education and industry have important implications for the education of adults. The significance of the relationship in terms of purposes of education, roles in education, and other consequences requires that the topic be given specific independent treatment in a separate chapter.

Six conceptualizations of adult education were noted. The ideas discussed include two of an ideological nature, one that relates to the practitioner and three that are structural in focus. Some questions about the concepts of adult education as a social movement, adult education as a voluntary activity, the adult education pyramid, and the marginal concept of adult education were noted. Other ideas included Moses' (1971) concept of the learning force that includes two educational systems, the core and periphery. Yet another concept of diffuse relationships in the education of adults was presented as a metaphoric contrast between the "vine" of adult education and the "trunk" of the traditional education system. It was observed that a structural change may be occurring. An alternative system that might be placed nearer to the core, but different from the traditional education system seems to be emerging. I have referred to this alternative system as the corporate system which is discussed further in chapter three.

PART TWO

CLIENTELE OF EDUCATION OF ADULTS

Three chapters in Part Two describe and discuss
three important foci of adult education programming
in the United States. As indicated in the
introduction to Part One and in chapter one the
kinds of educational programs provided through an
extensive network of agencies and organizations
defies comprehensive description. Therefore, for
the purposes of this book, one alternative was to
select one or more programmatic areas for
discussion. Three program areas that represent
three different kinds of clients and usually
different kinds of providers were selected for
discussion here.

Corporate education, gerontological education
and literacy education cannot be presented as
representative of education for adults in the
United States. But, perhaps, neither could any
other group of selections. Ultimately, these three
topics were selected because among themselves they
illustrate a range of philosophies, purposes and
providers of education for adults as discussed in
Part One.

Other candidates for possible discussion
include continuing professional education (CPE),
continuing higher education as distinct from CPE,
liberal education for adults, arts, crafts and
recreation or leisure education, personal
improvement or the human potential development
programs, corrections education, leadership
education and a host of others. The reader who is
interested in indepth discussions of the total
range of adult education programs, providers and
clients in the United States will need to dedicate

enormous time, effort and resources to searching out the literature.

In the meantime, most discussions of education for adults in the United States tend not to be encyclopedic but illustrative. This work, of necessity, follows that pattern.

Nevertheless, the three topics chosen are provocative. Issues abound in each area. Can government and schools solve the problem of illiteracy? How extensively can gerontological education be made available? and, what are the implications and consequences of corporate education?

Chapter Three

EDUCATION OF ADULTS IN THE CORPORATE IMAGE

Trying to make sense of the non-system of education
in which American adults participate is almost as
easy as unravelling a plate of tender spaghetti
with a pitchfork. As suggested in the previous
chapter, the many interests, institutions,
philosophies, purposes and actors involved are too
numerous to disentangle readily. No
classifications seem to be mutually exclusive. As
a result, all kinds of exceptions often exist to
most rules selected for explication and
clarification. Nevertheless, efforts must be made
to organize the chaos that characterizes the topic.
This chapter, thus, continues the attempt at
clarification initiated in chapter two.

A foundation for the discussion of corporate
influence was laid in the previous chapter. There
some of the important philosophies and purposes of
education of adults were identified and discussed.
Despite the absence of universal unanimous
agreement among the works cited and concepts
described, some consensus emerged. Moderate
agreement exists among the variety of philosophical
orientations reflected in the justifications for
the education of adults. There is also partial
agreement concerning the purposes of education for
adults. Thus, assuming rational human beings
devise and direct programs and activities that
contribute to the education of adults, some
agreement should exist among the philosophies,
purposes and program activity.

Philosophy contributes to purpose and purpose gives direction (or should provide direction) for the selection of a program design, format and consequences. None of the above is static, however. Each variable dynamically interacts with the other in a reciprocal fashion. As a result, the relationships among philosophy, purposes, programs and consequences are constantly being adjusted. Adjustment among the many parts that constitute the education of adults results in varying emphases and expectations concerning purposes of education and the nature of education institutions at different times.

The social context of the United States in the current decade is one where many changes are taking place at various levels among diverse segments of society. It is as difficult to agree upon the salient current event in the education of the adult as to agree upon the one purpose of education, but my vote is for what I have called education in the corporate image.

Conceptually, for purposes of simplicity, education of adults in the United States is the outcome of the interaction of four systems: the first is the postsecondary education system, the second is the corporate system, the third is the "other educative" system (really a non-system of numerous other agencies and organizations), the fourth system is composed on the consumers of the educational services and opportunities provided by the three educative systems. Each of the systems are open and dynamic systems that are sensitive to macro-social-political-economic input. The input from the macro-social level provides some kind of justification for education at all levels and for all ages. Following Moses' concept (1971), as discussed in the previous chapter, the learning force for the past 100 years was composed of two systems, the core (which would include the postsecondary systems proposed above) and the periphery (which would include the second and third systems noted above). The second system, which I have designated as the corporate system is an alternate to the postsecondary, core systemm, and will soon bridge the conceptual space between Moses' (1971) core and periphery. Unwittingly, it appears that the postsecondary system is providing important assistance to the development of the corporate system while simultaneously becoming increasingly competitive with it.

Figure 3:1 illustrates the relationship among the four systems discussed above. Solid lines in the figure represent direct relationships while broken lines suggest informal and indirect relationships. The so called nonsystem is that part of the educational environment composed of the numerous and varied agencies and organizations that are engaged in the business of education for diverse reasons and are not usually coordinated and/or regulated even though some of the agencies such as correspondence schools and some proprietary schools may be required to hold a state license or some other minimal requirement.

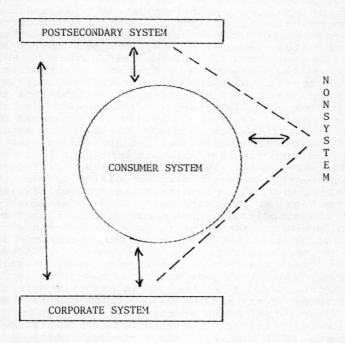

Figure 3:1. Four Inter-related Systems in the
Education of Adults in the United States

Three sources of energy are currently exerting pressure to give the alternate corporate system greater prominence, more power and a larger share of the education consumer system. The first of these sources of energy is the increasing focus on three activities: accountability, certification and measurement of competence in education of adults. The second energy source is the continuing loss of postsecondary education's monopoly on the college degree. The increasing acceptance of the concept of lifelong learning by the education consumer system is the third energizing element stimulating both systems.

It is helpful to examine each of the three energy sources in more detail. Let us begin with accountability, certification and measurement of competence. Accountability and the concept of competence are not new arrivals in the vocabulary of educators in the United States. The way in which the concepts are taking hold may be. It is obvious that the three ideas of accountability, certification and competence are, or could be, closely related. At this point in the narrative attention is directed to accountability and competence while a fuller discussion of certification follows near the end of the chapter. The growth of educational budgets and increasing public criticism of student and teacher performance, primarily aimed at, but not limited to the elementary and secondary schools, plus concerns about industrial production and national defense exerted great pressure to "prove" by examination that the schools were producing a product that met certain minimum standards. The wide differences of opinion that exists among citizens, educators and politicians concerning the objectives of childhood education does not deter the movement greatly. Perhaps the strongest source of the criticism of education was the declining SAT (Scholastic Achievement Test) scores between 1960 and 1980 and the interpretation put on them.

Briefly stated, the situation is as follows. Between 1963 and 1980 the SAT scores, often used for college admission, declined. The decreasing scores, in turn, were identified with a variety of other incidents concerning the verbal and math skills of young adults and were cited as evidence that the school systems in the nation were releasing an infirm product. Public concern about the academic abilities of high school graduates was easily translated into economic, and national defense questions. Numerous books (Flesch, 1955;

1981; Copperman,1978) addressed major educational concerns over the years. They in turn have been followed by an extensive list of reform oriented books and studies (Adler, 1982, Education Commission of the States, 1983, and Goodlad, 1984). Cetrone (1985) provides a handy analysis of the reform works.

Livingstone (1945) suggested the philosophy and expectations held for childhood education are reflected in what is envisioned for adult education. Stated in another way, if a society expects its childhood education provisions to emphasize occupational education and if that provision is marked by accountability and measurement, it is likely that the same characteristics will prevail in the education of adults. Often since the 1920s adult education in the United States has tended to be the conscience of education even though it has been in the periphery. But, if the periphery ceases to infuse the core and becomes only the recipient of ideas and philosophies that originate in the core, the historical relationship will change.

Recent developments in accountability and measurement in adult education confirms Livingstone's opinion. It is easy to see how corporations, which spend millions of dollars on educational and training programs for employees, desire to report to stockholders that a beneficial relationship exists between expenditures and corporation profits.

The second source of energy stimulating the growth of the alternative corporate education system is the result of postsecondary education's loss of its monopoly on certification via the college degree. For years higher education institutions were the only source of college degrees. The larger society accorded higher education the responsibility and authority to prepare young adults for their life's vocation and to certify their competence by a college degree. At a date yet hidden in historical archives, but perhaps within the past 50 years, a few corporate schools were given the authority to grant a "college" degree in specialized areas. Since then the trend developed slowly until the present. More is said on the topic of corporate college degrees later.

The third related energy source supporting the development of the alternative system is one that is also stimulating the traditional postsecondary system. It is the increasing awareness and

acceptance of the concept and practice of lifelong
learning. Evidence in support of the argument that
business management staff personnel are advocating
lifelong learning is provided by comments of a
corporate executive. John A. Young, President of
Hewlett-Packard Corp. recently said, "we should be
teaching our people how to learn. We can't
predict, with any certitude, exactly what skills
will be needed in the workforce of the future"
(1984, p. 72). He continued, "the age of 15 or 16
is just too young to effectively close off career
options and yet many of our young people have, in
essence, been allowed to attenuate their own
participation in a wide range of career options"
(1984, p. 72). To consolidate his position, Young
stated we need to examine the concept that learning
can be confined to just a short segment of our
lives. For example, a four-year period is simply
not enough time for the modern engineer to master
what he or she needs to know. The sheer bulk of
our knowledge has forced us to defer learning to
applications until later -- during the worklife of
the engineer. He also said . . . lifelong learning
is the only alternative to rapid obsolescence in
our industry. And the obsolescence of valuable
resources is a waste this nation cannot afford
(1984, p. 72).
      The development of the corporation college is
not incompatible with all of the philosophies,
purposes and conceptualizations of education for
adults as discussed in the second chapter. Its
emphasis appears to be incompatible with some,
however. The lack of philosophical consistency
does not necessarily arise from the sponsorship
difference, but emerges more directly from concepts
of purposes, goals and philosophy. Some of these
differences are discussed in the general discussion
section of this chapter.
      Several dangers are presented by the growth
and development of the corporation school for
adults. First, education increasingly may become
justified by the "bottom line" syndrome. (A
tendency to make all decisions based on the
relationship between assets and liabilities or
profit margins) Second, the traditional
educational system may be affected negatively
through competitive strategies that blur the
distinction between an education that at least pays
lip service to the wholeness of the human being and
an education designed only to equip the human as a
worker. Third, education of adults may become more
a means for constraining humanity than for

liberating it. The alternate system would find it difficult to serve the objectives of the American Idea as proposed by Kallen (1962) as discussed earlier.

The hazards noted in the above paragraph are not the rantings of a paranoid "educationist." The dominance of an exaggerated emphasis on the accountant's bottom line leads to a demonstrated direct relationship between an educational expenditure and an improvement in narrowly defined behaviors that account for an improved profit margin (or some other measurement in non-profit organizations). Such a view of education reduces the human to the status of a drone whose main purpose in life is to occupy a narrowly specialized place in a giant economic machine. Unfortunately, the pronouncements concerning education by the captains of American industry and even the U.S. tax laws concerning training expenditures reinforces the fears of the above rather than suggesting them to be the worst possible scenario.

It should be preferable to not be an alarmist as the long view indicates historically that even though changes in the popular mix among the purposes and providers of education for adults have occurred in the past, a reasonable balance has usually continued to exist. Yet, the evidence leads to the conclusion that the corporate approach to education is already well advanced and that the danger signals have substance. We should not panic, but should seek to become better informed about the development so that appropriate safe guards can be taken. Therefore, educators of adults and adult learners should find this topic instructive, if not a little disturbing. Four major elements in corporate trends in the education of adults lend themselves to provocative discussion. They are as follows: corporate trends in education, justifications of education, the corporate approach and corporate cooptation of education.

CORPORATE TRENDS

Having been unable to discover an old word or to coin a new one that adequately describes the philosophy and practice of adult education as perceived within the corporate trend, I have chosen to use the old familiar term, corporate. Corporate is used to connote an impersonal management approach to the education of adults. The focus is on results that are narrowly defined in terms of the primary goals of the organization. The enterprise that reflects the above characteristics need not be a profit making one, neither is it necessary for it to be legally constituted as a corporation according to state laws. For example, a professional association or a non-profit voluntary organization could meet the above criteria. In fact, one of the topics to be discussed later considers the possibility that many public and private postsecondary education institutions may be employing management procedures that apply equally well in the profit making arena.

Decisions within corporations are usually perceived to be logical, if somewhat mechanical formula based and devoid of emotion and altruism. Individuals noted as being successful leaders of corporations are often described as "hardheaded, no nonsense" types. They earn such flattering titles as the one Casper Weinburger received when, as a secretary of a large governmental department, he became known as "Cap the Knife." Decisions are perceived as being made with one question in mind, what is best for the organization? The meaning of that question may often also be translated into what is best for the officers of the organization, including academic adminstrators (Duggar,1974)? It is obvious that the stuff of corporate decisions is in stark contrast with the basis of decision making that characterizes a more humane philosophy. Individuals in such a context are not really regarded as people normally are, they are transposed into the category of resources. They are resources that are instrumental in the achivement of corporate goals. Goals, which may be, or may not be consistent with many social needs. Hence, people in the corporate context are equated with other resources such as wordprocessing equipment, heavy industrial materials, transportation facilities and capital. Unlike some of the other resources, however, people sometimes can be modified (through training or education) as organizational needs change. New skills can be developed among existing employees and when this can be done less expensively than by hiring new workers it is best for the company to sponsor the training. When new workers can provide the required labor less expensively than the older experienced workers can after training, the company decision often favors the decision to fire and hire rather than train.

As provided by the definition given above, corporate management behavior is not limited to the profit making sector of the economy. Government also has a similar perception of people as resources to be used in the achievement of specific national goals. The United States Federal government is not usually identified as a competent planner. Nevertheless, national policy decisions that have implications for educational goals concerning the role of people in the achievement of policy goals are made. Two examples that readily come to mind are goals on the areas of defense and space. It seems as if government learned attitudes and related strategies from the business community. Two of the most visible management specialists whose influence has been widespread in government are the late James Webb, former boss of NASA and Robert McNamara, Secretary of Defense during the administration of President Kennedy and Johnson. If the skills, knowledge and world view believed to be necessary for success in business are perceived to be appropriate in the federal government, is it not unlikely that they will also be duplicated in other forms of governmental and bureaucratic organizations such as education?

Thus, government and corporations are perceived to be controlled by accountants, or at least by the mentality of individuals whose decision making process is consistent from organization to organization despite differences in missions that may exist. Human capital is an important element in the corporate accounting procedures and education is a means of modifying the productive output of each individual. There is likely to be some special justification for education of adults in a society dominated by corporations. Additional comments on this important topic are provided later.

JUSTIFICATION

The justification for education in the United States is a continuing process. Each generation reviews and debates the goals of education in some shape and fashion. It is not always an organized debate but it is usually protracted and complex. The dialogue and the consequent justifications of education for all age groups are reflected in the change from religious motives of the seventeenth and eighteenth centuries to the current specialized secular rational for education. While the pattern from 1700 to the present has not been a harmonious one, certain elements in the warp and woof of the fabric of education have been more or less consistent. For example, education has become increasingly secular and less religious in justification, provision and content. The secularization of education has been paralleled by increasing occupational justifications. The theme of occupational education has been played on various instruments across three centuries with different volume and lyrics, but it has always been discernible. Earlier the theme was related to religion while in more recent times they have been based on national development and national defense.

To continue the musical metaphor, the melody in the education of children and adults in the United States in the current period is a derivation of occupational skill development for economic reasons and the harmony is provided by the national defense justification. The economic and political world climate since World War II has contributed greatly to the emergence of an economic-political coalition in the United States composed of business and industry, government and postsecondary education. Increasingly, the goals and motives of the members of the coalition have converged. Education of adults is, thus, increasingly justified in language that is common to this coalition.

As the interests of business and industry, government and postsecondary education converged, a high degree of blending has taken place. Specialists move among the three institutional forms with increasing ease and frequency. Managers and planners and scientists are equally at home in research laboratories, governmental bureaucracy, corporate offices and university administration. Presidents, chancellors and deans in education institutions employ administrative procedures and attitudes lifted directly from the board room and executive suite while executives of large corporations move freely from Wall Street to the White House and sit on higher education institution boards of control. Thus, it should be no shock to discover that higher education, one of the major providers of systematic education for adults in the United States, has adopted a corporate approach in resolving educational issues and in directing the mission and activities of its institutions.

The permeability of the boundary between educational and corporate administration is quite

high. Despite regular news reports of the
frequency of white collar crime and unethical
behavior within the corporate setting, Americans
greatly respect the successful business leader. As
a result, businessmen and women have long been
favorite candidates as board members and
policymakers for public schools and postsecondary
institutions (private and public). It is assumed
that these kinds of people have a particular skill
and gift for efficiency and cost containment, i.e.,
they can operate an educational institution and
show a profit.

The cult of efficiency is not a new or recent
phenomenon in American education. It emerged in the
early years of the current century and even though
some of the principles and procedures that were
typical of the early application to public school
issues have been discredited, the notion has not
faded from the American psyche. Evidence of the
faith that politicians and the general public
frequently place in the American captains of
industry is found in the frequency of their
employment as chief administrative officers of
higher education institutions. The following
excerpt of an editorial concerning the recent
appointment of a new President of the University of
Florida illustrates this point:

> . . . in searching for a replacement for
> departing President Robert Marston, they
> (Florida Board of Regents) passed over many
> candidates with academic backgrounds in favor
> of Marshall Criser, a UF (University of
> Florida) graduate who rose to prominence in
> Florida's political business-legal
> establishment. (Gainesville Sun, August 20,
> 1984, p. 10A)

Despite the apparent editorial approval of
businessman Criser, the newspaper cautioned that a
philosophical divide separates higher education
from the private sector. Consequently, Criser is
urged to avoid the temptation to de-emphasize
liberal arts as the university tailors its
educational programs "to better serve the needs of
business and industry" (p. 10A). Similarly, the
new administration is reminded that the teaching of
students, particularly undergraduates, is paramount
and must be kept in mind while the faculty are
encouraged to engage in more private research and
consulting duties. Finally, the editorial writer
warns that conflicts of interest must be guarded

against as the motive forces of industry and a university are not the same.

The relationship among business and industry, government and postsecondary education is not, however, absolutely harmonious. There is a constant tension among the three partners as each attempts to improve its position. Often, at the expense of one of the other partners. As a consequence, government seeks to regulate and control higher education and industry. Each of these institutions naturally resists the efforts of the other two. In turn, higher education and business and industry occasionally compete with each other for governmental grants and influence in other ways. Continuing education is one of those areas in which higher education and industry are competing with growing intensity. The competitive position in which postsecondary education and industry find themselves is one of the sources of pressure for education to adopt corporate strategies and behaviors as discussed in previous sections of this chapter. Yet, competition among government, higher education and industry has not prevented the three institutions from seeking common ground and cooperating in a number of areas that are perceived to be mutually advantageous.

COOPERATION AND COMPETITION

Anyone viewing the current relationship between postsecondary education and industry must observe that both cooperation and competition distinguishes the relationship between them, or else their perspective would be incomplete. Declining student enrolments and fewer federal dollars for research has stimulated postsecondary education administrators to turn to business and industry for additional students and research dollars. Simultaneously, consulting organizations and other entrepreneurial organizations have increased their competition for government money and for additional clients for expanding training and personal development schemes. It is no secret that higher education has stepped up its efforts to obtain assistance from business and industry. The competitive struggle is less obvious. Yet, examples of both are available should one care to search for them.

Cooperation

There is extensive evidence to support the contention of a merging of interests and goals among governments, higher education and industry. The following comments made by one large university president (Davison, 1982) is representative. Davison, President of the University of Georgia, had the following comments to make at a national meeting. Among other things he said: "Cooperation between institutions of higher education and the business world is an appropriate subject for discussion." (p. 1)

"Higher education has been hamstrung by inertia where its relationships with the industrial world are concerned. We have been timid in developing the kind of relationships with business that we eagerly embraced with government. And those relationships, as I have said, have been highly productive for the benefit of our citizens at large." (p. 2)

Davison's next remark is especially illuminating and supportive of the argument developed in this chapter. He said, "we must now develop and enhance our ties to the business-industrial world. We, as the land grant and publicly assisted institutions of higher education, must forge business links of the type we have had with agri-business for decades."(p.3)

In preparing this chapter, almost ten typewritten pages of suitable quotes in Davison's speech to support the thesis of enhanced efforts of higher education to win the support of business and industry were identified. They included such observations as "many higher education institutions see the corporate world as a new source of funding . . ." "higher education . . . should have moved to establish a strong interface with the business world many years ago . . ." ". . . our country can no longer afford the luxury of separate intellectual components . . . that do not communicate." Davison's speech is recommended reading for the unconvinced.

Davison is true to his beliefs. In April of 1985 the University of Georgia announced the appointment of a founder and former chief executive officer of Agrigentics Corporation, as Bicentennial University Professor in the Management Department of the University's College of Business Administration. His duties were described as follows:

He . . . will conduct a seminar . . . on the
need for strengthened relationships between
American universities and the country's
industrial community. He is also expected to
work with ...adminstrators and faculty...in
exploring ways the university can take a
leadership role in the advocacy of reform in
the U. S. tax laws which would favor
stronger ties between industry and university
research (Columns, 1985,pp.1-3).

Davison's view of the social context in which
universities are operating is reflected by others
(Adult and CE Today, 1984; Chronicle of Higher
Education, June 27, 1984a). Advertisements for
personnel appearing in the Chronicle of Higher
Education (August 1, 1984b, pp. 41 and 43) provide
interesting evidence of the trend.   Stephen J.
Trachtenberg, president of the University of
Hartford, is cited by the Gainesville Sun (August
20, 1985) as indicating the need for a new kind of
leadership in higher education is called for as
"educators . . .leave their towers and go
hat-in-hand to corporate boardrooms . . . ." (p.
10A).

Florida Board of Regents Chairman Robin Gibson
also looks to the business community as the savior
of American higher education. He is quoted in the
Gainesville Sun (August 20,1985) as saying "state
government can afford to give us a good university
system, but state government cannot afford to give
us an excellent state university system" (p. 10A).
To achieve greatness and a national reputation
Gibson believes the University of Florida must turn
to private business and industry for additional
research and developmental support.

Other evidence of the increasing interest of
educators in linkages with business is provided by
the numerous conferences being held on the topic.
A recent brochure to come across my desk that
illustrates this point. It advertises an "A to Z
conference on working with Business and Industry."
The conference title was "College and Business:
Building on a Successful Partnership." Conference
participants were scheduled to address the
following topics: (a) getting started: making it
work; (b) how to improve your marketing strategy;
(c) building quality assurance for training
programs; (d) expanding programs and opportunities
for training; and (e) combining resources for
better worker productivity. The proliferation of
conferences of this type designed for higher

education personnel supplements some of Davison's rhetoric quoted above. One interesting question facing higher education faculty, staff and administration is "when does marketing become soliciting?

Competition

The individual who has been sleeping away the past twenty years, as Rip Van Winkle, may be surprised to see the terms competition and higher education used in the same sentence. A more alert person would not be startled by the suggestion that higher education institutions compete among themselves in areas other than athletics (Deitch, 1981). But, a larger number may be a little amused and surprised by the suggestion that universities and corporations are engaged in a battle for students.

Competition between higher education and industry is primarily of two kinds: competition in instructional activity and research. While both kinds of competition have practical theoretical implications, the primary concern here is with their mutual interests in instruction. Some educators of adults have been sensitive to the implications posed by large scale involvement of business and industry in education and training for a number of years. More than twenty years ago White (1962) indicated that he was uneasy about the trend that he identified then. More recently Stern (1983) raised additional warnings about competition among providers of education for adults. Brickell and Aslanian (1981) observed "the 1980's may see 300 colleges... which are running out of high school graduates... close their doors while 300 company colleges open theirs. Had the railroads, it is said, realized their business was not trains but transportation, they would own the airlines today rather than being out of the passenger business. Some of the established colleges have not decided that their business is education, not 18 year-olds. Thus, they leave the companies to educate their own adult workers"(p. 37). Thus, two areas of competition among higher education institutions and corporations that focuses on students will probably become sharper in the next decade. Continuing education, a kind of education for adults, is one area of intensifying competition. For example, it is rumored that some of large private and even quasi-governmental organizations are planning to open their internal management education programs to outsiders. More large corporations are expected to follow their lead in specialized areas. A second area of competition was also noted by Brickell and Anslanian: competition in the awarding of college degrees.

More recent communication with Aslanian (1985) indicates that the above prediction was a valid one. More is said on this later in this chapter.

An uneasy truce between education and the corporation will probably exist as long as education can do the following: (a) provide education less expensively (through governmental support of the educational establishment) than the corporation; and (b) provide the specialized education that meets the needs of the corporation. When governmental support declines, or some other event occurs that weakens the cost advantage or when higher education can no longer adequately and effectively provide the specialized instruction desired by the corporation, the corporation will increase its continuing education activity. A second step in the process leads to the development of the corporate college in the very large business organizations.

Despite the increasing transfer of management strategies and attitudes from the corporation to education, education generally has maintained a competitive position. This has been so for at least three reasons: (a) education has a carryover impact into the corporation world, it continues to have the reputation as the main source of college degrees; (b) education has access to a multiplicity of specialists at a competitive price as a consequence of state and federal assistance, private institutions derive similar benefits from endowments; and (c) more higher education institutions are adopting various schemes to enrol more adults. Yet, it can be observed, in the language that is being used more frequently by both parties, the corporation has penetrated the education market. Demographic trends in the United States and formula funding schemes in public education based on enrolment stimulated postsecondary education to seek new consumers. Thus, the adult, 25 years of age and older, was identified as a consumer by institutions that previously had little interest in anyone over 23 years of age. At about the same time, the corporations began to more aggressively cast an eye at education for adults as a subsidiary area of interest. This has contributed to a trend of corporate cooperation. However, another development preceded the cooporation, that was the adoption of the corporate approach in the management of higher education.

CORPORATE APPROACH

A second element in the emergence of the corporate image in education of adults in the United States is the corporate management approach to education, as briefly noted earlier, but which requires additional elaboration. The corporate approach is defined as the adoption of decision making procedures, establishment of priorities, a product oriented climate and general management strategies based on concepts and principles of business and industry rather than education. The drift in the direction of the corporate approach to education of adults was signalled more than 20 years ago when Knowles (1962) identified six broad "genetic principles" that he believed to guide the development of adult education institutions.

Taken collectively, several of Knowles' genetic principles imply that needs for adult education emerge from society and that they emerge in an episodic manner. Furthermore, he indicates that institutional forms that develop in response to the erratically emerging needs are frequently short-lived unless they become attached to multi-purpose agencies. Higher education institutions and corporations are such agencies that can provide the kind of sophisticated structural and functional differentiation perceived as being necessary. Finally, the residual institutions fail to be centrally associated with any kind of generalized adult education movement, according to Knowles. The configuration of principles provided by Knowles is far from simple and it requires more than just a cursory observation; it seems to present a good explanatory structure for partially understanding the issue of education in the corporate image.

Three characteristics of education of adults as identified Knowles' principles are associated directly with corporate functions: stability of a market, needs of consumers and structural differentiation. Administrative and organizational similarities of corporations and education institutions are interesting, but the substance these structures represent are even more interesting. An immediate parallel is noted between Knowles' observations about the episodic nature of emerging needs in adult society and the needs of large organizations in education and business. The similarity between corporate goals of achieving stability between prices and production through detailed planning and marketing processes and related activities conducted by educational institutions is a significant topic for discussion.

Consider Knowles' suggestion that needs emerge from society and that institutions of adult education sequentially and logically flow from such emerging needs. Up to a point, one might agree with such a model that represents needs as an independent variable and institutions of adult education (and their programs) as the dependent variable. The model of emerging needs and institutional responses to address them is quite popular in adult education literature (Long, 1983b). For at least 50 years, leaders in the education of adults have promoted the idea that adult needs and wants provide the energy for educational programming for adults. A major enterprise of the adult education field has developed from this idea. Needs assessment is frequently a common buzz word in the conversation and papers of educators of adults. In keeping with the title of this book, it is appropriate to offer a different and possibly new perspective of the model.

A different, but not entirely original, point of view suggests that needs and wants are rather amorphous and malleable; because of their vagueness and sensitivity to suggestion needs are unstable sources of psychic energy. Consequently, decisions concerning needs and wants are often made for individuals by others who are in a position of authority or power where they command sufficient resources to mold needs and wants, if not correct them. As a result, what emerges may be related to the original psychic need, but not necessarily be it. An example at the physical level is to use advertising and social custom to modify the need for food until specific dietary patterns that favor certain food products are preferred while other foods are practically eliminated. Other illustrations of how the latent energy of needs and wants has been directed to selected and predetermined ends are provided in the kinds of automobiles we drive, the housing we expect and even what we believe to be important to know. The need to know about computers and how to operate them is closely associated with their increasing availability and production costs. The greater the need in society, real or imagined, for computers the larger the market. Profits and growth are, in turn, associated with how well the machines and software are sold to the general population. This position does not deny the importance of needs and wants as a source of energy. It does suggest that the individual may not be in control when needs and wants are supposedly used to develop products or educational programs that are designed to address them. Thus, it is possible that the energy produced by needs and wants can be successfully channelled or directed by others.

Therefore, if educational needs and wants are episodic in "their natural" state, and if they are sufficiently malleable to be directed, it is possible to use advertising and other means to develop a relatively stable need. Stability of the molded or the created needs is important to planners of education as it is to planners of other products. Consequently, the alternate view suggests that if needs do contribute to the development of selected adult education institutions and programs at a particular time, it is also possible that institutions eventually contribute to the identification and modification of educational needs. Subsequently, educational institutions design programs to address the modified needs. To the unconvinced, it need only be asked, if it works in the area of fashion is it realistic to deny that the same process cannot be used to influence education?

Elsewhere (Long, 1974), it is argued that pressures for acceptance of lifelong learning emerge from three sources (a) human characteristics, (b) social and technological change, and (c) institutional needs. Human characteristics that contribute to the pressures to accept the notion of lifelong learning are believed to be intrinically associated with being human (Fromm, 1955; Murphy, 1958). Many of the same qualities that contribute to the distinctiveness of homo sapiens-- those things that make us human-- contribute to a basic human need to learn. Actually, one might argue that more primitive forms of this organic need are found in other life forms as well. But, at least for humans, it exists at a level and intensity that requires fulfilment in some form for the maintenance and development of acceptable human qualities of life. This view

71

derives its support from a variety of religious and philosophical sources.

The idea that social and technological change exert pressures favoring the acceptance of lifelong learning philosophies and actions is rampant in the education literature in the United States. Social commentators such as Toffler (1970; 1980) and others have written at length on this point. It is evident in the continuing elongation of the period of schooling for American youth. It is the basic argument for all kinds of training and retraining schemes. Individuals and institutions justify educational activities for adults in language that emphasizes social and technological change.

Limited attention has been directed to the view that pressures for lifelong learning are stimulated by institutional motives. It is unlikely, however, that any reasonably comprehensive and accurate discussion of the education of adults in the United States could proceed without a consideration of institutional forces.

Institutional needs that result in the education of adults are of three classes: (a) the needs of social, political and economic institutions that demand knowledgeable and skilled personnel; (b) the needs of educational institutions that are associated with student enrollments and related revenue and growth requirements; and (c) the needs of the educational materials industry. Each of these classes of institutional needs are translated into activities designed for the education of adults. In turn, it is possible educational programs are often designed, first to address the three classes of institutional needs, and secondly, to meet the needs of individuals. Unfortunately, there is the possibility that Galbraith's (1967) description of planned needs may also apply to the educational sector.

Galbraith's (1967) popular book provides one view of modern economic life and changes that were then shaping the future. Even though it is said that the United States is now in the post-industrial age, many of Galbraith's ideas continue to be valid and perhaps even more so in some instances. In his book he begins with the world of advanced technology, highly specialized manpower, and the five or six hundred giant corporations that bring them into use. He illustrates how the firms supply themselves with capital, how the managers are motivated, and how organized intelligence replaced ownership as the source of power in the modern enterprise. Importantly, for our consideration, he shows how the market declined as a guiding influence in economic life, to be replaced in large measure by planned decisions concerning what will be produced, at what price and for whom.

Two major points are made by Gailbraith that support the thesis that postsecondary education, in its provision of education for adults, has adopted important strategies from business and government. He says "the need to control consumer behavior is a requirement of planning" (p. 201). Furthermore, he observes," . . . as the industrial system develops to the point where it has need for planning and the management of the consumer that this requires, it is also serving wants which are psychological in origin and hence admirably subject to management by appeal to the psyche" (p. 201). It might be useful to be reminded here of Knowles' fifth genetic principle noted earlier: planning is a central element in the contemporary educational administration. It is not illogical to see the parallel between planning processes in multi-million dollar businesses and multi-million dollar educational institutions. Neither can easily survive in an economy of wide episodic fluctuations in demands for their products and services.

Galbraith's second point that attracts our attention is his description of the governmental-industrial axis. His account is especially provocative and should be of interest to the administrator, planner, philosopher and provider of educational activities for adults. He is of the opinion that government in the industrial state can be understood only in light of the needs and goals of modern large scale organizations. Even though Galbraith failed to include the large scale educational institutions in his book, it is appropriate for us to include both individual institutions and systems of higher education in his concept. The needs and goals of large-scale organizations have significant implications for trade unions, political parties, education and the larger culture. We should be deluded if we failed to see the relationship between education and what Galbraith calls "technocrats." We should be extremely naive if we failed to recognize that education itself, while some individual institutions may be small, is collectively a very large-scale activity in the United States. Spring

73

(1976) notes after World War II education emerged as a national institution comparable to government. Furthermore, we should be amiss if we believe the administrators (managers) of the extremely large (and perhaps the small, as well) universities are radically different in motivation from their counterparts in business. At one large university they/faculty have suggested renaming it XYZ corporation (insert the name of the institution where I have written XYZ). If, then, the technocrats that manage the educational enterprise are not radically different from those in business, Galbraith's conceptualizations should enlighten understanding of such topics as educational planning and consumer (student or client) manipulation.

Finally, for the person who remains unconvinced that the ideas of needs and needs assessment as frequently discussed in the literature of adult education fail to reflect contemporary corporate reality, look to the marketing literature. If I understand Galbraith, marketing and planning are parallel activities in the large enterprise. Marketing is a means for supporting the planning goals associated with production and profits. Surprisingly, a review of literature in the 1950s and the 1960s revealed an absence of references to marketing education for adults (Long, 1983b). In contrast, marketing has emerged as one of the key terms among educators of adults in the current decade (Long, 1983b; Stern, 1983). Marketing is one way the corporations have attempted to gain control over prices and production, key elements in the industrial corporation's goals according to Galbraith (1967). Non-profit organizations, including postsecondary education institutional provisions for traditional and non-traditional education opportunities have responded to the piper of marketing strategies. The adoption of marketing schemes by educational organizations is symptomatic of the change that has occurred over the past 60 years in the education of American adults.

Postsecondary education has not only assumed some of the practices of business in recent years, the assumption of educational roles by business is equally important. This topic is discussed in the next section of this chapter.

CORPORATE COOPTATION

If education at all levels is increasingly justified in terms of certain goals supported by corporations, and if the environment of post secondary education is increasingly similar to that of industry, the next step in the emerging corporate image should come as no surprise. The third element in the process is the cooptation of education of adults by corporations.

Involvement of non-educational agencies and institutions in education of adults in the United States has a long and rich history. The multitude of agencies, institutions and organizations providing educational opportunities for adults complicates the conceptualization and discussion of the field. One can find numerous classifications schemes such as those offered by Liveright (1968) and Peterson (1979) and this writer (1983b). The following six part classification framework seems to adequately cover most needs for understanding: (a) educational institutions; (b) business and industry; (c) church and religious organizations; (d) governmental agencies; (e) professional associations, and (e) voluntary and civic organizations.

Recent moves of corporations into education of adults, however, appear to be of sufficient magnitude to represent a historical shift that requires comment. The involvement of business and industry in the education of adults has recently gone beyond its more or less traditional involvement in non-credit activity and on-the-job training. A variety of educational schemes abound in the corporate setting. They range from on-the-job training to staff development programs, from new employee orientation to tuition repayment plans, and from non-credit instruction to college degree programs. Companies involved in such educational activities range from small ones to the very largest corporations in the world. They include such giants as AT&T, General Motors, Hewlett Packard, Holiday Inns, IBM, National Cash Register and Xerox, to name a few.

Educational programs sponsored by business and industry are often well financed. For example, before the court ordered divestiture, AT&T spent over $1 billion on its vast education and training program. IBM's 1984 outlay for education is estimated at $700 million (Sirkin, 1985). The Xerox educational center in Virginia is reputed to have one of the most modern conference facilities in the U.S. Equipment used in educational programs at the General Motors Institute is more up-to-date than similar equipment found in most educational institutions. National Cash Register has found it necessary to develop a special computer program to maintain the education records of its employees.

The scope of the educational programs supported by corporations and similar business firms is broad. Eurich (1985) estimates nearly $60 billion a year is spent on corporate run education, making it similar to the cost of the nation's four year colleges and universities. Peterson (1979) estimated approximately 11 million students were enrolled in colleges and universities in 1979. It is believed that a larger number of adults are now annually participating in company sponsored education programs (Eurich, 1985). Thus, corporate education includes about the same number of individuals as are enrolled in all the American public and private higher education institutions from first year students to postgraduate students. Population projections suggest the very strong possibility that corporate education may soon exceed the size of postsecondary education in this country. The current estimate places the number served in corporate education and college and universities as being equal (Higher Education Daily, January 28, 1985). These projections indicate the relative size of younger population compared with the population of older adults will decline. Simultaneously, the saturation point in college attendance may have already been reached in most states. These forces will likely result in a rather stable or slightly declining higher education population in the foreseeable future. During the same period the number of workers and customers of the corporations will increase. Simply stated, the pool from which higher education institutions traditionally draw their students will not increase as rapidly as will the population from the business firms can draw their adult students.

The most radical development in corporate education for adults has taken place in the development of the corporate college. Information on this development is sketchy and difficult to acquire because of differences in accreditation procedures, but the limited information available suggests the trend may be much stronger than is commonly thought. One study has identified 18 accredited corporate colleges as of the end of 1984 with five corporations planning at least nine more (Eurich, 1985). The same report estimates that 20 more college level degree programs will be available by 1988. Even if a complete list of all corporate colleges in the United States were available, it would not be feasible to list them here. Additional evidence of the cooptation trend is presented by Brickell and Aslanian (1981) and Urich (1985).

Further evidence of the cooptation trend is found in the numbers of courses offered by business and government that are acceptable for college credit. According to one source, these kinds of courses increased from 0 in 1973 to 1790 in 1982 (U.S. News & World Report, 1982, p. 69). Trends reported are as follows: 1973, the number of courses was zero; in 1976 the number was 245; by 1979 the number rose to 962; then by 1982 an 86 percent increase was noted as 1790 courses were being offered.

GENERAL DISCUSSION

This chapter division includes a variety of subtopics related to, but not included in, the other chapter sections. Rather than discuss these items extensively, it seemed more appropriate to combine comments about them in a general category.

The trend to and penchant for some kind of certificate to confirm one's learning, for example, seems to be closely associated with changes occurring in education of adults since 1950. This phenomenon is somehow associated with two things, first the growth and expansion of the U.S. economy and big business following the beginning of World War II and the development of modern personnel administration practices. As the labor force expanded and employers were challenged to find new ways to screen and select employees for both employment and advancement, certificates attesting to one's education and training were useful documents. They became increasingly important testimony of an individual's abilities. As educational institutions were the primary agency in American society for the initial screening and selecting of individuals for the labor force, certificates from educational institutions were accorded significant recognition. Hence, certificates of completion, graduation and attendance of selected educational activities became valuable to both the individual who hoped to turn the document into an improved salary and to the employer who could base decisions on documented educational activity. Of course, the certificate syndrome was of value to the educational institutions who could use their authority to award such letters of achievement to consolidate their hegemony over education of adults.

Historically, educational achievement has been rewarded, though sometimes unevenly, in the United States. A doctrine instilled in almost every middle class family was "go to school and improve your income." After World War II the American's faith in the relationship between education and one's income permeated society. In the 1960s college retirement and programs designed to keep young adults in school were directly based on data that reported income advantages associated with persistence in education. High school diplomas were the minimum requirement for employment, then the baccalaureate degree became the key to better white collar jobs. As the years have passed since 1945, the pre-employment education level of education has continued to rise. An increasing interest in additional symbols of educational achievement became associated with rising educational levels. Occupational areas that did not formerly require degrees turned to certificates as a way of distinguishing individuals in fields such as insurance and real estate.

Postsecondary education responded to the drive for certified learning on two levels. The 1960s and the 1970s were a time when non-traditional degree programs expanded. All kinds of modifications were made to make it easier for adults to obtain college degrees. Parallel developments kept pace in the nondegree continuing education programs where diverse schemes were devised to award some kind of recognition for participating in noncredit educational activities.

As a result, today there are at least three streams in the education of adults: one stream is composed of degree work; another stream of certificate stream; the third stream is what I have called the noncertificate stream. The important point that emerges from this discussion is that economic reasons seemed to have stimulated the development of an attitude and a system closely associated with the provision of educational merit badges that are honored by the corporation. More is said about certificates and nontraditional approaches later in this book.

A second general topic related to corporate influence on education of adults is the distinction among the three systems that interact in the macrosystem of education for adults: the postsecondary education system, the corporate system and the consumer system. The first two systems have a major common element: the provision of certificates or degrees which have currency in the corporate economy and which are desired by many of the individuals in the third system.

The three systems reflect different foci in learning. The postsecondary education system is bifocal. By that, it is meant that learning activities are of two kinds. One kind is directly related to work or to corporate needs, whereas, the other kind is designed to help the individual become a better person who lives a fuller and richer life as a result. Postsecondary education institutions suffer from this schizophrenic division of purpose.

In contrast, the corporate system is monofocal, its interest is limited to better job performance, according to Theodore Settle, Director of the Management and Career Development Center at NCR's Dayton, Ohio headquarters. Quoted by Brickell and Aslanian (1981), he says, "colleges that want to work with companies will have to seek company business, study company needs, adjust curriculum content, modify time schedules, teach exceedingly well and remember that what a company values most is training that shows up in better job performance" (p. 37).

The difference between the two systems have important implications for the future. If postsecondary education makes the effort to develop the kind of relations that Davison (1982) encourages, as quoted earlier, and if Settle's description of what is needed is accurate, postsecondary education institutions will turn away from the general education that is narrowly occupational in focus to even more specific instruction that will vary according to the companies that education seeks to serve. Of course, the company colleges face a similar dilemma. In their origins they had to consider their instructional problems from only one company's perspective. As they "put their show on the road" and attempt to serve other companies, they many find that their narrow focus is too self-centered.

The third system, composed of the adult consumer of educational opportunity traditionally has contained two educational options. One possibility was to turn to the relatively rich, structured and organized opportunities provided by

postsecondary education institutions and other
sponsoring organizations. But, if the educational
goal included a degree or certificate the choices
were limited. The second option was learning free,
but that was often limited to a few sources of
print media and later the confining schedules of
educational radio and television. Autonomy,
however, had its costs. Opportunities, based on
independent learning, to obtain a recognized degree
were extremely limited or nonexistent.

The consumer system is no longer limited to a
few opportunities. Modern electronic technology
and print media have broadened the opportunities
for the person who wishes to control the time,
place and to a degree the content of learning.
But, there is a disadvantage when this person needs
a certificate to pass through a selection gate in
the world of work.

SUMMARY

Education of adults in the United States is a
multifaceted phenomenon. It is difficult to
describe, hard to classify and is constantly
adjusting to changing social, economic and
political realities. This chapter is devoted to
one of the major adjustments currently in progress.
It concerns the development of an alternative
system of education and the modification of the
existing postsecondary system. Different terms
have been used to refer to the alternate system.
The corporate or business identity is common to the
terms used, however.

Introductory comments attempted to place
educational programs and activities within
parameters determined by philosophies and purposes
of education as discussed in chapter two. It was
noted that the energy being exerted to modify the
existing postsecondary education system and to
create the alternative corporate system arises from
three sources: (a) trends in accountability and
measurement; (b) postsecondary education's loss of
its monopoly of awarding degrees; and (c) the
development of the corporate college.

Dangers associated with the emergence of the
alternate system (or even the extensive
modification of the current postsecondary education
system) are associated with the bottom-line
syndrome that reduces education to those things
that develop the human worker as opposed to
developing the human being. Six other major topics

were discussed in the chapter, they are (a) corporate trends; (b) justification of education; (c) cooperation and competition; (d) the corporate approach in education; (e) corporate cooptation; and (f) general discussion.

Briefly summarized, the above six topics were addressed by providing a description and discussion of the emergence of the corporate trend in education and the attitudes toward humans represented in the trend. It was noted that people are dehumanized in the process and become identified as resources that can be treated just as the inanimate resources that the corporation uses to achieve its goals. The major difference between the human resources and the capital and equipment resources is the renewable quality that the human possess. Renewal through education and training recommends their use in corporate strategies. It was suggested that business, government and higher education currently constitute a coalition wherein continuous tension for supremacy exists. Exchanges of personnel among the three units and the adoption of common management practices and philosophy often make them more alike than different. Competition and cooperation characterizes the relationships between the three, especially business and education. While postsecondary education has been emulating business, the corporation has pilfered some of what was originally postsecondary education's turf. In recent years more and more corporations have established their own credit and noncredit colleges. Postsecondary education institutions, to keep their corporate clients, have been challenged to modify their practices to meet the educational goals of the corporations and similar nonprofit organizations.

In the general discussion it was noted that the move toward some kind of certificate or eventually a college degree as a reward for adult learning expanded rapidly after World War II. The interaction between the corporation's needs and the fiscal and growth requirements of postsecondary education complemented each other. Finally, it was suggested that in reality there are at least three major interacting systems to be contended with in this discussion. They are the postsecondary education system, the corporate system and the consumer system. The educational goals of the first two are similar, but not identical. The postsecondary system continues to be more general in contrast to the company orientation of the corporate system. In turn they commonly control access to degrees to which the consumer (learners) system aspires. The individual members of the consumer system have a variety of choices in their educational pursuits as long as they have no desire for some kind of certificate. The other two systems continue to control access to the college degree.

Chapter Four

NEW PERSPECTIVES ON THE EDUCATION OF THE ELDERLY IN THE UNITED STATES

Bradley C. Courtenay and Huey B. Long

Perhaps the newest clientele with the greatest potential for the providers of education in the United States is the elderly. That assertion becomes even more significant if one includes education of the elderly in the concept of educational gerontology, "the study and practice of instructional endeavors for and about the aged and aging" (Peterson, 1980, p. 67). Thus, following Peterson, education for the elderly would extend beyond these individuals who are chronologically beyond 55 to individuals who are not yet "older adults" to individuals who work with older adults. In short, almost the entire United States population could be included in this clientele group.

To examine such a group in one chapter would be next to impossible, if not unfeasible. Therefore, the focus of this chapter will be education for the older adult. This definition includes any learning opportunity provided for or by the older adult. An inclusive, comprehensive perspective is suggested: formal coursework at an institution of higher education; informal, personal enrichment classes at a senior center; independent study; adult basic education classes to learn to read or receive a Graduate Equivalent Diploma (GED); workshops on retirement planning; skill development for a new job and so forth.

Two primary terms will be used to refer to this clientele: elderly and older adult. Both appear to be more acceptable to the clientele and avoid the condescending impression of senior citizen, aged, or old person.

Universally, elderly and older adults continue to be defined chronologically. Because of the need for compatibility in reporting data, the chronological definition will also be employed in this chapter. As noted earlier, an older adult is defined as the individual who is 55 years of age or older. The reader is cautioned against adoption of such a definition for general discussion of the elderly. Ideally and realistically, care should be taken to consider the physiological, behavioral and sociological dimensions when referring to older persons. Even a single chronological age is no longer reliable when drawing general implications about education for older adults. Recent published statistics on the elderly distinguish four groups (U.S. Senate Special Committee on Aging, 1984): older population (age 55 plus), the elderly (age 65 plus), the aged (75 years plus) and the very old (85 plus). The flexibility implied in the definition of this clientele reflects the theme of this chapter - conclusions about education for older adults must be made in context.

Donahue's (1956, p.200)) observation bears repeating:

The older group is not homogenous. It consists of at least two subgroups; those who
are to be classified as the aging and those
who may be considered to have become definite-
ly aged. It is non-profitable to lump these
two groups together for most purposes; and,
in particular, it seems undesirable when considering the psychological effects of aging.

Hopefully, the perspectives that follow will make the reader aware of the diversity of education for the older adult as well as the necessity for such a varied approach. That theme will be repeated in five sections. The first section provides an overview of why older adults are such an important clientele. In the second section, the participation characteristics of the elderly are identified and analyzed for program development implications. The variety and breadth of educational opportunities for older adults is revealed in the third section. How educational gerontologists might respond to the heterogeneity of the older student is examined in the fourth section. The final section projects to the future and identifies a few scenarios for the next decade.

IMPORTANCE OF THE ELDERLY AS CLIENTELE

Two factors suggest the significance of the older student as a potential client for providers of education. First, the proportion of older adults in the United States population continues to rise faster than other age groups. According to the U.S. Senate Special Committee on Aging (1983) report, "the older population has been increasing at a far more rapid rate than the rest of the population for most of the century. For instance, in the decades of the 60s and 70s the 65-plus population grew twice as fast as the rest of the population." (p. 4). In 1980, over one fifth of the United States population was 55 years of age or over. The trend is expected to continue into the 21st Century, realizing a growth rate of 113 percent for the 55-plus group between 1982 and 2050. That figure simply overwhelms the one-third increase expected for the total U.S. population during the same period.

Soldo (1980) compares the growth rate of the elderly in developed and underdeveloped countries noting the high rate in the former. In the underdeveloped countries, the populations are growing at about 2 percent a year. The annual number of births are on the increase, broadening the base of the population age structure. That factor is reinforced by recent reductions in mortality which have been concentrated in younger age groups. Thus, the median age is less than 22 years of age and nearly two of five people are under age 15.

In sharp contrast are the developed countries, where zero growth rate is a reality and life-span is age 72 compared to 59 in the underdeveloped countries. The concentration of older adults is also much greater in the developed regions - 11.4 percent compared to 3.9 percent.

However, as Soldo forecasts, "regardless of the policies adapted in developing countries, it is clear that their growing number of older persons will initiate social changes. In this respect, they will not differ markedly from the United States or other developed countries " (p. 43). Thus, what appears to be a trend only in the United States is in reality an opportunity for providers of education throughout the world.

The second factor supporting the importance of the older adult as a clientele for adult education providers is the diminishing gap in the educational level between older and younger learners. In 1940,

the median years of school completed by persons 65
and over was 8.1 years. (U.S. Special Senate
Committee on Aging, 1984). That statistic remained
under nine years through 1970 (8.7) compared to
12.2 years completed for the entire population. By
1980, for persons 65-plus the median years of
school completed had advanced to 10.2 years
(compared to 12.5 years for the entire population).
Ventura and Worthy (1982) project that by 2014,
approximately three fourths of the older adult
population will have graduated from high school and
less than 10 percent will have no high school
education.

Data from the U.S. Special Senate Committee
on Aging (1984) shows that in 1984 the proportion
of the population aged 55 to 64 which has completed
high school is nearly equal to that of the younger
population. Reasons projected for the reduction in
the size of the gap are a) the increased
educational opportunities that became available
after World War II; and b) the history of
immigration in the United States (a high percentage
of foreign born elderly in today's older
population).

The significance of the rise in educational
level is its usefulness in predicting participation
in educational opportunities. Ventura and Worthy
(1982), as well as others (Covey, 1980; and Graney
and Hays, 1976), observe that "all survey results
show a strong association between years of
schooling completed and participation in education"
(p. iv). Using the 1981 National Council on Aging
(NCOA) Harris poll data and the 1975, 1978, and
1981 National Center for Educational Statistics
(NCES) data, the authors support their finding
further. The Harris study shows that 16 percent
(360,000) of the population aged 65 and over who
have college degrees are enrolled in courses.
Enrolment declines noticeably for lower educational
levels. The 1981 NCES data indicates that 30
percent (2,842,000) of older adults with a high
school education were participants in adult
education. The authors conclude: "Succeeding
cohorts of older people will have more years of
formal schooling...Thus, because amount of formal
education is a significant predictor of
participation in adult education, future
generations of older persons will be more likely to
engage in educational activities" (p. iv). To the
extent that the educational level of the older
adult is known, better decisions may be made
regarding program development for the elderly.

Likewise to the extent that the educational level of the older population is increasing, expansion in educational opportunities for older students may proceed with expectations of success. Long's (1983a) interpretation of these data suggest the impact of rising educational levels for older adults on participation is not simply predicted.

PARTICIPATION CHARACTERISTICS

Then, may the continuing education staff in a community college surrounded by a large proportion of highly educated older adults assume that programs for the elderly are guaranteed to be a success? Based on the following data, the staff would be making a risky assumption. As will be disclosed below, having an educated clientele in proximity does not insure participation.

Drotter (1981) concludes that there are four types of older students:
1. Functional illiterates
2. Those who prefer classes of an informal nature, such as a reading group.
3. People who prefer consumer education courses.
4. People who prefer college courses, especially tuition waiver or Elderhostel programs.

Unfortunately, data gatherers have not classified participation rates according to Drotter's scheme; in fact, there appears to be no universal set of categories other than by age. There are a few participation data sets available, but each stands on its own providing little opportunity for cross-reference. Consequently, one must review several sources to obtain a comprehensive and more realistic perspective of the participation characteristics of older students.

Among the most recent and inclusive sources is the compilation by Ventura and Worthy (1982) cited earlier. Generally, the most frequent older students are women among the young old (65-69); there is a sharp decline after 75, with an educational level higher than the median for the total population of older adults, who are white and have an annual income of $20,000 or greater. In terms of both male and female students, older adults are participating in education in greater numbers and proportion than ever before. Nationally, only 5 percent of the elderly population took a course or were enrolled in an educational institution in 1981. That figure reflects a significant increase of three percentage points from 1974, however, definitional modifications may have influenced the increase. Citing studies conducted in New York, California and Virginia, Ventura and Worthy (1982) show that older adults represent less than 1.2 percent of adult education participants in 1980. Those studies were however, limited to formal higher education programs.

Ventura and Worthy (1982) cite other significant participation rates from the NCOA Harris poll and the NCES data showing that while the population 65-plus represents 11 percent of the total adult population, it constitutes only 3.6 percent of those who participate in educational activities. In spite of that small representation, the number of persons 65-plus participating in adult education almost tripled, growing at the average rate of 30 percent every three years compared to the average rate of 12 percent for adult participation of all ages during the twelve year period ending in 1981.

Encouraging as they may be, those figures are misleading because they reflect the participation of older adults in general. When one considers the participation rate of specific categories of older adults, it becomes obvious that the illiterate elderly are in the minority in participation: 2 percent compared to 6 percent for high school graduates and 16 percent for college graduates (Ventura and Worthy, 1982). Here again is another indication of the fallacy in generalizing a set of data to all older adults.

Given that older adults, at least middle class older adults, are participating in adult education, what motivates them to enrol and what are they interested in learning. Donahue (1956) correctly assessed the importance of motivation nearly thirty years ago: "Literally, at the present time much more is available to older people in the way of education, recreation, health programs, etc. than is being used by them. The task is how to motivate the aging person to want to take the initial step required to become a member of such groups and programs" (p. 206).

Motivation has not been without scrutiny in subsequent years. Ventura and Worthy (1982) citing NCES data and the Harris NCOA poll observe that two-thirds of the respondents in both data sets give personal interest in learning as the primary motivating variable. The authors conclude that "there is no question that the predominent motivation for older adults enrolling in education programs is to learn" (p. 28).

A similiar finding was reported by Kingston and Drotter (1983) who conducted a study of older adult participants in higher education courses in Idaho and Georgia. Intellectual stimulation, interest in the subject and a desire for more education were cited as the major motivating factors. Covey (1980) used a mail-out questionnaire and interviews with older adults in Colorado to determine the motivation variables of older adults involved in higher education courses. His findings confirm the above, although they were expressed differently: older adults are more likely to engage in learning by self-initiation than because of socially imposed reasons. In other words, older students do not enrol in courses because they are encouraged or expected to do so. Ventura and Worthy (1982) note one exception, namely a trend of pre-retired males (55-64) to take courses for job-related reasons. However, the number of men and women who take courses for job-related reasons drops dramatically after age 65 (41.4 percent to 15.8 percent).

Subject matter of interest to older adults is equally difficult to generalize about as participation rates. The findings from subject matter preference studies show no predominance of interest. The one possible exception would be interest in liberal arts courses by older college enrollees. Both Covey (1982) and Graney and Hays (1976) found Liberal Arts as the primary topic of interest to older adults enrolled in higher education classes.

Ventura and Worthy (1982) use the 1981 NCES data to support their finding by indicating that older students take courses that provide a sense of meaning (philosophy, religion, language art). However, they also indicate that 34 percent (compared to 39 percent for liberal arts) of participants in the '81 NCES data took courses that provided a sense of control or the ability to cope (physical education, health care, sciences, business courses, home economics). Heisel, Darkenwald and Anderson (1981) studied the 1975 NCES data for participation by type of course, age, sex and educational level and found:
1. older adults (60-64) took technical/ vocational, safety and managerial subjects more than others.

89

2. older adults (70-plus) took civic and
   public service courses and religious
   courses more often.
3. participants with college degrees are more
   likely to participate in professional,
   managerial subjects than participants
   without college degrees.
4. participants with high school diplomas are
   more interested in vocational/technical
   and sports/recreational topics.

Sheppard (1983) provides more specific data on
the vocational education topic. In a study of 143
older adults participating in senior centers in
Virginia, he discovered that older adults are
interested in courses that relate to skills,
competence and knowledge which can improve home
life, health, avocational interests and technical
expertise. Significant relationships were found
between females and interest in food services and
nutrition; high school graduates and interest in
merchandising and sales; and college graduates and
interest in consumer and homemaking education.
    This issue is expanded further by the results
of a 1982 survey conducted by the Teachers
Insurance and Annuity Association (TIAA) and cited
by Kearsley and Furlong (1984) in their work. The
primary activity pursued the most by the 2000 TIAA
respondents was reading (92 percent) followed by
socializing with friends (75 percent),
gardening/home improvement (71 percent) and travel
(66 percent). Formal educational programs ranked
last (28 percent).
    Studies conducted with undereducated older
adults extend the range of interests further.
McCluskey (N.D.) listed the need for basic skills
education first in his five major categories of
educational opportunities for older adults.
However, when Courtenay, Suhart, McConatha and
Stevenson (1983) asked a sample of 500 older,
undereducated adults what subjects they would
prefer to learn about, topics relating to health
ranked first (personal health care such as checking
vital signs and consumer information relating to
drugs). Learning to read and to write fell into
the bottom third of preferred study topics.
    The theme is repeated again: it is difficult
to generalize about older adults. True, many are
interested in college study, liberal arts courses
particularly; but many are also interested in
vocational subjects, business topics, health
issues, literacy, ad infinitum. Thus, the

generalization is that the nature of the group will dictate subject matter preference. Reality calls for sensitivity to context (nature of the older group) when subject matter preference is under discussion. Rather than posing a dilemma, that reality appears to expand the opportunity for educational providers interested in working with older students.

Motivation and subject matter preferences of the older student stands in contrast with the question of barriers to participation. As noted above, there are several studies available that have explored this topic (Courtenay, Suhart, McConatha, Stevenson, 1983; Sheppard, 1983; Kingston and Drotter, 1983; Fishtein and Feier, 1982; Kingston, 1982; Price and Lyon, 1982; Ventura and Worthy, 1982; Marcus, 1978; Graney and Hays, 1976; Goodrow, 1975).

As a result of their comprehensive literature review, Ventura and Worthy (1982) conclude that lack of interest is the major barrier to participation by the older student. That finding is both ironic and supportive in light of the fact that personal interest is the primary motivation behind the elderly participation in adult education. Graney and Hays (1976) Hiemstra (1976), March, Hooper and Baum (1977) and Wasserman (1976) all confirm lack of interest as the major barrier.

Being too old, having poor health, lack of time and costs have also been cited as major barriers to participation. Sheppard (1983) and Courtenay, Suhart, McConatha and Stevenson (1983) found fear of being out at night, lack of transportation and tired of school to be major barriers. Price and Lyon (1982) expand the list to include the absence of a companion and lack of information about the activity. Kingston (1982) discovered that for college-enrolled older students, parking was the major problem. He concludes: "Generally, however, the study reveals that many senior citizens can be accommodated in the typical college classroom without major curricular and administrative adjustments." (p. 87).

On the other hand, Fishtein and Feier (1982) uncovered psychological barriers in their study of potential participants to Union College. Respondents cited fear over competition with younger students, fear over exposure of inadequate background and fear over the unknown as reasons for little to no participation.

91

Goodrow (1975) conducted a study of limiting factors in reducing participation in Knox County, Tennessee. Because of its indepth analysis of the differences between male and female participation, the study is frequently cited in the literature. Generally, for both sexes poor vision ranked first and poor health second. Limitations peculiar to males involved the intrinsic nature of the educational opportunity rather than physical aspects: strict attendance, job responsibilities, and courses preferred were not scheduled. On the other hand, external factors limited participation by women, such as being out at night.

Finally, Marcus (1978) suggests that socioeconomic condition is a major barrier affecting participation of older adults. His study of the effects of age, sex and status relative to educational participation found that older adults with lower income and status were least likely to participate in educational programs, particularly for the purpose of meeting pressing needs. On the other hand, according to Marcus, older adults who have high income and status are more likely to participate in education, not to meet pressing needs, but to continue personal growth and for enjoyment.

The data on barriers to participate also suggests an individual approach to working with older students. It appears that there is a different limiting factor for each group, perhaps even each older student. This discussion adds to the proposition that a homogenous approach to program development with older adults is inconsistent with the nature of the clientele.

A final, major participation variable related to older adults is the location of the educational opportunity. Ventura (1982) has developed a catalogue of program profiles which identifies the several kinds of places offering educational programs for older adults. Although not considered an exhaustive list, the content is reflective of the current educational providers. Table 4:1, provided below identifies three types of institutions that are providing education services for older adults. Three sub-types are included in each of the three major categories.

Table 4:1
Categories of Institutions Providing
Educational Experiences for Older Adults

I. Educational Institutions and Organizations
    A. Community and Technical Colleges
    B. Colleges and Universities
    C. Non-profit, Independent Education Organi-
        zations (Elderhostel)
II. Community-Based Educational Programs for Older
    Adults
    A. Community or Senior Center
    B. Area Agency on Aging
    C. Public Library
III. Others
    A. National Voluntary Organization (<u>NCOA</u>
        Senior Center Humanities Program)
    B. State Department of Education
    C. Unions

Ventura and Worthy (1982) provide data from
the 81 NCOA/ Harris survey that indicate a college
or university as the place of greatest enrolment
(27 percent) in courses. Community or senior
centers (24 percent), Business (18 percent), High
School (7 percent) and Others (24 percent -
libraries, churches, museums) follow. The 1981
NCES data show a community organization as having
the highest percentage of courses, followed by
colleges and universities, governmental agencies,
employer, high school and private instructor,
business or industry, vocational or trade school
and labor or professional organization.
    In terms of specific enrolment patterns,
Ventura and Worthy (1982) summarize from the
NCOA/Harris survey:
    1. Older men (65-plus) enrol more at places
        of business or an adult education school.
    2. Older women (65-plus) enrol more at a
        college, university or senior center.
    3. Older adults with some high school
        education or less take courses at places
        of business or community/senior centers.
    4. Older adults with a high school degree are
        likely to enrol in courses at a college
        or university or community/senior center.
    5. Older adults with college degrees are
        likely to enrol in courses at a college
        or university followed by a place of
        business and community/senior centers.
    6. Older adults (65-69) indicate a preference
        for community organizations. This is

especially true for 70-plus older adults.

Price and Lyon (1982) provide one explanation for the diversity of locations chosen by older adults, namely the proximity and familiarity of the institution. Peterson (1981) lends support to this conclusion with his finding that the primary factor motivating a sample of older students to attend courses at the University of Southern California was familiarization with the institution.

As with the other data reported from these studies, the data reported here were obtained from formal educational offerings. The addition of informal experiences, were they available, could change these rankings. Thus, one must approach location of educational offerings with the understanding that the data are not reflective of older adults in general, particularly older adults engaged in non-institutional learning experiences.

SCOPE OF PROGRAMS FOR OLDER ADULTS

In 1952, the participants present at the Workshop on Education for Aging conducted as a part of the Adult Education Association annual meeting identified the need to know what educational programs were available for older adults throughout the United States. Out of that small setting in East Lansing, Michigan, Tuckman (1955) conducted a national study to identify program providers, how they served older students, initiation processes, recruiting techniques, finances, staff, volunteer input, program content, provisions for individual differences and special difficulties and evaluation. The results were printed in Wilma Donahue's (1956) work. The scope of the study is impressive, taking up 194 pages of the book. Even more noticeable is the range of educational providers available thirty years ago: public school adult education, opportunity schools (trades), universities and colleges, Cooperative Extension, correspondence courses, evening colleges, libraries, state agencies, welfare departments, recreation departments, churches, organized groups, voluntary social agencies, employment agencies, institutional agencies, business and industry, unions and government.

Similar, if not expanded, data are available on program vendors today (Ventura, 1982; Peterson, 1983; Lumsden, 1985) indicating the existence of numerous opportunities for the elderly. On the one hand, the current programs reflect the heterogenous nature of the older adult because the providers and subject matter are so varied. At the same time, older adults suffer from the absence of a unified system to advocate, coordinate, and assist to fund education for the elderly. Emphasis is on the younger student for whom education has been institutionalized in both the private and public school systems (K-12) and colleges and universities. Tuition waiver programs for older adults in colleges and universities reflect one example where emphasis is placed in serving the older adult at the college and university level. However, as reported in recent studies of tuition waiver programs (provisions of free or reduced tuition for older adults by colleges and universities) (Long and Rossing, 1979; Long, 1980; Romaniuk, 1982a, 1982b; Romaniuk, 1983; and Romaniuk, 1984) the provisions for participation of the older student are more restrictive than supportive. For example, Long and Rossing, (1979) note the rigorous entrance requirements (Student Achievement Test scores and minimum high school grade point average) adopted by some states. In a later study, Romaniuk, (1983) observes that participation in these programs remains low, due in large part to little to no marketing efforts by the institution. Consequently, tuition waiver programs in their present form lack the emphasis given to recruitment of younger students. These programs appear to be institutional responses to older students only on paper.

Nowhere is the disunity more evident than in Federal government programs for the elderly. Soldo (1980) reports that there are 48 major programs affecting the elderly and 135-200 programs that affect older adults indirectly. A total of 49 Congressional Committees and subcommittees, seven executive departments and five independent agencies are responsible for monitoring and managing the program. For the most part the program funds retirement and health care. There are no funds for educating older adults, even though in 1980 one-fourth of the Federal budget was allocated to the elderly.

The private sector response is equally dispersed. There are international, national, regional and state associations, lobby groups and even foundations concerned with the elderly. However, there is no coordinated effort among these groups to advocate for older adults except for the hearings to reapprove the amendments to the Older American Act.

Despite the uncoordinated nature of education for the elderly, there are some excellent programs available throughout the United States. Those frequently cited are the Herbert L. Donovan Scholar's Program at the University of Kentucky, Academy of Lifelong Learning at the University of Delaware, Institute for Lifelong Learning at Duke University, and Elderhostel (Long, 1983a). Only a few can be described in a single chapter, so the reader should avoid the asumption that those identified below are the only models. They do reflect a new group of successful programs omitted in previous listings.

Life Enrichment Center
Atlanta, Georgia

Established along the model of the Shepherd's Center in Kansas City, Life Enrichment was begun by a group of older adults in 1975. Reviewing the results of a survey of older adults in the target area, several local churches were approached to provide space and financial support. The response was immediate and generous. Life Enrichment is almost all volunteer in effort. Its impressive continuing education program is managed by an older volunteer who obtains instructors (preferably older) willing to donate their time and minds. In addition to the continuing education effort, the Center operates a meals-on-wheels program, a repair service (charges are for parts only), a telephone reassurance program, grief groups, widow-to-widow groups and workshops to help other communities establish centers.

Academy of Senior Professionals
Eckerd College

This program was begun, the second time, in 1981 by older professionals for older professionals. The first attempt in 1979 had been initiated by faculty of the College (Nussbaum, 1984). The Academy has a threefold task: "creating an environment of exploration and accomplishment that will attract members with a

history of distinguished achievement; providing a
climate of continuing intellectual and cultural
stimulation; and enabling members to work singly
and in groups on projects of personal and social
significance" (p. 76). Its membership includes
college professors and presidents, physicians,
dentists, artists, ministers, business executives,
authors, nuclear chemists, engineers, architects,
foreign correspondents and military officers. The
basic program consists of public lectures by the
members or their guests, colloquia, forums, and
luncheon discourses, which are supplemented by
social and recreational events.

A similar program, Institute for Retired
Professionals (IRP), New School for Social
Research, New York, is described by Hirsch (1978).
Hirsch along with other retirees started the school
in 1962. Classes are for members only. The
criterion for membership is retirement. The IRP is
designed to serve retired professional career
individuals; its major objective is to provide
opportunities for intellectual development and for
the use of creative abilities of retired persons.

Public Access Cable Television
By and For Elders (PACE)
Chula Vista, California

Ventura (1982) observes that PACE was
established in 1977 by "a coalition of institutions
of higher learning, social service agencies and
community groups" (p. 36). The two major
objectives of the program are to encourage older
adults to be major contributors to their own
post-secondary education, rather than passive
learners and to teach older adults how to produce
and videotape cable television programs. Initial
funding was provided by a three year grant from the
California Post-Secondary Education Department.

Waxter Center for Senior Citizens
Baltimore, Maryland

This program is a multi-purpose senior center
serving older adults since 1974 (Ventura, 1982). A
variety of classes including French, basic

97

education, music for listening, vocabulary building and needlework were offered initially. The program now boasts 6,500 members, up from 400 originally and includes over 90 classes the program operates seven days a week.

Senior Citizen Adult Education
Program for Monroe County
Moore, Michigan

As Ventura (1982) notes, the objectives of this program are to provide high shool completion opportunities for older adults and to provide continuing education opportunities to older adults with a broad educational background. Courses are varied, including "advocacy, changing values, creative writing, crafts, gerontology, nutrition fitness, tool shop, typing and weight watching" (p. 59).

District Council 37 Retirees Educational Program
American Federation of State, County and
Municipal Employees
New York, New York

Older retirees of New York's largest municipal unions expressed such intense interest in this program that the Executive Director of the union hired someone to establish it in 1976 (Ventura, 1982). Being a union-sponsored program, the activity includes recreation, social networking and political concerns. The educational program is diverse in an attempt to meet the needs of all kinds of backgrounds. Course areas include literature, history, symphony and opera, art, electric typing, health issues and self-help groups.

Readily evident from those descriptions is the variety of educational opportunities that exist for older adults, again consistent with the nature of the clientele. However, in order to provide better exposure for these efforts some form of coordination is necessary and it is suggested that greater attention should be provided in the literature for descriptions of the opportunities for older adults.

RESPONDING TO THE HETEROGENEITY OF OLDER ADULTS

Assuming that the elderly represent an important clientele in adult education and that participation characteristics of the elderly reflect a heterogenous group, what steps should educational gerontologists take to improve research and practice around the theme of individual differences? First, researchers need to examine the characteristics of the older student in the learning process. The state of knowledge in this area has progressed slowly, if at all in some cases. Donahue's (1956) observations now seem ahead of her times:

> Although adult education has been a field of growing interest for a considerable number of years, and education for older adults has attracted the attention of some teachers of adults during the last dozen years, few studies have been made as yet to determine the teaching methods and course content most useful in training older people (p. 205).

True, there is a host of research on learning and aging in terms of factors that may foster or inhibit learning (Hayslip and Kennelly, 1985), but little attention has been given to research that measures effective teaching methods and course content for the elderly. Most educational opportunities follow accepted but untested principles of program development described by Peterson (1983) and Knowles (1980). However, because there is little research, especially experimental, with older adults, it is difficult to determine if there is a better way to develop educational experiences for the older learner.

Similarly, the absence of experimental data relative to instructional methods prevents the determination of effective learning by older adults. This issue is compounded by the absence of cognitive evaluations of learning experiences for older adults. Evaluation usually consists of satisfaction indices, which are highly predictable (Knowles, 1980). Program offerors are at a loss to say with substance whether an older group has learned the content of an educational experience. And, as reported earlier in this chapter, it is the content more than any other variable that motivates the older learner. In their defense, program developers are following the advice of Goodrow

(1975) and Knowles (1980) to be cautious if not abstain altogether with respect to testing the elderly. However, as Courtenay and Moore (1985) discovered, older adults are not unfamiliar with tests and, when given in the right context, the older student responds positively.

Thus, principles of program development and principles of instruction need to be tested in order to know if there is a better way. For example, Anderson (1955) proposed seven principles of instruction for use with older adults. Although they seem reasonable, most do not have a substantial research base:

1. The learner should be a participant in learning.
2. Learning should produce a visible, tangible product.
3. Materials should not be too simple, but should pose a problem.
4. Group learning is more effective than individual application.
5. Materials presented through several sensory avenues are more effectively learned.
6. Have the learner practice what is to be learned.
7. Good teaching methods and subject matter presentation will assist materially the learning of the adult.

Reinforcement for these principles is provided by Glynn and Muth (1979) in their study of the aids that will enhance text-learning by older adults. The problem with the principles and the aids is that for the most part they are suggested from research findings with younger people, not older adults. But, the article has been effective in stimulating needed research in this area. For example, Taub (1984) designed a study to measure the effects of underlined cues in texts on learning prose material. Differences between experimental and control groups were not significant relative to the underlined cues; however, a significant difference did emerge with respect to the nature of the prose passage. The study calls into question the use of underlined cues in texts and raises the importance of the relevancy of subject matter to the older student. Taub's findings, as does most research, raises additional questions for study. It is a good beginning toward research on specific issues with specific older samples.

What is happening in program development and instruction is a generalized approach to planning and conducting educational experiences for older adults. As Knowles (1980) and Peterson (1983) observe, every group of adults, especially older adults, is different. Each must be approached in an open, non-generalizable manner. Following Lorge's (1956) admonition would serve program developers and instructors as well:

Many generalizations are based upon narrow tasks; we generalize to all tasks as though they were positively correlated regardless of complexity or duration. Our performance is limited. We do not realize in our tasks the impact of the previous practices upon the present (p. 209).

A second gap in education for older adults is the lack of recognition of and provision for self-directed learning by the older student. Hiemstra (1976) found, as did Tough (1979) with younger groups, that older adults are involved in a variety of learning activities on their own: "The picture is that of an active learner, frequently engaged in self-directed learning, and not very dependent on the traditional sources of information" (p. 336). Not only should self-directed activities be recognized as valid, they should be nurtured . Educational providers can assist the older student in these efforts by finding ways to facilitate self-directed learning, such as identifying and making available resources. Emphasis in this area could greatly expand the learning opportunities for those older adults who cannot or will not participate in group learning activities.

A third area of need in developing and implementing education for older adults is expanded emphasis toward the illiterate older student. Much is written and spoken about the anticipated increase in the educational level of the older adult, but, ironically,

the current population of older adults has higher rates of illiteracy, more predominent representation of people for whom English is a second language, a higher rate of failing health and a higher proportional representation of semi and skilled life occupations. Current programs will be needed at least to improve this group's ability to function

successfully in today's society (Ventura
and Worthy, 1982, p. 7).

But who knows what functional literacy is for
the older adult? In a comprehensive literature
study of literacy and aging, Courtenay, Stevenson
and Suhart (1982) discovered conceptual confusion
over a universal meaning of functional literacy,
and therefore, ask whether one can consider an
older adult who may have completed the third grade,
but who has lived 80 years - the last 25 alone - to
be functionally illiterate. The age bias present
in tests used with older adults led the researchers
to conclude: "In short, none of the studies
addressed the question of whether the demands for
literacy was the same for various age groups nor
whether various competencies were related to
adequate functioning in different ways among age
groups" (pp. 349-350).

Unfortunately, education for older illiterate
adults is characterized by such observations as
"one can find literally hundreds of articles
dealing with the reading of children, teenagers,
college students, and adults in Education Index and
the ERIC Index. If one finds even a handful of
articles or studies dealing with reading of the
elderly, one will be fortunate" (Rigg and Kazemek,
1983, 418). What appears to be reality to those
researchers is decision-making by gerontologists
and program developers without the use of empirical
data. Consequently, stereotypical assumptions such
as this abound: the older adult is "incompetent,
inadequate and in need of 'fixing up' by some
professionals" (p. 419).

Heisel (1980) is no more optimistic in his
observations of literacy and aging:

> Once past the information gathered by the
> Bureau of the Census, and national surveys
> documenting in detail that an overwhelming
> majority of older adults are educationally,
> socially and financially disadvantaged and
> that these same people are glaringly absent
> from the rosters of adult education, the data
> practically disappear (p. 134).

Perhaps this aspect of education for older
adults could be improved by concentrated efforts to
determine exactly the learning needs of the
illiterate older adult and placing emphasis in
learning experiences on those needs. Courtenay,
Suhart, McConatha and Stevenson (1983) report the

development of an instructional manual that is designed to teach older adults the basic skills by using subject matter that is of greatest concern to older adults. For example, maths can be learned while acquiring the ability to take one's temperature or blood pressure. Reading can be learned by focusing on Social Security and Medicare regulations. The heterogeneity of the older population includes the under-educated older person; if program developers are to be consistent in educational opportunities, efforts must be channelled in their direction.

PERSPECTIVES ON THE FUTURE

Whether or not education for older adults will exist in the future is aptly answered by the foregoing discussion. The current and projected population and educational attainment demographics provide ample support for its continuation. What is not so readily evident today, but sure to follow over the next few years is a positive attitude toward education for older learners. Havighurst (1976) and Covey (1981) have articulated the basic rationale for education for the older population, namely that the investment made in the economy by today's older cohort deserves some repayment. Havighurst concludes that "all people have a right as humans to the good things of life, whether or not they have worked to produce these goals. A quality of life society should provide the necessities for good living to all people in relation to their needs as far as is humanly possible" (p. 51). Covey is even more forceful: "The interest that older people have in learning whatever they choose is reason enough for us to allow them to be students whether or not it serves society directly" (p. 381). Thus, the future may be expected to reflect a more optimistic conception of education for the elderly.

That attitude will be bolstered by a second expectation in the future, the acceptance of lifelong learning as the predominant mode of education in the United States. Graney and Hays (1976) propose a progression of theory relative to education for older adults ranging from leisure interest activities to instrumental activities to education as a lifelong endeavor: "...educational gerontology is a normal extension of previously recognized concerns. Thus, education of the aged is destined to be eventually integrated into a continuous process of lifelong learning" (p. 349). As Peterson (1975) has observed, lifelong learning will promote a more positive image for aging in the long run, because citizens will recognize that eduction has a role in assisting people at all stages of life.

Akin to the emergence of lifelong education as a conceptual model is the development of a coordinated structure for education and the elderly. Like the establishment and maintenance of public education for children, adolescents and young adults, so will a system arise for education for the older persons. Its nature is likely to be different from the conventional structure of public and private education; in fact, it would not be surprising to realize a combination of both sectors given the differential nature of older learners.

In terms of programming, computer education opportunities will increase. Both Chin (1984) and Kearsley and Furlong (1984) report on successful experiences of older adults in computer education classes. A principle emerging from both reports is that no major differences were observed between younger and older learners: they learned at about the same rate, made similar mistakes and were equally enthusiastic or disenchanted about what they learned. Other observations important for program development include:

1. Instructors were older adults. It seemed helpful to keep classes free of computer whizzes.
2. Emphasis was placed on having fun with the computers and on the fact that people are superior to computers. This last emphasis diminished the attitude of "computer-phobia".
3. Socializing appears to be a major motivating variable.
4. The courses offer excellent intellectual stimulation.

Finally, the future must address programs and policy questions mentioned or implied in preceeding sections of this chapter if improvements are to be realized in providing education for older adults. Among the most significant questions are:

1. What supportive services foster successful learning experiences for older adults?
2. What are the preferred and the most effective teaching methods for various groups of older adults?

3. To what extent should and can new technologies be utilized in education for older adults?
4. What methods are available to gather data on informal learning by older adults?
5. Is the existing system of providers the best for future programming?
6. What are the advantages/disadvantages of developing a coordinated plan of education for older adults?
7. How can educational providers better serve the undereducated older adult?

SUMMARY

From both a demographic and a philosophical perspective, older adults represent a significant clientele for adult educators for at least the next several decades. Current participation data, though limited to institutionalized learning and middle class participants reflects the vivid differences among individual older learners. Unfortunately, the state of the literature has focused on the better educated, relatively income secure older person to the extent that generalizations are often made for all older adults from one-sided data.

This chapter attempts to reflect the theme that educational researchers and programmers must redirect their perspective on education and the older student to include the variety of backgrounds extant in the older population. Suggested principles of program development and instructional methods must be provided with a research base that accounts for the differential samples within the population. While there will be new developments in educational gerontology, such as the emergence of lifelong education as a conceptual and operational mode for all of education, education for older adults is no longer a future event. It is reality now; it is maturing rapidly; it requires a new perspective...

Chapter Five

NEW PERSPECTIVES ON LITERACY EDUCATION
IN THE UNITED STATES

Curtis Ulmer and Huey B. Long

Adult illiteracy has been in the forefront of
educational, social and political news for the past
two decades. Ironically this emphasis is due in
large part to the unparalled success in technology
which has resulted in the automation of farms and
industry. The situation has been described as
follows: "Within the United States today there are
a staggering 23 million Americans - 1 in 5 adults -
that lack the reading and writing abilities needed
to handle the minimum demands of daily living. An
additional thirty million are only marginally
capable of being productive workers" (U.S. News and
World Report, 1982a, p. 53). While this number is
possibly a smaller percentage of our population
than in past years, the tragedy in human terms is
illustrated by the high rate of unemployment among
undereducated adults. In social terms the lack of
productivity and the feeling of social inadequacy
in this segment of the population results in
increased welfare and unemployment costs to the
general public.

     Prior to the 1960s this undereducated segment
of the population constituted the "silent millions"
who performed vital work in tilling the fields,
working the assembly lines, building railroads and
helping to build a vital United States. Also the
eradication of illiteracy was often a matter left
to the church and volunteer agencies since the cost
was largely individual with little social and
economic cost to the country.

     A new perspective of literacy challenges the
basic structure of the social and economic future

of the United States. The future organization of
literacy education in the United States must
reflect the social and economic conditions of the
communities where the adult illiterate lives and
works. Thus literacy education becomes part
education program, part social and economic
program, and part integration of these forces in a
total community education effort. The problem of
illiteracy transcends educational policy and
becomes a problem of public policy. The passage of
the Economic Opportunity Act of 1964 and the
subsequent enactment of the Adult Education Act of
1966 provided continuing funding for adult
illiteracy and placed illiteracy in the public
domain. Education and public policy unfortunately
have yet to establish programs that attract a
significant percentage of the target population.
Several years ago the General Accounting Office
questioned the expenditure of funds for the Adult
Basic Education Act of 1966 by citing the small
numbers of the target population reached through
the program. As a result of the criticism, the
U.S. Office of Education and the states engaged in
curriculum reforms leading to performance based
curricula. However this emphasis, while
educationally sound, ignores the social aspects of
illiteracy and has not significantly changed
national enrolments in literacy programs. It
appears that illiteracy as a multi- dimensional
problem will not be advanced by measures that only
reach one dimension of the problem.

The modest purpose of this chapter is that of
examining the scope of the problem of illiteracy in
the United States. The chapter will also speculate
that a community based approach to literacy
education may be a viable alternative to present
programs.

OVERVIEW

Nature of the Target Population
Liebow (1967) and Kozol (1985) graphically depict
an American underclass who for many reasons do not
share in recent cultural, educational, and economic
progress. The illiterate do not reject the social
and economic systems, but for reasons they do not
clearly understand - nor are they equipped to
understand - they do not fit into the mainstream.
Not fitting, they form a large population surviving
by temporary jobs, welfare, or by skills in conning
the larger society. These are the people that

formal schooling has never been able to reach in any numbers including programs directed to them in literacy education by adult basic education programs. Their language, thought processes, and action proclaim them as being different and by implication uneducable. The social, political and educational mandate is clear - find ways to reach them or settle for a permanent underclass. It appears that it might be a permanent, growing underclass.

In a previous work the senior author (Ulmer 1968) described the characteristics of adult illiterates.

Somewhere between the impersonal statistics and the life stories of flesh-and-blood people lies the realm of the sociologist who describes the general characteristics of groups of people. His generalizations may be less precise than the statistics but they may give more insight into the illiterate living patterns than any other approach. A composite picture of the uneducated would show that they tend to have typical patterns of social and cultural traits.

More than likely they are poor, since level of education is usually correlated with income level. The uneducated are probably below average in aptitude to learn academic sub-jects. Both poverty and lack of scholastic aptitude are chicken-and-egg propositions. Poverty fosters cultural and educational deprivation, which in turn affect academic achievement, and so around again to poverty.

The illiterate are also low in motivation and confidence. Excessive failures in achieving the recognized American standards of success lead to discouragement which may amount to complete resignation to fate. Consequently, they are frustrated and may stop trying to im-prove life and live for today because today is enough of a challenge. Tomorrow is beyond comprehension.

Although help may be available through the so-cial service agencies of the community the il-literate (sic) probably do not know about them and might not use their services if they did.

Tired of trying to meet the expectations of middle class America, the uneducated join cultural sub-groups with a common standard of behavior and achievement. Having joined a culturally deprived, excluded group, they are no longer subject to middle class standards. In fact, their exclusion from the main stream of society actually prevents them from ever being successful, and thereby places the blame for failure on others.

Education, for example, is not readily available to adults or children in disadvantaged groups. The traditional middle-class school system, which emphasizes middle-class values and verbal skills, has tended to screen out those students who cannot conform to or keep up with its educational program.

Good jobs or social betterment are not available to the excluded group either, because education is the key to success in both areas. The uneducated person's exclusion from society and success is now complete. While they may want the same things from life as those in the main stream of society, illiterate persons have no means of acquiring them.

They live, instead, in their own world with its own set of values and attitudes.

The only aspect of middle-class life aspired to is the acquisition of material comforts and conveniences. Today is what counts, and today can be much more pleasant with a car, a television set, or a washing machine. Insurance, savings accounts, and medical check-ups belong to the age of tomorrow. And for those without hope, any investment in something as uncertain as tomorrow would be as speculative as an investment in a uranium mine on mars.

Most of the characteristics of the poor, uneducated, deprived person are not only different from those of the middle-class students or teachers, but are characteristics which would be considered undesirable by middle class American standards (Ulmer, 1968 pp. 28-29).

DEFINITIONS

The historical concept of literacy in the United States was based on the ability to read, write, and perform simple mathematical computations. A fourth grade education was often used as a standard for measuring literacy. Essentially a literate person could perform the reading, writing, and computational tasks required to survive in an agricultural and industrial society.

Functional Literacy

Functional literacy is a situational construct whereby people acquire the skills to train and/or retrain to fulfil their own goals and objectives for employment, or for various roles as parent, citizen, consumer and other roles perceived as important by individuals and their reference groups. Movement toward the concept of functional literacy in the United States has contributed to several broad, but related curriculum movements. Competency based programs which stress individualized instruction, programmed instruction, adult performance levels and contract learning have dominated the literature of adult basic education over the past ten years. This emphasis has resulted in a different focus from traditional education where group goals and individual performance based on group norms is the standard for instruction (Lyle 1977). The functional literacy programs focus on assisting individuals to set their own goals in learning and to measure their progress towards those goals based on individual ability and educational level.

Basic Education

Sections 301-318 of the Adult Education Act (PL 91-230) describes and intreprets the federal funded literacy program to the various states and territories. The following statement of purpose (p 37 appendix, The Adult Education Act, November 1, 1978) observes the national commitment to adult basic education and defines the term.

It is the purpose of this title to expand educational opportunities for adults and to encourage the establishment of programs of adult education that will:

1. enable all adults to acquire basic skills necesary to function in society, (p. 37)
2. enable adults who so desire to continue their education to at least the level of completion of secondary school, and (p. 37)
3. make available to adults the means to secure training that will enable them to

become more employable, productive and responsible citizens. (p. 37)

Essentially this act implies a legal definition of illiteracy; it suggests that high school completion is a minimum standard for literacy. The Act also indicates economic competence is a priority for literacy training and by implication mandates a curriculum for literacy training where the term "adult basic education" is defined as: "adult education for adults whose inability to speak, read, or write the English language constitutes a substantial impairment of their ability to obtain or retain employment commensurate with their real ability which is designed to help eliminate such inability and raise education with a view of making them less likely to depend on others, to improving their ability to benefit from occupational training and otherwise increasing their opportunities for more productive and profitable employment, and to making them better able to meet their adult responsibilities." (p. 37, November 1, 1978, The Adult Education Act Appendix)

The wording and substance of the act stresses economic concerns with a thinly veiled goal for the illiterate to become self sufficient instead of wards of state, local and federal governments. The adult basic education curricula of the state departments of education in the United States have been established in response to this act.

Broadly stated, basic education is that level of education where the individual acquires those skills needed to learn how to learn. The focus of basic education is that of acquiring verbal skills in standard English, skills in writing and reading standard English and computation skills. Needless to say, the more complex the culture, higher levels of communication are required to achieve a basic education. The concept of basic education requires a different philosophical approach than traditional education where facts are learned for future use. Basic education is a functional concept where skills are learned for immediate application in some facet of a person's life. This accounts for the emphasis on vocational concerns and life skills application in many basic education programs.

SCOPE OF ADULT ILLITERACY IN THE UNITED STATES

The illiterate adult in the United States is an enigma to the larger population since they are often difficult to identify. Their dress, language, and customs tend to reflect the values of the community making it difficult to distinguish them as illiterates. Most tend to conceal their educational limitations through various excuses such as "I left my glasses at home" or by developing various ruses to conceal their inability to read and write. A larger number have limited skills in reading and writing, but lack the education to train or retrain for employment or to fill out the multitude of forms required for job applications, tax forms, etc.

The fact that adult illiteracy has reached alarming proportions is suggested by the following estimates. "Sixty million adult Americans cannot read a daily paper, a tax form, or the warnings on a can of pesticide," says Jonathan Kozoll, futurist, educator, and author. (Christian Science Monitor, 1985 p. 23).

Ulmer and Dorland (1981) state that between 50 to 65 million adults in the United States (age 18 and above, out of school) lack sufficient educational skills required to participate fully as workers and citizens. According to the U.S. News and World Report (1982a, p. 53) 13% of high school students graduate with the reading and writing skills of sixth graders. More than one third of adults have not completed high school."

The 1981 Census reports that 16.8 million adults had eight years or less of education (Bureau of the Census, 1982). Two factors illustrate the severity of the problem in the United States. Demographers state that illiteracy is steadily increasing by nearly one million school dropouts a year and by immigrants who cannot read or write in English or their own language (U.S. News and World Report, 1982a, p. 53). Adult basic education programs serve approximately 4 percent of the target population with volunteer programs adding a fraction of a percent to this total. Compounding the problem is the fact that many who are being served leave the programs before making significant progress.

Previous Efforts (20th Century)
Illiteracy is a social and class phenomenon for the most part in the United States. It is characterized as much by social and cultural

113

attitudes as by lack of education. Stated another way, lower class neighborhoods, pockets of poverty, and areas of high unemployment, are also places of high concentrations of illiteracy and prevailing customs and attitudes that practically guarantee that the succeeding generation will become the adult illiterates of tomorrow.

The current emphasis on adult illiteracy may lead one to believe that illiteracy is a recent problem in the United States. Such is not the case. Long (1984b) provides evidence that provisions for literacy education for adults was made by the British and Dutch Colonists. As in modern day United States, literacy was seen as a key to advancement in the social and economic life of the cities while few, if any, programs were available on the frontier and plantations. The history of education in the United States reveals waves of literacy education, Americanization classes beginning in Colonial United States and extending to this day.

One significant difference between illiteracy prior to the 1960's and today is the fact that the consequences of illiteracy were perceived as being largely personal prior to 1960. More recently illiteracy has been identified in personal, social and economic terms. This fact is best illustrated by the Economic Opportunity Act of 1964 which called attention to the fact that poverty and illiteracy hindered the growth of the economy. Thus illiteracy programs which had largely been a volunteer activity now became a matter of public policy with partial governmental financing. Social scientists, economists, and educators are still searching for a coherent public policy and educational organization to remediate the problem of illiteracy.

Voluntary Literacy Programs

For practical purposes there are two largely unrelated types of programs of literacy education in the United States. The oldest, one that practically spans the history of the United States is volunteer activities conducted by local, regional, and national organizations. The Moonlight School Program and the Laubach Literacy programs are perhaps the best known, although there are many others.

The Moonlight Schools (Stewart 1922) began in Kentucky following World War I and quickly captured the imagination of the American people. As the name implies, the schools were held on moonlight nights when volunteer teachers could find their way on mountain trails to a school cabin where literacy classes were held. The movement spread over the southeastern United States with notable success.

The Laubach Literacy program was also a large scale program that followed World War II and quickly became a world wide program under the guidance of Frank Laubach (1960).

Today the volunteer movement is more focused, better organized and in most instances has a paid professional staff with national and regional headquarters. The Laubach Program continued as the National Affiliation for Literacy Advance (NALA) and conducts extensive campaigns to recruit volunteer teachers and students who are unable to read. The NALA conducts training sessions for volunteer teachers and has developed extensive training materials for tutors and work/texts for adult students. NALA has a network of affiliates across the United States that certifies volunteer tutors and recruits teachers.

A second national volunteer program, Literacy Volunteers of America (LVA) is the lifework of Ruth Colvin. It consists of a national network with the general purpose of tutoring the nonreader for placement in a public school or community based program for advanced training.

Both programs are founded more on the community based service to humankind rationale than they are on the concept of 'schooling'. They tend to represent their activity as a Christian act provided for the individual rather than as a larger service to society. Volunteer programs have made significant contributions to national literacy efforts by keeping the problems of literacy before the American public, through the development of significant materials for training volunteer teachers and students and by maintaining the organizational flexibility required to remain relevant. The publication of a newspaper geared to elementary reading levels (two levels) on matters of adult interests was an early innovative teaching development by NALA. Volunteer literacy programs depend on community based local groups to organize and teach the illiterate, generally on a one-to-one basis.

For the purpose of this section, community based literacy education will be discussed within the framework of volunteer movements that date back to the early 1900's and extend through today. Those movements have provided the continuity of program, teacher training and materials preparation

to this date. <u>Mother's First Book</u> written by Cora
Wilson Stewart and published in 1930 was a primer
for women that embodied the latest in literacy
materials while it taught simple vocabulary and
sentences. Each selection concerned health,
religion, cleanliness, diet etc. in addition to
spelling and sentence construction. Sad Sack, Joe
and Willie became legends during World War II with
their simple messages designed to teach survival
skills to military personnel. Leon Sullivan and
Associates' Opportunities Industrialization Center
(OIC) became famous during the 1960s and 70s for
programs that reached into the core of the
inner-city and taught employment skills and basic
literacy to ghetto residents. OIC recognized a
basic fact of life that in some populations it is
necessary to attend to pressing human needs before
attempting to teach literacy.

In a New York Times article of December 27,
1984 about an Atlanta, Georgia volunteer program,
Literacy Action, a spokesperson explained,
"Illiteracy among adults is not primarily a reading
problem." He continued to explain that adults who
cannot read does not process information like the
rest of America does. Literacy Action hopes to
teach 1000 Atlantans to read in 1984-85, preferably
parents, since "illiteracy breeds illiteracy" the
report continued.

Multiply these programs by the hundreds
sponsored by the National Affiliation for Literacy
Advance and Literacy Volunteers of America as well
as the local and regional literacy volunteeer
groups and one will find a formidable national
network of volunteers dedicated to teaching
illiterates. However, volunteer programs currently
reach only a small part of the total population of
illiterates.

The national volunteer literacy programs have
budgets derived from private donations,
foundations, sponsored projects and sale of
materials. According to Hunter and Harman (1979 p.
63), NALA had a budget of $1,759,850 in 1976-77
while LVA's budget was about $382,000 (Hunter and
Harman, 1979). While the organization of these
national associatons differ, their vitality comes
from a network of local organizations.

Mezirow, Darkenwald and Knox (1975) say,

"There has been a continuing debate about the
relative advantages and disadvantages of
community outreach classes. Advantages in-

clude (1) extension of ABE opportunities to the hardest to reach and most disadvantaged portion of the target population; (2) a learning environment enhanced by the social cohesion that results from common membership in a church or other organization; and (3) greater visibility for ABE in the community and broader community support. Among the disadvantages are (1) higher per-student cost; (2) problems of coordination, communication, and logistics; (3) poor facilities; (4) lack of instructional equipment and limited choice of materials; (5) lack of means for grouping students by achievement level; and (6) diffi-culty in providing counseling services" (p. 146).

Governmental Literacy Programs

The second and larger literacy program, conducted by public schools, emerged from the Economic Opportunity Act of 1964. Since that date Federal funds have been allocated to the states and territories to conduct programs for literacy programs generally referred to as Adult Basic Education or ABE. These programs are conducted for persons 16 years of age or older, out of school and who did not complete high school. The 1964 allocation of 14 million dollars increased to approximately 200 million dollars in 1985. These funds are distributed by the U.S. Office of Education to State Departments of Education who disburse them to local programs based on a state plan for eradicating illiteracy. Many states supplement these funds through state funds and 'in kind' services such as free use of facilities, janitorial services, utilities, etc. The local programs have achieved varying degrees of success with many conducting exemplary programs. The U.S. Office of Education, Division of Vocational, Technical and Adult Education has copies of each state's plan for Adult Basic Education as well as numerous reports from school districts and agencies reporting on funded experimental and demonstration projects.

Each state Adult Basic Education program has a staff, several consultants who provide teacher-training, material resources and administrative support to local coordinators. At the local level the funds are allocated by the state to a local school district, and in some instances to community college districts where the program is administered by a local coordinator

employed by the school district on a part-time or
full-time basis. The teachers whose full time job
is usually in the local elementary or secondary
school are generally employed on a part-time basis.
In recent years there has been a tendency to employ
more full-time teachers. This trend accelerated as
more districts moved to individualized instruction
utilizing learning laboratories and programmed
instruction programs.

The Federal-State organization appears to
facilitate the flow of funds from the federal level
to local programs efficiently. In terms of the
history of literacy movements and the philosophical
orientation of the public school to the education
of youth, however, it may not be the most efficient
or effective way to attract adult students. A
number of reasons are suggested by the facts. In
most instances illiterate adults have rejected
public school education as a relevant factor in
their lives. Indeed, in some cases the adult
illiterate was alienated from the public school as
a child and continues to be. Also public school
teachers have prepared for their vocation through a
process of subject matter specialization, teacher
education programs and experience. As
professionals they find it difficult to adapt to a
new subject matter, clientele, and teaching methods
that should vary from their day school model.

For these reasons it seems feasible to
consider a different funding and organizational
pattern that could be administered through the
public schools or a local agency. Obviously such
an agency should be representative of the total
commmunity including the illiterate population.

CRITIQUES OF THE EDUCATIONAL ESTABLISHMENT

Distinguished panels, such as the Faure Commission
in 1972, the Congress of the United States in
enacting the Economic Opportunity of 1964 and
dozens of noted authors such as Toffler, Naisbitt,
Hunter and Harman and Freire have called for
educational reform including literacy education.
Most have cited cultural, social, economic factors
in the age of technology and communications as
sources of educational changes. The idea of
education as an instrument of national policy is
not new. The Morrill Act of 1862 is well known to
most students of American education. The emphasis
on science in the late 1950's began a progression
of Federal mandates and funding as national

interests and defense dictated new thrusts. Most of these programs were successful as typified by the so-called GI Bill of Rights which provided benefits to veterans to continue their education. However, in spite of 21 years of funding, the national imperative to eradicate illiteracy appears further from reality today than it did in 1964.

Ulmer (1974, p. 54) made eight recommendations about basic education programs and stated, "The important decisions about education are out of the hands of those being educated. Remedial adult education is generally led by conservative educators with little, if any, training in adult education." His recommendations were as follows:

1. The various local, state and national governments should change their priorities and allocate more funds to remedial continuing education programs. It is expected that the gross national product will continue to increase. Therefore, the United States should easily be able to finance the educational programs required to keep pace with the economy and to eradicate poverty.

2. A comprehensive national policy should be formulated for continuing education programs as an integral part of the educational system. Such a program would obviously not be based on present elementary and secondary education programs.

3. More planned and organized efforts to motivate people to work as volunteers should be started by the government and other adult education agencies.

4. The needs of the participants as they perceive them should determine the priorities in the educational program.

5. Self-realization of adults should be enhanced through a process of responsible and self-directing decision making.

6. Organizations should be created for the purpose of developing programs more relevant to the needs of remedial education.

7. Universities and other agencies of continuing education should encourage, plan and conduct research projects in various fields of continuing education to find better methods of teaching, more efficient organizational structure, methods to motivate people to participate and to motivate people to work as volunteers, etc.

8. New approaches to remedial education such as the methods used by Paulo Freire (1968) should be tried. This method has potential applications in American society such as:

   a. It might help in transforming present adult education programs from a middleclass operation to an approach that will also serve the poor or marginal groups.

   b. Alternative organizational methods, or agencies, may develop a new vitality in the remedial education movement.

   c. An extensive program cannot be developed without the intense interest of the target population. Perhaps the interest and vitality of the labor union movement among the poor could be replicated in the remedial education movement if the poor worker becomes involved.

   d. The para-professional movement can be utilized in remedial educational movement as one alternative to our present dependence on elementary and secondary teachers for the instructional program (p. 54).

More recently Hunter and Harman (1979) in an important book funded by the Ford Foundation made a similar point in their principle conclusion when they stated, "A major shift in national education policy is needed to serve the educational needs of disadvantaged adults." (p 133) They proceeded to make eleven specific recommendations which are not greatly different from the ones listed above.

A UNESCO commission report on Education (Faure et.al. 1972) seems to support the call for change with the statement, "The aim of education is to enable man to be himself, to 'become himself'. And the aim of education in relation to employment and economic progress should be not so much to prepare young people and adults for a specific, lifetime vocation, as to 'optimize' mobility..." (p. xxxi) Faure, et al further supports the thesis of this chapter when they state that education is no longer focused on the learner, nor anyone, nor anything else. It must necessarily proceed from the learner.

Two principle recommendations of the Faure report that have specific relevance to Literacy Education programs are:

1. Educational institutions and means must be multiplied, made more accessible, offer the individual a far more diversified choice. Education must assume the proportions of a true mass movement (p. 183).
2. Each person should be able to choose his path more freely, in a more flexible framework, without being compelled to give up using educational services for life if he leaves the system (p. 186).

Freire, (1968) emphasizes the uses of the problem posing dialogic method in adult education. Through this dialogue with people their needs can be found and those needs should be studied and amplified.

SPECULATIONS ON A NEW APPROACH

Based on one of the author's experience of some twenty-one years of literacy programming in public education agencies, several assumptions about illiteracy in the United States can be posed.

1. Based on the small percentage of adults who attend literacy programs, it appears that the illiterate does not see continuing his education as a viable alternative to improve his condition in life.
2. The pursuit of education has not been a tradition for lower class citizens as children or adults.
3. The educational establishment has failed to provide instructional programs that are appropriate to the needs and interests of the adult illiterate.
4. The educational establishment has not accepted adult illiteracy as a priority of public education. Consequently in most instances there is no established career track for adult teachers and the program remains primarily part time after twenty-one year's operation.
5. Adult education for the adult illiterate is a complex social, economic and public education program and federal funding and public education practices must be restructured before an effective program can be implemented.

Two largely unrelated social efforts have dominated the continuing quest for literacy for those who for some reason did not receive a basic education in their youth. The public schools have had continuing involvement in educating adult immigrants, adults who failed to complete high school and more recently vocational education for adults to prepare for entry into war industries and other vocations of national defense and interests. However, public schools have been slow to accept the education of adults as an integral part of their purpose. Evidence is provided by the fact that most adult education projects are based on external funding by the Federal government or some other agency rather than state and local funds.

The second social force has been the literacy volunteer activities with roots that are as long as the history of public education. The volunteer program has been resiliant and successful. Notable success was achieved following World Wars I and II. Until Federal funding was provided for adult literacy programs in 1964 volunteer programs were often the only resource for the illiterate who wished to learn to read and write. The strengths and weaknesses of both programs have been discussed in previous sections of this chapter; however, it appears that the major strength of public school adult literacy programs reside in their Federal support, an administrative organization throughout the United States, and their success in the high school equivalency programs where adults with a basic education can obtain the high school credential.

It appears the major strength of the volunteer programs reside in the community approach to education and their success in teaching the adult illiterate to read and write. Further, the volunteer movement has retained a vitality which appears to be derived from the inherent interest of volunteers to help those less fortunate. This is accomplished in an informal setting where there is little concern with certification and other restrictions necessarily imposed by the bureaucratic nature of public education.

It seems volunteer agencies function best on a one-to-one basis while public schools traditionally employ group instruction methods that facilitates learning for those who read and have a basic knowledge of computation.

The review of the work of Faure, Hunter and Harman, Ulmer and Dorland, and others lead to four conclusions:

1. Literacy education must be community based and,
2. The organization and funding of adult literacy education must be changed to a structure and administrative organization that supports and facilitates community based literacy education and,
3. The illiterate population must be involved in developing the curriculum and instructional strategies for a community based literacy program and,
4. Support must be generated for a public policy designed to furthur these goals.

Before discussing these conclusions, it should be noted that public school adult education has been moving in the direction of these goals although they have not significantly increased the numbers of the target population reached. Their primary success has been in the high school equivalency program where their principle expertise and perhaps interest lies. On the other hand the national volunteer agencies appear to be most successful in tutoring the non-reader in spite of a combined national budget that is smaller than the budget of several states for literacy training. One may speculate that the emphasis on group instruction by public schools and individual instruction by the volunteer agencies accounts for these facts.

The illiterate adult cannot distinguish between these approaches and fails to see that continuing education is a viable alternative in life. A change in national policy towards community based literacy education has been recommended by panels and scholars for more than twenty years. As noted previously literacy education is a complex social and educational phenomen and it is likely that it will have little success when addressed as the exclusive domain of one sector or the other.

An ideal community adult literacy education approach should involve three broad sectors of life, social agencies, educational agencies and the infrastructure of the target population. Each is dependent on the other to achieve the goals of the various agencies. Such an approach would reduce the efficiency and standardization that each agency has strived to achieve, at least initially, but over a longer term should prove more beneficial in economy and the numbers reached by each agency. In practice this recommendation has been achieved by progressive adult literacy programs over the United States. However, it appears that new funding approaches for social programs and adult literacy programs must be initiated at the Federal level to implement this goal.

Administrative changes should be made in public school adult education programs. Adult education has and will likely continue to be a secondary interest of public school officials. Adult literacy education has little representation in the various state governments where appropriations are made for funds. As a result; it, substantially, has remained a federal program in terms of funds expended. For many reasons it appears feasible to change the Federal funding patterns for literacy education. Alternatives that appear practical include the following: fund local community organizations, or fund an autonomous agency connected to the public schools similar to the vocational technical schools in terms of clarity of mission. In any event, the purpose of the administrative organization and funding patterns should be that of facilitating community based adult literacy education. A second purpose of the administrative organization should be to address the social, educational and occupational problems of the target population. While these dimensions were addressed in the Federal legislation creating the adult basic education program, they appear to have been largely lost in the programs of 1985. Given the nature and mission of public school education, it is highly unlikely that they can be accomplished without modifications such as those discussed above.

A first step towards developing community based adult literacy education should be a continuing dialogue by representatives of social agencies, volunteer educational agencies, public school adult education, social agencies and representatives from the illiterate target population. The federal government or an educational foundation should convene such groups and continue them until a viable national policy begins to emerge from the meetings and public support is assured. Such a process may take several years to achieve significant results. Inaction may be devastating to an emerging adult literacy education program that is the only hope left to as many as fifteen to twenty-five percent of the adult population of the United States.

SUMMARY

This chapter has recounted some of the problems of illiteracy and literacy education among adults in the United States. More than 20 million adults, or approximately one of every five, are identified as lacking the reading and writing abilities needed to address the minimum demands of daily life in contemporary society. Illiteracy is not a new phenomenon in the United States; despite decades of compulsory school attendance the problem persists.

The authors challenge the efficacy of the traditional school based literacy education programs that emerged following the adoption of the 1964 Economic Opportunity Act. The chapter is divided into the following topical sections: overview, definitions, scope of adult illiteracy in the United States, criticisms of the educational establishment and speculations on a new approach.

It is recommended that greater emphasis be placed on the use of volunteers and volunteer agencies in literacy education. As it is believed that a number of factors associated with the public school establishment are impediments to the effective delivery of literacy education services to adults it is posited volunteers in the local community may be more successful.

PART THREE

RESEARCH AND THEORY

For at least three decades educators of adults in
the United States have been anxious about the
status of inquiry and explanation. The search for
meaningful structures in research and theory are
apparent in the literature of adult education from
the classics, including Brunner and Associates,
(1959) and Jensen, Liveright and Hallenbeck (1964).
The search has generated a volume of criticism
of both research and theory that has been
predominantly negative. Only occasionally has the
youthfulness of the filed been cited as a
mitigating factor in the critcial literature and
even less frequently has there been any kind of
theorizing about the research of adult education
Maturity of the field optimistically has been
cited as a major factor in the eventual improvement
in theory and research or vice versa. The decade
of the 1980s marks the fifth decade since the first
doctoral degrees were awarded. The provision of
college courses in adult education has only a
slighly longer history. Less than 75 years ago
education of adult immigrants was given national
attention and agricultural education for adult
farmers became a national policy.
Thousands of men and women have taken courses
in adult education and more than 3,000 doctoral
degrees have been awarded. During the period the
knowledge base of adult has increased steadily.
The direction of growth has not always been
apparent and even the validity of some of the
knowledge generated by adult education research can
be challenged.

Yet, there is reason to believe progress in theory and research is discernible. Chapters six and seven provide additional comment and criticism of the developing theory and trends in research. Indirectly, a theory of adult education research itself is suggested in chapter six. Explanations for the nature and status of adult education research have traditionally been like much of the research : atheoretical. Chapter six begins what will hopefully become a larger conversation on the theory of adult education inquiry. For example, is the current condition of adult education research explained best by the personalities and backgrounds of the early leaders in the field, the nature of adult education as a field of service, by developmental structure, the nature of the subject of inquiry, by the research base, or by some combination of two or more of these constructs?

Chapter seven presents an array of what are referred to as microtheories that are popular or which have potential. They will not be listed here, but they range from andragogy to evaluation. Adult education theory, like adult education research is presented as being weakly conceptualized.

Chapter Six.

NEW PERSPECTIVES ON THE STUDY OF ADULTS

Increasing popularity of lifelong learning as
reflected by public attention to the topic, large
enrolments of adults in learning activities and a
growing population of professionally prepared
educators of adults combine to challenge those who
are concerned with the knowledge base of adult
education. As there are a variety of ways by which
humanity has attempted to create knowledge over the
years understanding of a phenomenon is legitimized
in diverse ways: authority, philosophy, experience,
intuition, and science. Concern, here, is with a
scientific basis of knowledge. We are interested
in what is referred to as research: a practice
that usually includes stating a question, making
observations, collecting, analyzing and
interpreting data and drawing conclusions. It is
through this process that we have improved
knowledge about adult learners and have arrived at
some helpful conclusions as the following:

1. Educational achievement levels are
   associated with participation in lifelong
   learning activities.
2. Entitlements appear to be positively
   correlated with participation.
3. The ability to learn does not necessarily
   decline during the first six decades of
   life.
4. It is not possible to predict "motivation"
   for participation by knowing the content
   of a learning activity.
5. A large proportion of participants in

lifelong learning activities seem to
identify some life change with their
enrolments in a learning
activity. (Long, 1982)

Despite increasing knowledge about the adult
learner and the context for educating a number of
important questions have yet to be addressed. For
example,

1. What kinds of associations exist between
   specific learning styles and particular
   educational techniques?
2. Is age associated with learning styles?
   If so, how and why?
3. Why is educational achievement associated
   with adult participation in educational
   activities?
4. Can attitudes toward education be changed
   during childhood? If so, how? What
   variables and processes are useful in
   bringing about positive attitude changes?

Additional and different questions are
concerned with programming processes, the social
environment, the physical environment, promotion
and marketing, the development of adult educators,
and so forth. The literature is replete with
numerous examples of efforts to develop inventories
and agendas of needed research. More is said on
these inventories later as this chapter is
developed. Seven major topics concerned with New
Perspectives on the Study of Adults are discussed
in the following pages: (a) some new perspectives;
(b) status of research; (c) research approaches;
(d) needed research; (e) research needs (f)
observations and speculations and (g) summary.

SOME NEW PERSPECTIVES

The literature on adult education research reveals
two related, but sometimes distinct views on the
purpose and role of research (Long, 1983b; Long,
Hiemstra and Associates, 1980). One view
emphasizes research as a means of answering
questions about practice, the other approach is
more theoretical and the emphasis is more upon why
than how. In other words, research in adult
education is often a practical applied activity.
Additionally, for some, there is an emerging or
expanding interest in research as an academic

activity, i.e., as a means of generating new knowledge or 'understanding' even if it has no immediate application to an education 'problem.' An even yet undeveloped area of concern includes a theory of adult education research. This area should include questions and hypotheses concerning the reasons for adult education research as indicated above as well as postulates concerning the nature of the subjects , i.e. adults, the characteristics of the discipline and so forth. Therefore, several different subtopics relating to the study of adults are explicated in the following pages. They include questions emerging from the two major tendencies noted in adult education research: research for application and research for theoretical purposes. Topics more directly related to issues of research theory itself include a discussion of the distinctive characteristics of the adult as a subject of study and comments concerning the implications of the structure of the field and/or developmental status of prior research. The possibility that the developmental status of the field of practice is approached from two different directions. The first focuses on the field from a historical perspective. The second, while related, comes from a more structural foundation based on the work of Knowles (1973) and Long (1983e).

One reasonable way to explain the two main streams of adult education research interests is in terms of the development of the field of and the kinds of people (institutional bases) attracted into adult education graduate programs. Furthermore, the following periods in the recent history of adult education in the U.S. (a) the early years - 1920-1949, (b) the middle years - 1950-1964, (c) the current years - 1965-present, are used as hypothetical development time frames for understanding the field. From the above hypothetical position two sets of questions were recently presented to a select group of reputational leaders in the field as follows:

1. What are the significant trends/events or characteristics that may be useful in arriving at a concept of the modern era of adult education, similar (or different from) the concept statement proposed above? What changes would you suggest in the above concept by periods and how would you describe each period?

2. What kind of research "tradition"
characterizes adult education? Is there
more than one "tradition" concerning
the philosophy, purpose and methodology of
research in adult education? What seems
to be the source or explanations for
either the stability or change in
traditions?

Replies to the questions were stimulating and
informative even though agreement among the
correspondents was limited.

One of the respondents, referred to here as
the first professor, said "When I entered the
field of adult education in 1934 and for a long
time thereafter, it was a kind of summit meeting of
leaders or representatives of various institutions.
Librarians, public school people, general
university extension directors, and representatives
of the Cooperative Extension Service were most
prominent but many other agencies were represented
as well. The research tended to suit the interests
of these several entities, although there were many
efforts to bridge them. The first major break came
with the growth of group dynamics beginning in
1947. Adult education started off in a wholly new
direction, the inter-relationship of an academic
discipline -- in this case, social psychology -- to
adult education as a field of practice, with adult
education making a greater contribution to the
discipline than the discipline (social psychology)
did to adult education.

. . . Before long, adult education was tending
toward an almost completely derivative status, the
beginning point being some principle or construct
drawn from an aspect of one of the social sciences,
chiefly sociology or psychology. What came to be
called 'research design' was elevated to an
important status, a position which was partially
won because almost all the research in the field
was carried out in academic settings by graduate
students. A gulf grew up between graduate
education and adult educational practice; the
people who worked for graduate degrees were trained
to be researchers, not professionals (First
Professor,1982).

Another colleague also indicated three
different groups historically may have been
involved in the development of the field of adult
education since 1920 even though he did not agree
with the index years used.

An even more recent circular letter sent to all current members of the Commission of Professors of Adult Education, a sub-unit of the American Association of Adult and Continuing Education, generated a similar divergence in views concerning the kind of research needed (Long, 1984d). One group of respondents favor more attention to the theoretical underpinnings of education of adults. This group is interested in understanding why something seems to be so. In contrast, another group of professors of adult education is equally interested in empirical and practical research. They want to know how to do something.

Problems with the research concerning education of adults are not limited to only the historical traditions and the relative emphases on how and why questions. These two factors are little more than symptoms. Conceptualization is the larger problem area. Of course conceptualization is associated with the above factors, a discussion limited to historical traditions and the practice-theory dichotomy fails to get at the heart of the problem: conceptualization, integration and synthesis are generally weak or absent. This problem seems to unlie the criticism of Bittner (1950) and Brunner and associates (1959) noted later in this chapter.

Reflecting upon this state of affairs in the attitudes and preferences of adult education professors and the characteristics of research in the field, a comparative analogy with medicine can be drawn. The analogy goes something like this, instead of studying the questions of the circulation of blood from the view of the circulation system, or reaction to stimuli based on a perspective of the nervous system, educators of adults have tended to study a limited part of the system. Their behavior would be likened to a study of only the heart, of the lungs, of the blood vessels or of the capillaries while attempting to explain the phenomenon of blood circulation by an extremely limited perspective of the selected part of the system. Thus educators of adults talk and write about such diverse topics of military education, credit courses, non-credit activities, nutrition education, satisfaction and achievement, personality and development, self-directed learning, participation in group learning and so forth without comprehensive theories or careful consideration of alternative frameworks. See chapter seven for observations concerning a

Newtonian view of science versus a perspective based on quantum mechanics.

For example, turn to two of the more productive research topics in U.S. adult education: participation studies and self-directed learning. Inquiry concerning each of the topics has proceeded as if there were no relationship between them despite the reality that a good argument can be made for the thesis that participation in group learning and participation in self-directed learning theoretically may be closely related phenomena. Being "closely related" does not necessarily suggest that they are identical, neither would one suggest the lungs or heart are identical, but both are necessary in understanding many questions of the human circulation system. Would it be incorrect to suggest that learning is learning whether pursued in a group setting or an autonomous mode? Could one defend the suggestion that explanatory motives, obstacles and precipitators of learning generally may be similar for both group learning and self-directed learning? If not, how can the manifest or latent differences that might be identified be explained? Furthermore, is it plausible to suggest that individuals may use different learning resources according to some kind of rational scheme (Houle, 1984)? If so, is such behavior normative? Is it restricted to certain kinds of individuals? If so, what kind of people use a variety of educational media or modes and what kind tend to limit their learning activity to one or two media or modes?

The tendency among educators of adults to focus on the adult learner as a unidimensional being has recently elicited another set of criticisms. Some believe that adult education research has focused too heavily upon psychological studies (Rubenson, 1982). In contrast, these individuals call for more sociological analyses. This writer is not convinced that the emphasis on psychological explanations is sufficiently heavy to "tilt" theory away from other explanations. Nevertheless, the observation is suggestive; certainly, if the psychological explanations dominate the literature and if they fail to explain and predict adequately in important areas, then educators should search for other explanations. The argument about dominant disciplines in adult education research is similar to the debate over dominant research methodology. What is needed is a recognition that more of some kinds of research rather than less of other kinds is needed.

Questions should be asked why researchers in adult education departed from the sociologically based investigations that were popular at an earlier time. Is the answer to be found in the nature of the field as identified by the first professor cited earlier? Recall he suggested interest in social psychology that was paramount about 1950 may have been an influential factor. But also it was after this period that London and Verner made their greatest contributions. Or is the answer to be discovered in reputational analysis. A preliminary study conducted by this writer indicates that the research of professors of adult education may be strongly influenced by sociological relationships that exists among the professors themselves. No special review of the sociologically based research was specifically conducted for the puposes of this book, but it appears that the sociologically related body of literature available between 1960 and 1975 was not a small one. For example, Coolie Verner's work is too extensive to list here. According to Dickinson (1979) Verner authored almost 400 items, many of which were based on his background in rural sociology. Jack London's work, cited in this book and in Long (1983b) was also of a sociological nature. Verner's student, Dickinson, also published a number of similar studies. A careful review of the literature may generate a much larger body of sociological work than Rubenson's criticism would suggest. Nevertheless, the criticism, even if completely unfounded raises questions concerning research proclivities of adult educators. A major question that bears repeating is why did the psychologically based research become prominent while the sociological work became less visible?

Elsewhere (Long, 1980a) it is argued that the study of adults is different from other research in some specific ways. Suggestions on this topic have been criticized, but it appears they have sufficient merit to observe that conceptually and procedurally the research is influenced by the characteristics of adults.

Distinguishing Characteristics

First, it is generally recognized that a range of differences distinguishes research in the natural sciences from inquiry in the social sciences. If this is not the case, how does one explain the many books on research that are designed to communicate how to conduct social science research (Gibson,

1960)? To suggest that there are features that distinguish the two kinds of research does not suggest that assumptions on which statistical analyses proceed, or the way hypotheses are stated, or even that research reports are written or structured differently. It can be argued that the human and the monkey are both mammals, but to say that they have no distinguishing characteristics is foolish. Social science and education research have some special features associated with the objects of study just as the natural sciences have some special features associated with their objects. Furthermore, the objects of research in the study of education of adults are often different from the objects of research in childhood education. For example, despite a large body of childhood research concerning morphological readiness, adult educators have not been overly interested in such explanations for learning behavior in adults. The idea of learning readiness in adults seems likely to be more associated with emotional, affective or personality variables, experiences and social variables than with morphological developments.

Just as humans and monkeys are both mammals, adults and children are both human, but to deny they are different in substantive ways is illogical. For some purposes their similarities may be more important than their differences but for other purposes the differences may be more significant. For example, studies of medical treatment may be based on similarities while behavioral studies may require very different research designs. Differences among objects of study present the researcher with research challenges concerning strategies, procedures, logistics, and design. Questions posed by childhood and adult educators concerning learning, cognitive styles, cognitive development, memory, recall, personality and so forth, sometimes may be similar. They may also differ (White, 1962). The extensive debate concerning andragogy tends to confirm this view (Carlson, 1979; Elias, 1979; Knowles, 1979; Knudson, 1979; McKenzie, 1977; McKenzie, 1979). Furthermore, the investigator's problems of obtaining a sample, issues of validity, questions of levels of sophistication, effects of maturation, etc. can differ according to the ages and research problems studied.

Similar concerns have been expressed in the psychology of aging literature (Birren and Cunningham, 1985). Birren and Cunningham, for example, suggest the Cascade model of analysis may be useful in the study of aging as "it is particularly germane to research situations that are not ripe for experimental manipulation or that are intrinsically unsuited for meaningful or ethical manipulations" (p. 23). In another place they indicate "the nature of the phenomena being studied (in human aging) may limit the extent to which meaningful, ethical manipulations are possible or technically feasible" (p. 23-24). They continue, "certainly, controlled experiments are preferable. . . . Unfortunately, not all topics within the area of behavior lend themselves readily to their approach" (p. 24).

Contrasts in the status of inquiry between scholars primarily identified as adult educators and gerontologists appear to exist. However, based on recent reviews of research by Birren and Cunningham (1985) and Birren, Cunningham and Yamamoto (1983), it appears that gerontologists have been more actively engaged in developing, modifying and testing research procedures tailored to the basic characteristics of their subjects and theory. In contrast, Adult education research literature does not seem to reflect a similar vitality.

Seven characteristics appear to have implications for designing, conducting and interpreting research in adult education:

1. The length of the adult period of life.
2. The various definitions of the adult.
3. The various definitions of adult education.
4. Ethics and values in adult education.
5. The nature of adult samples and sample sizes.
6. The sophisticated nature of adult subjects.
7. The pluralistic, naive and incomplete nature of theoretical paradigms.

Figure 6:1 conceptually illustrates just one of the distinguishing features of adult life that may affect concepualization , design and implementation of research using adult samples. Figure 6:1 depicts life as expansive, both horizontally and vertically. Individual differences, biologically and socially provide opportunity for ideosyncratic ontological development. Childhood represents a time of life when individuals are likely to be more similar and as they advance through life they become more different.

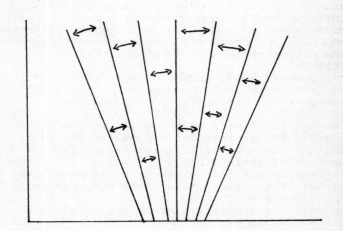

AGE

Individual Differences

Figure 6:1   A Model of Individual Differences across Life - A, B, C, Illustrate the hypothesis of explanding differences among individuals with increasing age.

Bergevin (1967) reminds the educator of adults that experience, as illustrated in figure 6:1, differentiate adult and child learners. It is important for both practitioners and researchers, if they are different, to be aware that adults have a greater history of experiences, different kinds of experiences, and that they interpret their experiences differently than children (Bergevin, 1967). Equally important, a range of differences exists among adults (Long, 1972). A group of adults is likely to have a greater variation in skills, interests, experience and education than a similar group of children. In essence they are more highly differentiated (Bergevin, 1967). These social and psychological facts are important for both research and instruction.

To reiterate, to observe that investigators who study adults must contend with research problems that are different from problems encountered by childhood investigators is not the same as saying that transductive reasoning replaces inductive or deductive reasoning in adult study (Baltes and Schaie, 1973; Murgatroyd, 1977). Neither does the observation suggest that Mill's Cannons or other principles of research do not apply in the study of adults. The major point is investigators who study adults must be aware of the characteristics that distinguish research in adult education and be prepared to plan their research accordingly. Some, as attested by the recent comment of a colleague, believe for example, quantitative research cannot address the basic issues in the education of adults. While this writer does not agree totally with that position, it indicates a view that research designs and procedures should reflect the distinguishing characteristics and nature of adults and their education. Support for the validity of this view can be found in a number of places, but Silverman (1985,p.2) says it as well as any. He says "...it is an increasingly accepted view of a science that work becomes scientific by adopting methods of study appropriate to the data at hand.".

Sources of Influence

Are there other sources of influence on the nature of adult education research than those discussed above? Knowles (1973) suggests there are. He theorizes that research methods in adult education may emerge from structural properties of the field associated adult education as a field of social practice. Long, (1983e) suggests that resting the theory of adult education research on the developmental stages of the field is attractive, but unwieldy as conceptualized. Therefore, a different approach is recommended. Long (1983e) proposes that the evolving spiral as offered by Knowles is more closely related to the corpus of knowledge available to (a) the entire field of research in adult education, or (b) to specific limited areas of inquiry. Evidence presented by Long (1983e) is supportive of the latter. Using articles published in Adult Education (Dickinson and Rusnell, 1971; Long, 1983c) he concludes the general research literature does not reveal a sequential spiral. In contrast, when the theory was applied to the research on participation and self-directed learning it was concluded that evolutionary developments in methodology was suggested. Further investigation of the research literature is recommended before the question can be answered with finality. However, since Long's (1983e) study additional work in the area of self-directed learning indicates that Knowles' original proposition was at least partially correct. If one assumes that the developmental stage of the field of adult education can be equated with the status of any one or two areas of research the proposition can be accepted. On the other hand, if that assumption is too generous, then the partial confirmation is the most that is likely at this time. Even the partial explanation as noted by Long (1983e) provides an opportunity for the development of a new perspective on the nature of adult education research methodology in the United States.

STATUS OF ADULT EDUCATION RESEARCH

The status of research concerning the education of adults, especially the research labelled as adult education has been described by numerous writers (Dannenmaier, 1962; Grabowski, 1980; Kreitlow, 1964, 1964, 1970; and Long, 1983a Long, 1983b and White, 1962). Also, it has been compared with research in other countries (Brookfield, 1982). Generally, most of the published comments have been critical and negative. In 1962, Dannenmaier observed "adult education has not been noted for its meticulous attention to self-study of its theories and practices" (1962, p. 9). He tempered the severity of his criticism some by noting that there were good reasons for the state of affairs in adult education research: "a thing must exist before it can be examined, and it must exist in considerable quantity before it can be studied with precision" (Dannenmaier, 1962, p. 9).

In recent years some of Dannenmaier's justifications for a weak research base in adult education have been negated. Following World War II the field began to grow at an unprecedented rate. By 1980 it is estimated that approximately 3,000 doctoral degrees in adult education had been awarded in the United States (Long, 1983b). The nature of graduate study, which requires a research dissertation, is an important factor in the expansion of the research base. During the same period, estimates of adults involved in educational activities ranged from less than 20 million to 90 percent of the adult population (Long, 1983b). Thus a reasonable body of practitcioners and subjects for study was developing.

Two polar perceptions of the status of adult education research are discernible in the U.S. literature. Bittner (1950) and Brunner and his associates (1959) and White (1962) made comments not unlike those of Dannenmaier (1962). Bittner was pessimistic about the ability of adult educators to conduct useful research whereas, Brunner and his associates implied that, at least up to 1957, adult educators had not conducted much effective research. White (1962) indicated that adult education research had limited significance. In contrast Knox (1985) and Long (1983b) comment more favorably on the status development of research in adult education.

The contemporary status and criticism of adult education research seem to be better understood within parameters set by Brunner and Associates (1959); Jensen, Liveright and Hallenbeck (1964); Long, Hiemstra and Associates (1980) and Long (1983b).

Bittner (1950), Brunner (1959), Dannenmaier (1962) Griffith (1979) and Kreitlow (1960, 1964 and 1970) have discussed the weaknesses of adult education research. They are in some general agreement concerning the nature of the problem: inadequate research procedures; inadequate research skills; unevenness in topical coverage; and limited utility. Others such as Matkin (1980) and Long (1983b) have been less critical. Long said,

My perception of the vast array of research reviewed for the purposes of this volume leads to ... an optimistic view. This perception

is ... influenced by appreciation for some of
the issues that confront the older disciplines
. . . . Yes, adult education as a field is
challenged to clean up its terminology, to
establish parameters, to.improve the rigor of
its research and practice. (1983b p. 308).

Several important events over the 26 years
that intervened between Brunner's book and Long's
work altered the field of practice, research and
study concerning education of adults in the United
States. The important events contributing to an
improvement in adult education research are
associated with the expansion of adult education as
a field of practice and the increasing numbers of
graduate programs of study in adult education.

A direct relationship appears to exist between
the establishment and expansion of graduate
programs of adult education and research
productivity. Long's (1977) study of the
publication practices of professors of adult
education suggests the field began a rapid
expansion about 1966. Between 1950 and 1973, 81 of
the 172 members of the 1972 Commission of
Professors of Adult Education (CPAE) produced 2,098
publications. In his review of research for his
book Long (1983b) examined an estimated 6,000 -
9,000 pieces of research. The annual production of
adult education research in the United States in
the last decade was probably close to the total
body of research reviewed by Brunner and his
colleagues (1959). In the ten years 1971-1980
numerous articles and research papers were
published in Adult Education or presented at the
annual Adult Education Research Conference and the
Lifelong Learning Research Conference. Recently
other regional research conferences have been
established in the mid-west and Texas.

Even with the phenomenal growth in the number
of researchers, numbers of media for reporting
research and the rapid expansion of research
bibliographies, some problems continue to plague
the study of adults in the United States. While
all of the reasons for limited progress in
knowledge of adult learners cannot be explained
historically, explanation and justification for the
current state of affairs can be partially explained
and justified by knowledge of the historical
structure of the field of adult education.

RESEARCH APPROACHES

In the previous section, some distinguishing characteristics of adult education research were discussed. That section did not elaborate on the characteristics of the research approaches, or types of research, used in the study of education of American adults. This section is designed to further develop the topic in a two-step procedure. First, three major subtopics are examined; they are studies of research, descriptive research, and calls for different approaches. Secondly, some concluding and interpretative comments are provided.

Studies of Research
Research concerning the education of adults in the United States has been a topic of numerous studies. Some of these have been reviews of the research, others have addressed issues of quality (Matkin, 1980) and others have examined questions of procedures and topics (Dickinson and Rusnell, 1971; Long and Agyekum (1974). Other investigations included DeCrow and Loague (1970) and Grabowski and Loague (1970).

The above investigations focused on one of two major sources of research: doctoral dissertations (DeCrow and Loague, 1970; Grabowski, 1973; Grabowski and Loague 1970); journal articles (Dickinson and Rusnell, 1971; Long and Agyekum, 1974; Long and Fisher, 1979). The authors are in remarkable agreement concerning the distribution of research by types and the dominance of description in the two bodies of literature studied.

DeCrow and Loague (1970) reported abstracts of 505 doctoral studies completed in adult education 1963-1967. They reported 17 methodological designs, 34 historical studies, 97 experimental investigations and 357 descriptive dissertations. Grabowski and Loague (1970) reported a similar study of 297 dissertations completed in 1968-1969. They identified 5 philosophical studies, 9 methodological investigations, 16 using the historical approaches, 47 based on experimental designs and 200 were descriptive dissertations.

The studies of journal articles by Dickinson and Rusnell (1971), Long and Agyekum (1974), and Long and Fisher (1979) provide similar results. Collectively the studies confirm descriptive designs as being the dominant research type

143

employed by adult educators between 1950 and 1980. Studies of adults conducted in the fields of gerontology, educational psychology, psychology, instructional designs, and other disciplines have not been analyzed. Thus, it is difficult to assert that the emphasis on descriptive research by graduate adult educators and those individuals who choose to publish in the adult education journal is either typical or atypical. Therefore, comments here are limited to the research identified as adult education research rather than the broader topic of research concerning the education of adults.

If research in adult education primarily is based on descriptive designs, does that mean that it is all of one kind? Not at all! The range of approaches used in descriptive research is discussed in a later section.

Meta-Research. Sork (1980) has identified a typology of meta-research that includes six forms of systematic study of adult education research. They are as follows:

1. Type I.   Inventories of Research
2. Type II.   General Reviews of Research
3. Type III.   Critical Reviews on Specific Topics
4. Type IV.   Research Agenda or Taxonomies of Need Research
5. Type V.   Focused Critiques of Research Methodology
6. Type VI.   Framework of paradigms for Understanding and Improving Research

Each of the above six types of meta-research are briefly described below.

Type I. -Inventories of Research. There are a number of examples of this type of meta-research in adult education literature so an exhaustive list of such inventories will not be provided here. For illustrative purposes, reference to the three books published on adult dissertation abstracts by the Adult Education Association seems to be adequate. Other lists of other research activities have been published in journal articles and by ERIC. These lists are usually limited to providing simple bibliographic information on the research. They are occasionally supplemented with an abstract.

Type II. -General Reviews of Research. This type of meta-research is designed to provide a general overview of adult education research, usually within a given time period. Examples of this type of research are more abundant in the 1950's and 1960's and were published in the Review of Educational Research of the American Educational Research Association.

The classical example of Type II meta-research is provided by Brunner and Associates (1959). Long's (1983b) work is the first and most recent comparable effort of this kind since 1959.

Other illustrations of this type of research are found in the 1969 and 1970 handbooks of adult education.

Type III. -Critical Reviews on Specific Topics. This type is self-explanatory. Research on a specific topic is intensively and extensively reviewed to determine the status of knowledge on a specifically defined topic. In a sense, Brunner's and Long's (1983b) overview books contained a number of such reviews of this nature in each chapter. Other illustrations of Type III meta-research are to be found in the pages of adult education journal articles. Verner and his students were frequent contributors to the literature of this type. More quality reviews of this kind are desirable.

Type IV. -Research Agendas or Taxonomies of Needed Research. Discussion of meta-research Type V, Research Agendas or Taxonomies of Needed Research, is not very productive. This is not to suggest that research agendas are not needed. Rather, research agendas are seldom developed for the field as a result of general writing and by speeches. Research agendas are perceived to be very personal. Professors and others engaged in research may be encouraged to develop an agenda for research by the presence of funds and local institutional pressures. But without such external pressures it is likely that they study topics that are of personal or direct interest to them with limited reference to the opinions of others. Related comments on research agendas are shared later.

Type V. -Focused Critiques of Research Methodology. Type V research is also self-explanatory. It is research that focuses on the methods of research. Examples of this kind of research are to be found in <u>Adult Education</u> and in papers presented at research conferences.

<u>Type VI.</u> -<u>Framework of Paradigms for Understanding and Improving Research</u>. Type VI meta-research is designed to go beyond the methodological inquiry of Type V to look at research in adult and continuing education from a broader perspective. This chapter serves as an illustration of Type VI meta-research. Studies on the content analysis of <u>Adult Education</u> are additional further examples of this type (Dickinson and Rusnell 1971; Long and Agyekum 1974).

<u>Descriptive Reseach</u>
Studies of adult education research by Dickinson and Rusnell (1971), Long and Agyekum (1974) and others support the view that published adult education research is dominated by descriptive methods. These studies, however, have tended to lump descriptive research together without concern for differences within the category. As a consequence, descriptive research may have taken on the image of a monolithic concept based on one research procedure and very simple statistical or deductive analysis. Long (1983d) demonstrated that adult education descriptive research in the United States is multifaceted and includes numerous data collection activities that employ diverse sophisticated procedures. He cautioned "failure to recognize this inhibits the development of an awareness of the richness and diversity of procedures currently in use to better understand adult education" (p. 372).

Long adopted four objectives for his study of descriptive research in adult education in the United States: They were to: (a) determine the frequency of use of descriptive research designs, 1971-80; (b) identify the range of topics examined by use of descriptive designs, 1971-80; (c) identify the procedures used to collect data in descriptive studies, 1971-80; and (d) determine if there is any conspicuous trend in the publication of descriptive research, 1971-80.

A summary of the findings indicates the frequency of descriptive studies in adult education does not appear to have changed significantly since the work of Dickinson and Rusnell (1971) and Long and Agyekum (1974). Recent work by Long and Fisher (1979) revealed 39.4 percent of the articles published during 1973-80 were descriptive. A similar analysis of research papers presented at

the Adult Education Research Conference (AERC),
1971-80, shows 55 percent were descriptive (Long,
1983d).

Eleven different topical categories of
descriptive research were developed by Long and
Agyekum (1974). They include adult learning;
program planning and administration including
participation and evaluation; institutional
sponsors; adult education as a field of study;
instructional materials and methods; program area;
personnel and staff; international perspective;
particular group; and other. Descriptive research
published in the journal 1971-80, most frequently
concerned program planning and administration
topics (36.7%), specifically participation issues.
In comparison, the topic addressed most frequently
at the AERC in the 1971-81 period was the program
area topic (22.9%) with program planning and
administration (18.6%) a close second.

Perhaps the most interesting finding reported
by Long (1983d) concerns the variety of descriptive
research procedures employed in adult education
research. He identified six broad categories of
research procedures: (a) questionnaires, scales
and other instruments; (b) interviews; (c)
observations; (d) studies based on documents and
other records; (e) delphi techniques; and (f)
grounded theory, an interview and/or observation
based procedure.

No distinct trends were apparent in the
sources studied by Long. Differences between the
two sources concerning possible trends made
conclusions difficult. For example, the percentage
of descriptive research in the journal remained
fairly stable over the ten year period, whereas the
percentage of descriptive studies reported at AERC
increased dramatically. The AERC papers also
revealed an increasing use of delphi and grounded
theory procedures; but no such increase was noted
in the research articles.

The investigation of research in adult
education using AERC papers and journal articles
as sources indicates that descriptive research
procedures are more diverse than commonly might be
believed. Some of the research is also believed to
be well designed and has been subjected to analysis
by sophisticated statistical treatment (Matkin,
1980). The sophistication of analytic procedures
such as ANOVA, split-plot analysis, factor analysis
and multiple regression is sufficient to be
separated conceptually from traditional studies

based on common descriptive statistics such as means, medians, models and percentages.

Other Research Studies

Several studies of published adult education research have been reported in the recent past. Dickinson and Rusnell (1971); Long and Agyekum (1974); Grabowski and Loague (1970); Long and Fisher (1979) and Long (1983c) agree on the dominance of descriptive research in the field. Yet as noted, Long (1983d) reports it would be incorrect to assume that the descriptive research is of one kind.

A number of educators of adults have issued diverse calls for emphasis on different kinds of research such as historical studies and experimental designs. Others have expressed disappointment with what they perceive to be an overemphasis on quantitative research procedures. These individuals believe that much of the quantitative work has degenerated to an overemphasis on procedures at the expense of substance.

Data are not currently available to prove the assertion, but it appears that an expanded use of qualitative methods of research has developed recently. These kinds of studies include the use of grounded theory, anthropological and ethnographic approaches and related research methods that place an increasing dependence upon rationality and logic in observations and interpretation.

It is difficult to establish cause and effect but one explanation for the domination of descriptive research in adult education and the disaffection with quantitative methods may be associated with the distinguishing characteristics of research noted earlier. Ethical considerations and personal values of adult educators interfere with the process of designing investigations that must depend on manipulating subjects in some way in an effort to overcome their sophistication. Problems in obtaining large samples and the criticism of small sample research in quantitative research compels the researcher who must use small samples to use different strategies such as meta-research (studying and reanalyzing an existing body of previously conducted research), grounded theory, which seldom requires more than a dozen subjects, or conducting secondary analysis of data collected for other purposes. Of course, other explanations for the adult educators' fascination for the descriptive qualitative research methods can be defended logically. One such suggestion is that the graduates of advanced study in adult education generally duplicate the kinds of research values and methods of their professors and that it would be illogical to suggest that the choices of methods are always rationally based.

Different Approaches. Despite the apparent progress noted in the study of adults in the past 30 years, a number of calls have been issued for new and different approaches to research. These calls usually have been pleas for more qualitative inquiries contrasted with quantitative research. There are those who believe the currently perceived stress upon quantitative empirical studies ignores other conceptual inquiry. As a consequence, the appropriateness of the hypo-thetico-deductive model has been questioned.

Acceptable approaches recommended as alternatives to quantitative studies include a variety of qualitative methods such as grounded theory, observation and ethnographic studies. Such proposals also legitimize small samples, down to the individual level. Grounded theory and ethnographic studies seem to have been the most popular of the new approaches. Examples of the grounded theory approach are rather easily found in published materials. Mezirow, Darkenwald and Knox (1975) is one of the most conspicuous examples. Marieneau and Klinger's (1977) study of participation is a good example of an anthropological approach.

Elsewhere, (Long, 1980c) this writer has rejected the idea that adult educators have overemphasized any of the approaches and methods of research. Rather, they have underutilized many of the available approaches and methods.

NEEDED RESEARCH

There is apparently no limits to the educator's interest in needed research concerning the education of adults. My files reveal the topic is a recurring one at adult education conferences and that it has been addressed in both published (Brady, 1982; Knox, 1977; Long, 1982, 1983b) and unpublished sources. Brady's (1982) report is

149

based on a review of selected literature and responses from thiry-six professors of adult education. According to Knox (1977), his publication is based on his familiarity with relevant research reported in the fifteen years before 1977. Long's (1983b) comments resulted from his review of hundreds of research articles and papers in preparation for his book.

Brady (1982) reports his survey revealed some consistent recommendations for research. His respondents seemed to have focused on research needs in the following topical areas: adult counselling, career change, creativity, delivery systems, effective adjustment to physical and psychological change, effective evaluation, international adult education, needs assessment, new techologies, learning strategies, longitudinal studies on adult learning and intelligence motivation, teaching styles and changes needed in many colleges and universities to provide effective education for adults.

Knox (1977) divided his research questions among three categories: adults as learners, program development, and organization and administration. Approximately 125 different research questions are recommended in his thirty-nine page booklet.

Long (1983b) selected nine topical classifications to include research questions identified in his research review. They include participation, attitudes concerning education, learning, programmatic questions, social environment, physical environment, socio-physical environment, teaching, and general topics. In addition, he identified thiry-five questions, some of which are multiple questions such as the following: are there common basic variables associated with both educational achievement levels and participation in adult education? If so, what are they? What are their origins? How are they developed? How can the negative effects be mitigated? The above questions illustrate the limits of current research and inquiry in adult education. Answers to such questions are needed but it is unlikely they will be forthcoming as a response to taxonomies like the above. Given the limited usefulness of taxonomies of needed research let us turn the phrase around and examine research needs.

RESEARCH NEEDS

Need
Before discussing specific areas of need, let us
turn our attention to the concept of need. The
concern, here, is with what has been defined as
normative, prescriptive or real needs. According
to Monette (1977) "a need may be called normative
when it constitutes a deficiency or gap between a
'desirable' standard and the standard that actually
exists" (Monette, 1977, p. 118). Others call such
a construct a prescriptive or real need. Following
McKinley (1973), two models were used in the
identification of the research needs discussed
here. They are the problem-need model which is
derived from diagnosing a deviation from a standard
of adequacy and the goal-identification model which
contributes to a general improvement focus rather
than just a remedial focus.
     Five general research needs have been selected
for limited development. Each of the needs are
worthy of much fuller discussion than can be
provided here. The needs include the following:

1. Needs associated with conceptualizing
   research.
2. Needs associated with the integration of
   adult education research.
3. Need for programs of research.
4. Need to improved dissemination of
   research.
5. Need for improved research-reporting
   skills.

Research Concepts
The assumption about the instrumental purposes of
research noted earlier should be borne in mind
here.   There are at least two different
philosophical perspectives of knowledge, one sees
knowledge as requiring no further justification, it
is good because it is true, the other represents
knowledge as being functional, the goodness or
value of knowledge is derived from its usefulness.
Comments are based on the assumption that knowledge
about adult education is valued because it is
useful in some way.   It may be useful in
contributing to theory or it may be useful because
it directly helps to resolve some problems.
     Research needs concerning conceptualization of
investigations in adult education concerns are
associated with ways that research is

151

conceptualized. The conceptual need exists on at least two levels, the general level and the specific level. At the general level we are concerned with the big picture that includes such issues as the nature of knowledge, what constitutes knowledge, what are the relative merits of different ways of knowing, how do we relate the results of different approaches to studying a topic?

Apps (1972), Knowles (1973), Long (1980a) and others have addressed the broader conceptual research needs. If Apps and Knowles have been interpreted correctly, it seems they have advocated different ideas. Apps appears to recommend a broader framework within which knowledge may be created. His conceptual parameters include thinking, sensing, synthesizing, and accepting. Knowles' spiral concept is perceived primarily as providing a vertical dimension for the development of a scientific empirical concept. Perhaps, in some way, these two concepts can be integrated.

The important element in the comments of Apps, Knowles and Long that attracts attention is the encouragement for investigators to consider a range of alternative ways of knowing. The exhortation differs among the three, yet the theme is one that says adult educators should not worship at only one alter as far as research philosophy is concerned. Long pleads for using "appropriateness" as the criterion for the selection of a research method. Apps encourages us to consider a number of alternatives and Knowles encourages us to think developmentally about research methodology.

Conceptual needs also exist at the specific level. At this level concern is with issues associated with precisely conceived inquiries or questions peculiar to the problem. An example from another field illustrates this point. Certain chemicals such as pemoline, pictrotoxin and mentrazol have been associated with memory and learning. Most studies in the area have cast these chemicals as independent variables and memory as the dependent variables. Accordingly, research designs typically include a treatment by which one or more chemicals are inserted into the subject's bloodstream and the effect of the treatment on behavior is measured. In contrast, David Krech (1968) has hypothesized that intellectual activity may stimulate the physiological production of such chemicals. Hence, his research designs have inverted the typical dependent-independent variables, thereby behavior is the treatment and independent variable and the chemical is the dependent variable.

The inverting of independent and dependent variables is not within itself particularly innovative in conceptualizing research. However, the development of nomological structures that result in such reversal of variables may be the result of a new conceptualization or fresh approach to long standing concerns such as learning, program development and instruction.

Some research needs appear to require that adult educators develop longitudinal studies that include long-term observations of participants and non-participants, persisters and dropouts. Such designs may well begin with some subjects as early as five or six years of age. Others may begin after age eighteen, even after age fifty. But there is strong reason to believe that some useful answers to some important questions will not be available until such studies are done and done well. This point is illustrated by the impact that longitudinal studies have had on knowledge concerning adult learning ability (Long, 1983b).

There is clear and compelling evidence of the ability of adult educators to accept and use different research procedures as the anthropological, ethnological and grounded theory approaches. There is a need for the continued use of such approaches along with critical incident analysis, path analysis, loglinear analysis and multivariate statistical studies. In other words, adult educators should be as creative and innovative as possible in the design of research. There is no disagreement among us concerning the challenge of devising optimal research procedures on extremely challenging issues.

Integrative Efforts

Activities designed to integrate, consolidate and synthesize advances in knowledge of the education of adults need to be strengthened and encouraged. University Microfilms at the University of Michigan reports over two hundred dissertations in adult education were completed annually in 1978, 1979, and 1981. Bachus (1981) reports over 1100 adult education dissertations were completed in the period from 1970 to 1977. Collectively these two sources indicate more than 1700 adult education dissertations were written in the eleven year period. During the same time more than 600 research papers were presented at the two main

153

adult education research conferences and/or published journal articles. Some of the articles, dissertations, and papers are duplications. Nevertheless, the publication of more than 2,000 research reports during 1970-1980 is encouraging. Yet, it contains elements of a problem. How can we systematically refine our knowledge base so that the incremental value of numerous research projects accumulate in a meaningful manner?

In one way this problem is associated with the first research need identified in this paper. Reviews of research are not always accorded the status they deserve. Research and practice potentially can be improved more by good solid reviews of previous research than by a research project that has a limited research review base and which has limited generalizability or external validity.

Of course, the value of the reviews will depend upon adequate rigor, logic, and adherence to the highest standards of scholarship applies. It is especially important to be reminded of this expectation in this discussion of research reviews. Good reviews can be extremely helpful in illuminating several areas of concern such as gaps in the research, conflicts or contradictions, points of agreement, trends and additional hypotheses.

Cross (1981), for example, has provided one such review of the numerous participation studies. Through the reviews of the research literature on this topic, one of three explanations for participation become evident. Explanatory frameworks are based on (1) personal qualities or characteristics, (2) social characteristics and (3) institutional variables. Usually investigators have conceptualized their research to limit consideration to only one or two of these explanatory frameworks.

Other recent works are also useful in providing a good point of departure for drawing inferences for practice or for deriving ideas for future specific research direction. These include Anderson and Darkenwald's (1979) analysis of participation and persistence and Irish's (1978) dissertation on persistence studies. The work of Verner and his students illustrate early work on integrative analytical reviews. Unfortunately, we do not have the means by which we can integrate findings of the X number of investigations conducted in a given year on any topic such as associations between personality variables, instructional procedures and achievement.

Programs of Research

A third research need in adult education is related to the two previously discussed ones. There is a need for programs of research (Easting, 1979). In programs of research institutions and individual professors and practitioners are encouraged toward systematic approaches to selected issues. Advantages of developing programs of research are numerous. Some of them are as follows:

1. Institutional resources could be developed in depth. For example, library holdings and departmental resources on a given topic such as cognitive structure in adults or history of adult education or teaching techniques and personality traits could be strengthened.
2. Beginning from a given position research in the selected areas could proceed in a linear fashion.
3. Student-investigators would benefit from the regular involvement and with other researchers and would possess a greater level of sophistication prior to initiating their own research.
4. Student-investigators could cooperate in research activities in such a way as to improve the substantive, methodological and applied aspects of research.
5. Through greater specialization individual faculty members would strengthen their own scholarship and improve their abilities to lead and direct and supervise unfolding research.

Reviews of the research contributions from the major producers of published research in the United States and Canada do not reveal the current existence of research programs. There are a few instances where there are suggestions of the possibility of a kind of informal effort in this direction. Tough's personal investigations concerning the self-directed learner is associated with a number of similar investigations conducted by students at the Ontario Institute for Studies in Education, Boshier's follow-up to Verner's interest in participation and other studies of this topic are identified with the University of British

155

Columbia. Dickinson and his students, also formerly at the University of British Columbia, have been identified with teaching issues. Knox, currently asssociated with the University of Wisconsin, has been identified personally with a number of investigations related to the adult learner and adult development and administration. Long, at the University of Georgia, has contributed to historical studies of the colonial period in America and reviews of research in adult education. Even, at the University of Nebraska, has focused on the adult learner and teaching questions.

Comparative analysis of the publications based on the research of individual investigators, however, do not result in conclusions that specific institutions have tended to focus either on topic or methodology.

The proposal is not without its disadvantages. For example, it is not unusual for professors of adult education to feel that individual students should be given great freedom in the identification and selection of research topics for dissertations. Limiting the opportunities for research topics is perceived to be inconsistent with a basic philosophical position concerning the importance of personal choice, self-direction and human worth. Somehow, the automatic requirement that a student would be required to conduct research in a pre-selected area is offensive. A second disadvantage is associated with the possibility that faculty members would become too narrow in their specialization and hence lose a broad perception of the field of adult education.

Taking both the advantages and disadvantages into consideration, it seems that the development of research programs in graduate departments of adult education is commendable. The two major disadvantages identified can be addressed. First, students can be well informed of the focus of a department and individual faculty members prior to admission. If the program is not consistent with the student's academic and professional goals other institutions that specialize in the appropriate areas (as far as the specific student is concerned) can be identified. The prospects of over-specialization by an individual faculty member can also be addressed by the opportunity to have a major area of specialization such as adult learning and a minor area of inquiry such as history. One topic could be used by the individual professors as an alternate area when they temporarily become fatigued through emphasis in one area.

Improved Dissemination

Closely connected with the need for better integration of previous research is the need for dissemination. Somehow, ERIC, Dissertation Abstracts and the main adult education journal and the increasing numbers of research conferences fail to satisfy the needs of the investigator and it is even more likely that the needs of the practitioner are even less well served.

ERIC contains some useful information, but one has to wade through material of quesionable values that it is of limited productivity. Similar criticisms apply to Dissertation Abstracts , however, the problem here usually is one of too little or too much information. A provocative abstract may encourage the purchase of a dissertation copy and only then does the investigator discover the research design to be flawed to such an extent that the conclusions are highly questionable. A few costly experiences like that lead to disillusionment.

The editors of the Adult Education Quarterly are greatly challenged to mitigate a situation that will become more severe in the future. Only approximately 16 articles are published annually in what is the single most important research publication in the field, especially for adult education. About 240 pages are devoted to the journal annually, hence the mean article length is 15 pages. Other journals such as those published by the American Psychological Association usually provide 4-8 page articles.

Finally, the two main research conferences are now providing a forum for 80-100 papers annually. The personnel responsible for the conferences are encouraged to consider ways of improving the dissemination of more useful summaries of the research, to consider the issue of resource allocation where duplication is not strongly discouraged. For example, it is possible for the same paper to be presented at both conferences and published in Adult Education Quarterly. The relative quality or significance of the research so reported does not always justify such exploitation of scarce resources.

Research-Reporting Skills

A virulent attack on the field by generalized sweeping condemnation of methods used in research or weaknesses in reporting ability is not appropriate, because adult educators are not unique among the academics. However, there is always room for improvement. Negative destructive criticism is not the best path to that goal. Continuing encouragement and open dialogue are the better procedures.

According to a survey conducted among A.E.A., U.S.A. members who had served on editorial and publications committees during the 1970's the following descriptions could be used to describe research:

1. Adult education research in the ten years including 1971-1980 was described as good.
2. Improvement over previous time periods was noted.
3. Improvement was accounted for by the following:
   a. Improved theoretical foundations
   b. Rigor of research designs
   c. Sound data collection procedures
   d. Relationship of research problems to previous research is clear. (Long, 1982, pp 259-260)

Note areas of weakness cited by the respondent also include some of the above reasons for improvement. This suggests that the respondents see improvement, but also believe additional improvement is justified. The weaknesses cited are as follows:

1. Theoretical foundations
2. Conceptual ability of investigators
3. Validity/reliability of instruments used
4. Relationship of research problems to previous research is not clear
5. Statistical analysis procedures (Long, 1982, p. 260)

OBSERVATIONS AND SPECULATIONS

Perhaps there is greater agreement among educators of adults concerning the immaturity of the status of research or inquiry in adult education than any other single feature of the field. Individuals who disagree on the definitions of adults, adult

education or the critical elements of program
planning are apt to agree that research needs to be
improved. Yet, there is some disagreement on the
acuteness or severity of the problem: some are
more optimistic than others.

This writer is of the opinion that research
quality has improved as adult education has matured
as a field of graduate study and as practice has
been institutionalized. Naturally, as the number
of practitioners has increased, the number of
poorly designed studies, as well as the number of
well designed investigations, has grown. In other
words, with more people doing research in the
field, the total body of literature has been
enlarged. Some of the literature is bad, but by
contrast some is quite good.

The main villain in adult education research
is not methodology, which usually receives the
greatest attention, but conceptualization! More
investigations are employing better research
designs and more powerful statistical and
qualitative analytical tools. Yet, the
sophistication of theoretical conceptualization has
not paralleled that of the analytical modes. As
Mezirow (1971) observed a number of years ago, much
of the research of adult education remains
atheoretical. Despite the negative consequences of
this fact, the more optimistic can be comforted.
More is said about theoretical developments in the
next chapter.

Speculations

Six developments that will have significant impact
on the study of adults are converging. They are
(a) aging of the American population; (b)
increasing interest in adult learners by
institutions and individuals who previously
emphasized childhood learning; (c) availability of
high speed technology to process masses of data;
(d) technological advances in model development and
testing; (e) use of large data bases developed for
other purposes; and (f) new analytical procedures.
Each of these developments is briefly addressed
below.

The aging of the American population, as
discussed in chapter four, is a well-known reality.
More than one-half of the nation's population is
now more than 30 years of age. The trend toward an
adult population is expected to continue into the
future unless some currently unidentified event
such as increased rates of immigration (legal and

illegal), war or a major change in fertility rates brings about a dramatic change. The proportion of adults in the population will contribute to political and social activities designed to develop human resources in many ways. Continuing education of one kind or another (corporate training or liberal education) will be ways of developing the adult human resource.

Because of the demographic changes, all kinds of agencies and individuals will turn more of their attention away from childhood programs and activities. Adults will be identified as new targets for these agencies and individuals. Some scholars previously interested in research problems associated with childhood will bring their skills and expertise to bear on issues of adulthood.

Development in computer technology, hardware and software, will bring enhanced capabilities within reach of most researchers. Large scale studies, or studies of a large number of variables in small populations will be more easily analyzed. Various permutations and relationships can be analyzed relatively inexpensively and with great speed.

Educators will be able to use technology to more easily create and test more easily various models of human activity. Such refinements may facilitate second and third generation investigations in ways not currently imagined.

The collection and storage of masses of data for purposes other than education is already underway. Continued advances in technology are likely to open this rich resource to the creative genius of a few scholars. The model is already available in adult education literature (Anderson and Darkenwald, 1979; Saindon and Long, 1983). Anderson and Darkenwald (1979) re-examined the statistics of the National Center on Educational Statistics. Saindon and Long (1983) made use of the Quality of American Life, 1978 survey collected by the Center for Political Studies of the Institute for Social Research, University of Michigan.

Trends in statistical treatment and analysis will continue to provide a variety of new and different approaches such as power analysis, linguistic and syntactic interpretations and triangulation methods, as discussed by Dickinson and Blunt (1980) are just a few of the promising developments in this area.

SUMMARY

This chapter provides some new perspectives on the study of adults in the united states. Seven major topics are discussed in varying detail. A brief summation of each section follows.

Some New Perspectives

This section contains two main themes. The first reveals how research interests have changed as the field of adult education has changed in the last fifty years or so. The second reiterates the point that the study of adults is marked by certain important distinguishing characteristics. It is argued investigators of adult related topics are challenged to design research procedures and formulate concepts appropriate to critical distinguishing characteristics.

Status of Research

This section reports and discusses selected critical views of adult education reported in the literature from 1959 to 1983. The bulk of the criticism is negative, especially the views published in the 1960's. More recently, Knox (1985), Long (1983a) and Matkin (1980) have shared more positive views.

Research Approaches

The section on research approaches summarizes the main research into the kinds or types of research reported in selected adult education literature and research conferences. Subdivisions of the topic include a summary of meta-research, adult education inquiry and descriptive research.

Needed Research

The fourth major chapter section provides a brief comment on needed research as reported in the literature.

Research Needs

The idea of needs of adult education research is conceptualized differently from the traditional needed research approach discussed in the fourth chapter section. As a result five research needs are reported and discussed. They include needs associated with conceptualizing research, needs associated with the integration of adult education research, need for programs of research, need for improved dissemination of research, and need for improved research reporting skills.

Observations and Speculations
The final chapter topic shares some observations concerning the status and condition of adult education research and some speculations about the future.

Chapter Seven

THEORETICAL PERSPECTIVES

Education of adults in the United States has
proceeded for three centuries without any grand
theories and few minor ones. Several explanations
for this state of affairs are available. First,
education of adults has lacked a singular patron
discipline. It was only in the past half-century
that the study of adult learners, providers of
learning resources, and instruction of adults
became objects of academic study. Second, the
practice orientation of the first wave of
individuals described as adult educators in the
1920s through about 1950 worked against the
development of theory in adult education. Third,
educators of adults are divided on the issue of
borrowing from other disciplines such as
psychology, sociology and social psychology.
Fourth, difficulty in conceptualizing the education
of adults as a distinctive field of practice and
study also has been an obstacle. For example,
adult education graduate programs are most
frequently located in colleges of education with
some also having some kind of relationship with
colleges of agriculture. Yet, many of the
individuals who enter graduate study in adult
education come from disciplines other than
education and agriculture. They have previously
earned degrees in fields as diverse as agriculture,
business, education, engineering, history,
journalism, psychology, sociology and theology.
Adult education graduate programs are thus often de
facto interdisciplinary; as a result scholars
identify, define and describe their practice in the
language and theories with which they are familiar.
Consequently, the development of theory is retarded

163

by the above diverse, but powerful sources of influence.

Professors of adult education, the logical contributors to the development of theory, are often hindered by the historical practice orientation of their field and by internal university work conditions. They are also distributed all along the continuum concerning the issue of borrowing from other disciplines. Mezirow (1971) is the most outspoken champion of the need for adult education to develop its own theory. Jensen (1964) is perhaps the most ardent defender of the borrowing strategy. Verner (1978) would fall somewhere between these two, he did not object to borrowing, but he did specify some criteria that should apply. He suggested the following should be used to determine the appropriateness of using knowledge from other disciplines:

1. It helps to explain some phenomenon encountered in the field or discipline.
2. It helps in the solution of practical problems encountered in the field.
3. It can be translated into operational principles that will contribute to greater efficiency and effectiveness in adult educational programming.
4. It contributes to the development of essential attributes, values, or skills important to the field.
5. It can be reformulated so that it is applicable to adult education.
6. It is derived solely from adult populations.
7. It relates to systematic education of adults.

As argued elsewhere (Long, Hiemstra and Associates, 1980) as well as in this book, this writer is of the opinion that adult education and the learning activities of adults have, or should have some distinctive or differentiating characteristics. If not, adult education has difficulty qualifying as a field of study. On the other hand, to suggest that the learning processes of adults are unique goes beyond the state of current knowledge. Therefore, Verner's position seems to be the stronger one. We should not reject appropriate theory from fields such as biology, psychology and sociology. Neither should we accept all theories from the related disciplines without careful reflection. As the boundaries of disciplines become less distinct and rigid this central position will be justified even more strongly.

SELECTED DEVELOPMENTS

As noted in the discussion of research in chapter six, adult education research and conceptualization (theory) has tended to focus on microelements with limited effort to relate the many elements to any kind of general organizing structure. Interestingly, Birren and Cunningham (1985) have recently made similar comments about contemporary psychology of aging. They said it "is a collection of segments" which "implies that most theories in the psychology of aging are actually microtheories" (p. 18). Birren and Cunninghamn further observed that microtheories do not embrace large amounts of data from different domains of behavior. Subsequently this implies different levels of explanation are used by investigators and that their explanatory positions are very close to observed data with little reference to the kind of comprehensive concepts that would be involved in viewing human adults as a constantly transforming biological system moving forward in time with interactions within their own organism as well as within their social and physical environment.

Following Birren and Cunningham (1985) it is suggested the theoretical developments in the education of adults cited in this chapter are microtheories, if they can be labelled as theories. They are also incomplete and diverse. No effort will be made here to consolidate them in any systematic way. Even though the following theoretical positions may lack the desired standards of rigor and systematic character of formal theory, they are efforts to explain certain attributes or elements of education of adults. Several criteria were used in the selection of the microtheories discussed in the following pages. First, they had to be relatively recent (in keeping with the thrust of the book). Second, they had to be relatively popular or visible. Third, a balance among important sub-areas or topics was sought. Accordingly, the theoretical topics selected include a theory of the field of adult education, structural concepts such as participation, learning versus education, perspective transformation, program planning and development, general models, evaluation and continuing professional education.

Boyd and Apps

Boyd and Apps (1980) have proposed a conceptual
model of adult education (as a field of practice).
They describe it as a three dimensional model;
which represents basic elements: (a) transactional
mode, (b) client focus and (c) system. The model
is presented as a cube with each plane representing
one of the educational dimensions. Using this
system, Boyd and Apps, say that one may locate a
given program in terms of its three coordinates;
its transactional mode, client focus, and
predominant system. Each of the three elements
contain three parallel units.

The transactional mode is defined as the
character of the learner's situation: are they
working independently, in groups or classes, or as
members of a community? The client focus concerns
individuals, groups or communities served by adult
education. The system dimension is also
conceptualized as a three-part structure consisting
of personal, social and cultural systems.
According to Boyd and Apps the model makes several
contributions:

1. It contributes to the establishment of a
   conceptual structure of the nature and
   parametrics of adult education.
2. It provides a framework for identifying
   and organizing problems in adult
   education.
3. It is based on the structure of adult
   education rather than on other
   disciplines.

Carlson's (1980) criticism of the model
includes the following plea:
> We need definitions of the field that do not
> rely solely on such terms as change, growth,
> progress, and problem solving. We need a
> theory that honors the orneriness that is
> humankind, that provides an esteemed place for
> unorganized and unplanned adult education,
> that accepts conflicts of interests inherent,
> in all societies, that recognizes the finite
> nature of planning, and that taken account of
> the limits both to man's rationality and to
> his scientific technology . . . (p. 183).

Such a definition as desired by Carlson has
not yet been identified.

Structural Concepts

Mainline adult educators, i.e., professors and students in graduate programs have tended to focus on microsocial elements such as the family and small units of the world of work for explanations of adult occupational socialization and participation in educational activities. Diffusion theory from the field of sociology also has been frequently used. Other possibilities, as discussed in the following paragraphs, are beginning to be addressed by some adult educators and scholars from other disciplines, however.

Saindon's (1982) dissertation on differences between blue collar and white collar participants, moved the study of participation into a new arena. Most participation studies have been atheoretical and have been conducted with little consideration for differences in participation by major variables other than age, sex, income and geographic region as discussed in chapter one. Saindon's work provides a new dimension to the issue that relates participation to occupational characteristics not previously or widely examined in American literature.

Her dissertation on differences between blue collar and white collar adult education participants, as reflected by their working conditions, moved the study of participation with a new arena in the U.S.A. Previous studies have reported an association between participation and occupation (Anderson and Darkenwald, 1979; Johnstone and Rivera, 1965; London, et al, 1963). Despite the general observations concerning the association between participants and occupation, few studies have been conducted to determine how occupation influences the relationship. As a result, Saindon's study provides an original departure from previous investigations by examining particular working conditions and their relationship to participation.

Drawing from sociological literature (Blauner, 1964; Kornhauser, 1965; and Kasl, 1974;) Saindon moved beyond the work of Bergsten (1977), Botsman (1975) and others. Using the Quality of American Life 1978 survey as her data base, her study includes 3,962 individuals. Eleven work factors were examined: (a) work is perceived to be interesting; (b) pay is perceived to be adequate; (c) work surroundings are pleasant, (d) opportunity to develop abilities on the job is available; (e) chance to use skills on the job exists; (f) promotion is perceived as possible; (g) there is adequate time to finish the job; (h) satisfaction with the job; (i) perception that the job is secure; (j) work-travel conditions are convenient; (k) opportunity to make friends on the job is available (Saindon and Long, 1983).

Based on the results of her analysis, Saindon concluded that participants in general education and participants in vocational training differed in their background characteristics. Furthermore, the association between working conditions and participation also differed between the two employee groups. Participation in vocational training is associated with the opportunity to develop abilities on the job. Participation in general education is not greatly influenced by any of the identified work-related factors.

Saindon's work increases knowledge concerning the potential effects of occupation and working conditions on participation in adult education. Findings of this nature should contribute to a refinement of participation theory.

Perhaps one of the most promising areas of theory and research concerning structural elements will emerge from demography. Easterlin (1980) has proposed a general demographic theory that has implications for the education of adults. His theory, for example, explains population variations in terms of broad and general social conditions; good economic conditions contribute to larger cohorts while poor economic conditionns contribute to smaller cohorts. The cohort size, according to Easterlin; will in turn contribute to various events and conditions across the life span of the different cohorts. For example, the cohort born in the mid 1930's in the U.S. was one of the smallest cohorts of the century. They reached adulthood about 1953-58. Family size, occupational achivement, and so forth were associated with the economic environment and cohort size. In contrast, the 1950's cohort reached adulthood between 1970-75 in large numbers; they had competed for space, recognition and achievement most of their lives, due to the cohort size. Their economic advancement and other achievements have been slower to obtain, according to Easterlin.

In the 1960s onward, adult educators had access to a population whose ideas and philosophy concerning schooling (education) may be quite different from the life views of the 1970-1980 cohort. The implications of these structural and personal variables for the practice and study of adult education have yet to be adequately conceptualized and organized.

Participation
Despite the limited character of much of the earlier work on participation, attention has recently sharpened theoretical conceptualization. Elsewhere (Long, 1983b) this writer has described several major theoretical positions. Three of the most recent formulations include the idea of Bergsten (1980) and Rubenson (1979), Cross (1981) and Darkenwald and Merriam (1982).

The work of the above scholars reflects a deductive analytical approach to explaining participation, whereas much of the earlier work was more of an inductive approach. Only the Swedish model (Bergsten, 1980 and Rubenson, 1979) provides a theoretical exposition on which research has been reported. Cross (1981) and Darkenwald and Merriam (1982) have contributed inductive theoretical models. However, this writer is not aware of specific research that tests either of the models.

PARTICIPATION THEORY

Microtheories of participation of adults in education have emerged from two different orientations reflecting sociology and psychology. The work of Verner, (Dickinson, 1979) and London (1963; 1964; 1970), and their students, generally followed sociological lines while Houle (1961) and his students sought psychological explanations. Over the years the psychological approach has dominated recent participation theory. The work of Rubenson (1979) in Sweden and anthropological work (Marieneau and Klinger, 1977), however, encourages consideration of wider concerns.

Verner and his students sought sociological explanations for participation. Variables studied include age, education, family, income, learning location, marital status, occupation, race and sex (Long, 1983b). Houle and his students searched for psychological explanations. Stimulation for much of this work came from Houle's (1961) work that identified three learning orientations: activity, goal, and learning orientations. His students, principally Burgess (1964) and Sheffield (1964) extended the original inquiry by developing survey instruments and through the use of quantitative analysis.

169

Boshier (1964) raised questions concerning Houle's original typology and began his own line of inquiry in New Zealand and later in Canada. Even though this book concerns the education of adults in the United States, it would be erroneous to neglect either Boshier's work that is related to Houle's psychological concept or Rubenson's Swedish work that extends the sociological based approach. Boshier's continuing study of participation generated a number of facts that seem to be associated with participation. A recently (Boshier and Collins, 1982) reported analysis of 12,000 learners indicates a factor solution as "the most psychologically and psychometrically defensible solution" (p. 29). The factors identified by Boshier are social contact, social stimulation, professional advancement, community service, external expectations and cognitive interest. Socio-economic and life cycle variables associated with participation include education, occupation, income, and previous participation. Boshier's work over the past 15 years has been characterized by two elements (a) data collected via his Educational Participation Scale (EPS) and (b) a factor analytic statistical analysis procedure. In contrast to Boshier's methodology, Rockhill (1982) has argued for more qualitative approaches.

Aslanian and Brickell (1980) have offered a social psychological explanation. They speculate that participation in learning is triggered by some kind of crises or other similar life events. In some way, education provides a socially approved strategy for addressing some of the stress and anxiety often associated with some important life events. Mezirow also implies this kind of explanation in his theory on perspective transformation discussed later in this chapter.

Over the years six types of research into participation have been identified in the literature (Burgess, 1971; Long, 1983b) as follows:

1. Conducting an analysis of activities in which the learner participates.
2. Asking the adult learners to state in their own words why they engage in learning activities.
3. Asking learners to select from a prepared list of reasons why they participate.
4. Analyzing the adult's orientation to education.

5. Conducting studies of self-directed learning projects.
6. Conducting analyses of previous research.

Based on the research and discussion generated, five major models of participation have been identified (Long, 1983b):

1. Miller's Force-Field Model
2. Boshier's Congruence Model
3. McClusky's Margin Model
4. Expectancy Valence Model
5. Cross' Chain-of-Response Model

Additional models such as those proposed by Darkenwald and Merriam (1982), Berry (1971) and others are available. The five major models noted above, however, appear to contain the greatest potential for testing and further development.

Common to most if not all of the participation models is the assumption of universality. The value of a theoretical model depends upon the extent to which it can be generalized. Hence, educators of adults are most interested in a universal paradigm that permits prediction in all circumstances. Unfortunately, such models are few and far between in the area of social inquiry (Gibson, 1960). Therefore, it may be more productive to initiate a series of models that are population specific. Saindon and Long (1983) report important differences in participation by occupational groups. Theory development that focuses on occupational groups and other important variables may eventually contribute to a grand theory of participation.

Interest in retention and dropout among American educators of adults traditionally is high. Despite some logical speculations that dropout behavior and failure of adults to initially participate in education may be similar (Long, 1983b). Only Boshier (1973) has theoretically linked the two phenomena. Relatively recent work by Darkenwald (1981) has identified and criticized four theoretical models of dropout and retention: Boshier's (1973) congruence model, Rubenson and Hoghielm's (1978) expectancy-valence theory, Irish's (1978) reinforcement of attendance concept, and the cost-benefit model described by Tinto (1975).

Space does not permit a comprehensive explication of the above theories. Therefore, only a few general descriptive comments and criticisms are provided here. The reader who has interest in more detailed information should refer to the works cited. Boshier's congruence model is derived from the theory of Abraham Maslow and purports to consider the interaction of an individual's internal psychological variables and external environmental variables (Boshier, 1973). Boshier appears to use the concept of congruence in two different ways: intraself congruence is a function of psychological adjustment which is characteristic of growth-motivated or self-actualizing adults. In contrast "deficiency motivated," other directed and neurotic adults are characterized by intraself incongruence. Boshier hypothesizes, but provides no evidence to support his position, that intraself incongruence leads to self-other incongruence (incongruence between the individual and other students and teacher). Ultimately, this incongruence along with social, psychological and classroom variables leads to dropout. In essence, "the model asserts that 'congruence' both within the participant and the educational environment determiners . . . dropout/persistence" (Boshier, 1973, p. 256). Unfortunately, the model does not provide clear and unequivocal results. The probability of misinterpretation is high and critical variables are not specified.

The expectancy-valence model (Rubenson and Hoghielm, 1978) adopted expectancy-valence theory to explain and to predict dropout. Simply stated, the theory asserts that learners will persist if they believe a specific learning activity as meeting an important need (positive valence) and if they expect to be able to compete or cope with the activity in question (positive expectancy). Results appear to be easily predicted when both valence and expectancy are strong or weak. Mixed results, however, present difficulty in prediction. Darkenwald (1981) observes "the model is deficient, however, in that it fails to specify the factors that influence valence and expectancy" (p. 10).

Irish (1978) developed a model to predict dropout from evening classes based on reinforcement theory and the functional analysis of behavior. Three sets of variables were identified as reinforcers: those behaviors that occur in the classroom (ten items); those that may take place while the student is attending the class, but which occur outside the classroom (fifteen items); and those that may take place on the job as a result of skills acquired in the class (nine items). The total strength of the reinforcing variables was determined for each individual by multiplying importance and frequency of the occurrence ratings for each variable (34) and summarizing the results. Those students who experienced greater positive results did persist and Irish developed a prediction equation that accounted for 72.3 percent of the subjects (Darkenwald, 1981).

Darkenwald (1981) indicates Irish's model has the virtue of including three major kinds of variables: phenomena that occur inside the classroom, those that take place outside the class concurrently with attendance anticipated consequences. The in-class variables appear to be better predictors than either of the other two classes of variables. Yet, the model's simplicity is perceived to be a major weakness.

Reinforcement theory fails to provide satisfactory explanations of the process or dynamics that result in overt behavior (Darkenwald, 1981).

A similar model is offered by Tinto who acknowledges its close relztionship to cost-benefit theory. He, thus, relates the decision of a student to persist on dropout to perceived benefits reative to the perceived costs says little, however, unless someone is able to specify the actual costs and benefits and why and how they influence specific behaviors, such as dropping out of an adult education activity.

Each of the above models include, in some degree, some cost-benefit concepts relevant to dropout behavior; congruence or fit between the learner and the learning environment; expectancy and valence; and reinforcement of class attendance. But, the models are incomplete and insufficient representations of complex and diverse faces that cause dropout behavior in adult education (Darkenwald, 1981)

Educators have turned to psychology, social psychology and industrial psychology for theories of motivation that might explain participation and retention. The quest, however, is far from complete and additional theoretical work is required in both areas. A yet unexamined theoretical framework is provided by the hypothesis that projective techniques of analyses may be more useful than the current rationally based self-report approaches (Long, 1983b).

ANDRAGOGY

Flowing out of the broad philosophical and social ferment of the 1960s andragogy was popularized by Knowles (1970). The term meaning the art and science of helping adults learn (Knowles, 1970,p. 31), was not a new one as it had been used by Lindeman in the 1920s and in Europe prior to Knowles' 1970 publication (Brookfield, 1984). Nevertheless, Knowles, more than any other person in the United States, is correctly identified as the spokesperson for andragogy. The emergence of andragogy as a popular concept among adult educators is not surprising. First, adult educators needed some tangible rationale for their argument that the education of adults differs in important ways from education of children. This theoretical position is found in a number of publications released in the 1960s when the education of adults experienced rapid growth in the United States (Jensen, Liveright, and Hallenbeck, 1964; Kidd,, 1963; Knowles,1960). It was also during this time that the number of graduate programs in adult eduction increased significantly.

According to Knowles' (1970) position, andragogy is based on at least four critical assumptions about the characteristics of adult learners that differ from assumptions concerning childhood learners: (a) as people mature their self-concept changes from a dependency personality toward one of becoming a self-directed person; (b) as people mature they accumulate a growing reservoir of experiences that becomes an increasing resource for learning; (c) as people mature their readiness to learn becomes oriented increasingly to the developmental tasks associated with their social roles; and (d) their time perspective changes from one of postponed application of knowledge to immediacy of application, accordingly their orientations toward learning shifts from one of subject-centeredness to one of problem-centeredness.

It is not possible to exhaustively discuss here all the evidence that either supports or refutes the above assumptions. It is important one, however, to observe that several of the above "crucial assumptions" (Knowles, 1970:39) require critical examination. Assumption (a) for example, does not respond to the extensive literature on cognitive style or learning style, dogmatism and rigidity, and locus of control. While it is generally accepted that one's concept of self matures into early adulthood and that one anticipates and perhaps expects increasing autonomy in adulthood (Patterson, 1979), this does not mean that all adults become self-directing as implied by the first assumption. It is possible that one's level or degree of self-direction may increase with age and experience, but this does not assure that all adults reach an optimal level of self-direction. In fact, the literature on cognitive style and personality theory indicate that the attributes of independence-dependence are distributed among the population. Age, per se, is not identified as a discriminating variable. Hence, the assumption of an increasingly independent personality across the life span is open to challenge.

The role of experience in learning is also a debatable issue. Adult educators make much of experience. But, the negative aspect of experience such as an incorrectly learned procedure or a biased attitude to an important topic or field of endeavor has seldom been considered vis-a-vis the positive dimension (Kallen, 1962). Awareness and extensive rich experience certainly provides a framework for a more interesting and even perhaps potentially productive learning activity, but where negative elements contend with the learners' energy and attention the results may be less than hoped for (Bergevin, 1967).

The third assumption also lacks clear unequivocal support in the literature. Merriam and Mullin's (1970) study of differences among adults in different developmental task age groups indicates the problem is a complex one. They observed that many of the developmental tasks were not simple unitary ones. Instead, the tasks could be described as complex and correlated. Other reasons for questioning the universal application of the third crucial assumption upon which andragogy are based are provided by the work of Marcus (1977). His work also questioned previous positions concerning expressive and instrumental kinds of educational activities. As a result, his findings suggest that attempting to label an educational activity as instrumental or expressive is not a simple task. These few, but important studies indicate that additional study is required before the assumption concerning developmental tasks can be accepted without caution.

The fourth assumption, concerning changes in time perspective and application of learning to problems as opposed to learning content is like the first one. There is general acceptance that people's time perspective changes with age. However, the change is perceived to occur most significantly in later life whereas the bulk of participants in adult education are young and middle aged adults. Furthermore, the assumption implies that children prefer or adopt by choice an orientation of postponed application manifested in most school programs. In contrast, it could be argued that children are as interested in application as are adult learners.

Comments are not meant to suggest that the four crucial assumptions are completely untenable. They do, however, imply that the assumptions should be accepted only with caution, that further study is required, and that they represent complex concepts that require additional specification and description.

Andragogy as promoted by Knowles has stimulated an interesting and continuing conversation among adult educators in the United States and elsewhere (Davenport and Davenport, 1985; Elias, 1979; Jarvis, 1983, Hartree, 1984; Knudson, 1979; McKenzie, 1977; Yonge, 1985). Both critical and supporting positions are available for the interested reader.

Davenport and Davenport (1985) perhaps provide the most supportive recent contribution. In concluding their article they urge scholars to move their debate to a higher level, i.e., one based on what they perceive to be a growing empirical base. In contrast, Hartree's (1984) incisive critique neither extols or condemns andragogy. She logically reasons through some of the difficulties posed by Knowles' language and logic in Knowles' (1978). She concludes that while Knowles may have provided an important service by popularizing andragogy (a position also taken by Davenport and Davenport (1985, p. 209), "it is unfortunate that he has done so in a form which . . . is likely to lead to rejection . . . ." While agreeing with many of Hartree's observations, it appears the above conclusion is too severe, particularly if Davenport and Davenport's (1985) assessment is just one-half correct.

Finally, while agreeing with Davenport and Davenport's (1985) call for the debate to move to higher grounds based on empirical results, the existence of an adequate base may be questioned. More than ten years ago this writer challenged colleagues to initiate systematic study of the "principles" of andragogy. As yet, only a few such systematic and focused efforts have been identified (Arnold, 1985; Beder and Darkenwald, 1982; Darkenwald, 1982; Gorham, 1985; and Rosenblum and Darkenwald, 1983).

Another, related component, in the andragogy debate has received much more research attention than the global concept. Perhaps, this is to be expected, especially when that component strikes a philosophical cord as has the idea of self-direction in learning.

LEARNING VS. EDUCATION

One of the major theoretical developments to occur in the past twenty years is the inclusion of independent learning in the definition of adult education. In 1964, one of the most widely accepted definitions of adult education was provided by Verner (1964).

Verner defined adult education as ". . . a relationship between an educational agent and a learner in which the agent selects, arranges and continuously directs a sequence of progressive tasks that provide systematic experiences to achieve learning for those whose participation in such activities is subsidiary and supplemental to a primary productive role in society" (1964, p. 32). In contrast to adult education, Verner defined learning as ". . . the acquisition of information and the mastery of that intellectual behavior through which facts, ideas, or concepts are manipulated, related and made available for use" (1964, p. 30).

Following Tough (1965; 1966) whose dissertation stimulated the topic, study of adults' learning projects has more often included the self-directed, autonomous or independent learning activities traditionally associated with schooling (Johns, 1973; Hiemstra, 1975; Tough, 1971; Tough, 1978). Often the key to the inclusion of self-planned learning in definitions of adult education is the systematic criteria, i.e., the learning activity must be planned and pursued in a systematic manner in contrast to random and unintentional learning. However, Spear and Mocker (1984) have recently moved away from this criterion. In an article based on a qualitative analysis of self-directed learners they identified four types of learning according to environmental circumstances: Type I, single event/anticipated learning; Type II, single event/unanticipated

177

learning; Type III, series of events/related learning and Type IV learning, which as described by Spear and Mocker appears to be a kind of random fortuitous learning that individuals combine post hoc into some kind of meaningful structure. If this assumption is correct, then Type IV learning appears to be as significantly different from former definitions of self-directed learning (that required purpose) as learning is from education. For example, learning as defined in Tough's (1965; 1966; 1971; 1978) work and others (Johns, 1973; Hiemstra, 1975) focused on learning projects, i.e., activities purposely devised for particular learning objectives. Education is also traditionally defined as learning being holistic, organized and purposeful (Jarvis, 1985). In contrast, type IV learning as proposed by Spear and Mocker (1984) reflects the random and fortuitous accumulation of experience and knowledge rather than the purposeful structured connotation of previous uses of learning as in learning projects. Note Jarvis' (1985,p.25) description of learning:

> Clearly learning, which is a basic human capacity may be seen as a universal process, even though its definition has not been universally agreed, changing from behavioral to a broader perspective (sic).

Others (Houle, 1980 and Oddi, 1984) have conceptualized self-directed learning activities to include the unintentional learning that characterizes human behavior. Houle's (1980) contribution emerges from his model of learning based on three major overlapping modes of learning: instruction, inquiry and performance. Offered as a model of continuing learning of professionals it has been extended to learning processes in general (Oddi, 1984). A detailed description of Houle's three learning modes, is not possible here, however, it should be noted that the instruction mode conforms most closely with the systematic, planned and intentional characteristics frequently included in definitions of self-directed learning. Oddi (1984) appears to have been influenced by the work of Houle (1980), Mocker and Spear (1982). She has reconceptualized self-directed learning from a description of a process to a personality construct. Giving limited attention to Guglielmino's (1977) work she drew on Houle (1961) Kasworm (1982) and others (Knox, 1973; Skager, 1979) and arrived at a conclusion similar to the position implied by Guglielmino, self-directed learning is an attribute of personality. She argues that the personality construct approach is an improvement over the process orientation.

The phenomenon could be studied regardless of the mode of learning preferred or available to the self-directed continuing learner. Since psychological attributes of an individual tend to persist, such a conception should offer a relatively stable indicator of the phenomenon. Finally, conceptualization of self-directed continuing learning as a personality construct offers a unified and comprehensive focus for the characteristics leading an individual to persist in learning overtime, rather than on discrete episodes of learning activity.

The idea that motivation to be self-directed in learning is psychologically important is not a new one. Guglielmino's Self-Directed Learning Readiness Scale (1977) is heavily based on psychological items. Long and Agyekum's (1983, 1984) validation studies of the SDLRS were designed to include other personality variables such as agreement response, dogmatism and locus of control. The main difference in Oddi's work is her explicit effort to define self-directed learning as a personality construct rather than a process. Others have been less explicit in their position.

Conceptualization of self-directed learning as a psychological construct has not necessarily clarified the phenomenon. Guglielmino's (1977) Self-Directed Learning Readiness Scale is based upon psychological attributes such as independence, initiative, task orientations and so forth. Others (Long, 1985) have noted the importance of factors such as creativity, independence and self-concept (psychological constructs) in self-directed learning (process). Currently this writer is attempting to disentangle the concept of independence. For example, is independence, an important factor associated with self-directed learning readiness, a cognitive attribute or a personality attribute?

Long and Ross (1984) have conceptualized self-directed learning in terms of "forces." Four distinctive forces that influence self-directed learning are believed to exist: personality , social,situational,and contextual. Personality forces are conceived of as psychological attributes as discussed earlier. Social forces are identified as being related to one's position in society and relationships with other human beings. The third and fourth forces are environmental in nature. Contextual variables are related to the milieu in which the individual lives, works and plays. These contexts may provide much or little stimulation and opportunities to learn. Situational variables are those that relate to or arise from a given set of circumstances at a specific time. Beginning a new job, beginning or ending a personal relationship such as in a divorce or, death or experiencing severe illness or disability.

Long and Ross' (1984) concept is not vastly different from the one proposed by Spear and Mocker (1984), however the emphasis is not the same. Spear and Mocker have approached the topic from the perspective of learning types, whereas Long and Ross are exploring the possibility that different types of variables (forces) are important salient features in self-directed learning. It is easy to speculate that a combination of the two theoretical models might be useful. For example, one could raise the following question: what kinds of forces are identified with which type of learning? Questions concerning the productiveness of the new concept (Houle, 1980, Long and Ross, 1984, Spear and Mocker, 1984 and Oddi, 1984) remain to be answered. For example, Spear and Mocker's definition, despite the inclusion of unintentional learning is more consistent with the existing paradigm. They provide evidence that self-directing learning behavior may be episodic; or it may be cast as a dependent variable with other circumstances of the life field serving as independent variables. Oddi implies that self-directed learning is an independent variable (a psychological construct) that is a persistent personal attribute.

The idea that adults routinely engage in planned learning activities in some kind of patterned or systematic manner has been a long time interest of C. O. Houle. A contribution to this concept was published in 1961. Another was the direction provided to Tough's (1965) dissertation on adults' learning projects. Yet a third is Houle's most recent work (1984). The key element or idea that distinguishes Houle's latest work is the proposition that adults develop some kind of pattern or system in their use of different kinds of learning resources. Houle's recent work will contribute to the on-going discussion about the legitimization of various media in learning. The diverse and numerous opportunities for electronically assisted learning and the traditional media are noted by Long (1983a).

The trend noted here is important from both a practical and theoretical view. Despite the historical evidence (Long, 1976) that much of the education of adults prior to 1900 was a kind of free learning, i.e., not focused on a particular institution and not certified, the recent traditional view ties education of adults to some kind of schooling format. It is likely that both modes of adult learning will increase in the future. One challenge for theory will be to explain the similarities and differences between these two contrasting approaches within some kind of organizing structure. For example, what are the critical psychological and sociological variables that effect learning choices and behaviors? are they the same, or do they effect learners in the two kinds of learning activities (certified vs. free learning) in different ways? Why do some people choose or develop one pattern of learning rather than another? Are patterns influenced by age, developmental stages, family circumstances, macro-social events, etc.?

As noted by Long (1983b) research in self-directed learning in the education of adults seems to be surpassed in quantity only by the research in participation in learning. The extent of the research is illustrated by recent efforts to organize it by types. Brockett (1985) has described the research as reflecting the following characteristics: (a) descriptive research based on Tough's (1965) learning projects interview schedule and its diverse modifications; (b) research designed to identify relationships between self-directed learning readiness and other psychosocial variables, usually based on Guglielmino's (1977) Self-Directed Learning Readiness Scale (SDLRS); and (c) research designed to examine "questions most appropriately addressed through various qualitative methodologies"(p.56).

Caffarella and O'Donnell (1985) have identified five categories in which research on self-directed learning might be placed: (a) verification studies (following the Tough tradition); (b) nature of the method of self-directed learning (the how questions); (c) nature of the individual learner (the who and what questions); (d) nature of the process itself (perspectives on the process); and (c) policy questions (the role of education, institutions and society).

181

My own view of the research suggests two additional categories: (a) historical research and (b) methological research. Long's (1976; Long and Ashford, 1976) research concerning the education of adults in colonial America discusses self-directed learning during that historical period. Also, Brockett (1985) and Long and Agyekum (1983; 1984) and others (Fox and West, 1983; Hassan, 1981) have made contributions to methodological issues such as the validity and appropriateness of Guglielmino's Self-Directed Learning Readiness Scale.

Self-direction in learning is a highly complex construct that is too often submitted to overly simplistic analysis. Discussions of the topic too often falters because they are based on only one or two of the conceptual dimensions of self-direction. For example, self-direction in learning is easily limited to a structural concept that focuses only upon issues of autonomy of control in such areas as who sets the objectives (goals) of learning?, who determines the content?, who determines the activities? and who evaluates the learning? Or, perhaps the definition is limited to a sociological one that emphasizes the social character of the learning activity. This approach identifies three types of learners: (a) the learning hermit (the learner pursues learning independently and in isolation); (b) the plugged-in learner (the individual who studies alone or who is connected with others via telephone lines, etc., with computers and/or print media as the primary interface; and (c) the learning groupie (this individual is like Houle's activity oriented person who uses the learning activity to meet social interaction needs).

A third conceptual base of self-direction in learning is provided by psychological constructs. For example, self-direction may be a personality (Oddi, 1984) construct or a cognitive one (Long, 1985). Despite the interest in the nature of the learner as identified by Caffarella and O'Donnell (1985) research in this conceptual area is limited and should be strengthened.

PERSPECTIVE TRANSFORMATION

Mezirow (1978a, 1978b, 1981) has been developing a critical theory of adult education and learning under the label of "perspective transformation." Fundamentally his theory proposes three kinds of learning, which he derives from Habermas' (1970) three primary cognitive interests: the technical, the practical and the emancipatory. Mezirow's terms for these three kinds of learning are (a) instructional learning, which he defines as task-oriented problem solving relevant for controlling the environment or other people; (b) dialogic learning, which is that kind of learning by which we attempt to understand what others mean in communicating with us; and (c) self-reflective learning by which we come to understand ourselves (Mezirow, 1981). The later kind of learning, according to Mezirow (1981), is most directly related with what he calls perspective transformation which he defines as "becoming critically aware of how and why the structure of psycho-cultural assumptions has come to constrain the way we see ourselves and our relationships, reconstituting this structure to permit a more inclusive and discriminating intergration of experience and acting upon these new understandings" (1981, p. 6).

"Meaning schemes" constitute an important construct in Mezirow's perspective transformation theory. Meaning schemes are elements of an individual's meaning perspective or "the structure of psycho-cultural assumptions within which new experience is assimilated and transformed by one's past experience" (Mezirow, 1981, p. 6). According to the theory, perspective transformation includes three different kinds of learning processes: Learning within meaning schemes, learning new meaning schemes and learning through meaning transformation. These three processes are reminiscent of Piaget's concepts of assimilation and accommodation, which through dialetical process yield new or different schema.

Mezirow's theory seems to have emerged from or to have been influenced by his work in women's re-entry programs (1978a). Therefore, much of his writing on the topic emphasizes a dramatic or radical change in perspectives as a consequence of involvement in programmatic activities. Mezirow's explanations and descriptions is reminiscent of some of the work of Paulo Freire, Kurt Lewin and Jean Piaget and group process literature.

Even though Mezirow goes to some length in a recent article on the topic (1981) to defuse ethical criticism of perspective transformation, the issue has not been resolved. The neutral stance of the educator proclaimed in the article is not reflected in the language used in an earlier article (1978a). The article (1978a) implies a particular activist orientation and a bias toward radical change. Women who did not radically change were described in less favorable language than those who did. For example, "many women in re-entry programs find they can't stand the heat and go back into the kitchen" (1978a, p. 11). The use of the above cliche implies that women who "go back into the kitchen" do so as a result of some personal weakness. In reality, is it not possible that the "kitchen" (which also appears to be a loaded term) can be chosen just as well as the office or construction site? The option of choice appears to be denied if the woman makes a traditional choice. A comment on the results of a re-entry program in Illinois also implies that the sine qua non of perspective transformation was a shift from traditional views.

Mezirow's theory is like a fresh breeze blowing upon the face of adult learning theory primarily because of his attention to the peculiarity of adult learning. Not all adult learning tasks are of the instrumental or technical kind. Despite the increasingly pronounced vocational emphasis in adults' education, learning tasks and learning processes continue to require awareness of a different kind of learning. A related position is found in the writing of Flavell (1970), an adherent of Piagetian theory who emphasized experience and "the types of cognitions one would think of here are not of the psychometric or learning task variety . . . they have to do with judgments, attitudes, and beliefs rather than skills . . ." (1970, p. 250).

As Mezirow develops his theory he should be encouraged to also address that kind of learning Kilpatrick (1951) described as associated learning. New vistas and different worlds are often opened to individuals through associated learning as unintended consequences of the primary learning activities. As a regular practice, this writer has encouraged graduate students to be sensitive to all three kinds of learning and to be prepared to discuss and examine them. Today, most American adults' introduction to education is likely to be through programs of courses that emphasize primary learning. Few special programs such as The Women's Re-entry Project at Columbia will provide direct opportunity for perspective transformation. In most instances awareness of the other kinds of learning must be developed by sensitive educators.

Kilpatrick (Tenenbaum, 1951) identified three types of learning that occurs in classroom settings. He labelled them primary, associated and attendant learning. <u>Primary learning</u> comprises of those specific direct learning goals such as skills, knowledge and appreciation. <u>Associated learning</u> comprises of learning that is "related" to the former, i.e., French conversation is a primary learning goal, but in the process of learning French for conversation some people may also become interested in and learn about French architecture, cooking, geography, history, and so forth. <u>Attendant</u> learning comprises of new attitudes (or changes in existing ones), dispositions and standards of reference that redirect the development of personality.

Perhaps the most important conceptual contribution of Mezirow's perspective transformation is the reiteration of the position that much of an adult's learning or education concerns areas that are not commonly identified with education of adults. The premise that adult education has more than one function has sound historical roots. Bryson's (1936) typology of purposes of adult education is well-known to students in the field. Less well-known, but equally supportive is Long's (1984c) historical analysis that identifies the following purposes of education for adults:

a. Americanization education
b. Education for application
c. Education for personal liberation
d. Education for social liberation
e. Education for literacy

PROGRAM PLANNING AND DEVELOPMENT

Program is used in American adult education in a manner similar to the way terms such as course and curriculum are used in other levels of education. Program is not synonomous with either of the above terms, however. As a result, educators of adults in the United States frequently experience difficulty in communicating about one of the field's basic constructs. A number of years ago Thomas (1964) illustrated the difficulty when he observed no term or idea throughout adult education is so widely used, nor quite so elusive in precise meaning. Great liberty is taken with the term in adult education and there is limited insistence that people agree completely on its exact usage. Some of the more commonly accepted characteristics of a program include the following: (a) it is an activity; (b) it has order and continuity; (c) it includes more than one item or event; (d) it includes educational objectives, and events within the activity are related to every other event (Long, 1983a).

Recent theoretical and applied work concerning adult education programs reflect the pluralistic nature of education of adults in the United States. Schroeder's (1980) concept is general compared with Long's (1983a) model that emphasizes adult and continuing education, and Boyle's (1981) model which emerges from his long association with the Cooperative Extension Service. Continuing professional education (CPE) is perhaps the area currently experiencing the most active scholarship in both applied and theoretical issues of program planning. While a detailed discussion of many of these developments are reported by Long (1983a), brief comments on some of them are shared here. Two general classifications are used: (a) general; and (b) CPE models, discussed a little later.

GENERAL MODELS

Even though Long's (1983a) model was used to illustrate an approach to program building in higher adult and continuing education and Boyle's (1981) model grew out of his Cooperative Extension Service experience, they are both amenable to general application. Thus, the three models noted here include the contribution of Boyle (1981) Houle (1972) Long (1983a) and Schroeder (1980).

Boyle's (1981) concept is founded on a conceptualization of program types which he defines as (a) development; (b) institutional; and (c) informational. The primary goals of the three program types differ as follows: (a) developmental programs define and solve individual, group or community problems; (b) institutional programs are designed to achieve growth and improvement of an individual's basic abilities, skills, knowledge and competencies; (c) informational programs are designed to exchange information. Other differences include source of objectives, use of knowledge involvement of the learner, role of the programmer and standards of effectiveness. As impact evaluation is one of the developmental areas noted elsewhere in this chapter, it may be productive to note how Boyle describes the standards of effectiveness according to the three program types: (a) developmental-effectiveness is based on the quality of problem solution and the degree to which individuals, groups and communities develop problem solving skills; (b) institutional-effectiveness is determined by how well the client masters content or desired competencies; and (c) informational-effectiveness is determined by the number of persons reached, and how much information was distributed.

Boyle's (1981) more recent model is more abstract than his earlier (Boyle, 1985) program planning principles. The trend toward abstraction and generalization is also noted in the models of Houle (1972), Long (1983a) and Schroeder (1980).

Houle's (1972) model includes seven major decision points with two of them containing ten and four substeps, respectively. The major element in Houle's design of education model are (a) a possible educational activity is identified; (b) a decision is made to proceed; (c) objectives are identified and refined; (d) a suitable format is designed (this step includes ten other decision points); (e) the format is fitted into larger patterns of life (includes four substeps); (f) the plan is put into effect and (g) the results are measured and appraised.

Long's (1983) model is more abstract, or deals with a higher level of abstraction than the previous ones. Like Houle (1972) Long identifies seven components in the program planning model. Even though the components are discussed in a linear fashion, the model is an interactive concept employing continuing use of feedback loops. The seven components are (a) philosophy of basic purposes and character of adult and continuing education, (b) historical characteristics of adult and continuing education; (c) structural factors in the environment (revealed through social, psychological and technological analyses); (d) organizational mission and readiness; (e) interpretation of environment; (f) needs of specific target groups in specific areas of interest or location; and (g) specific program planning and implementation procedures as noted by Houle (1972) Boyle (1965) and others.

Schroeder (1980) conceived of the program planning process as a two-tiered concept including macro and micro level elements. Each of his two levels also contains two major systems: The agent system and the client system. The two systems differ as follows: the agent system tends to include the more institutionalized and traditional

social organizations that are usually task
directed; the client system, in contrast, is
composed of the more flexible, transitory and
person-centered groups. Control emerges from the
judgments concerning discussions about educational
needs, program objectives, procedures, learning
needs, objectives and experiences.

EVALUATION

Following the enactment of Title I of the 1965
Higher Education Act, the Department of Education
specifically encouraged state agencies receiving
funds to provide impact evaluation data on their
projects. Over the recent decade additional
efforts to address issues of accountability through
evaluation schemes have been made. The general
status of research and theory concerning evaluation
is reflected by this writer's decision to delete
evaluation as a category analytical in a recent
paper (Long, 1984). A review of articles published
in the adult education research journal between
1974 and 1982 revealed that only one evaluation
article had been published during the review
period. In contrast, 21 papers were presented on
the topic at the Adult Education Research
Conferences over the ten years between 1971-1980.
These 21 papers represent only 5.9 percent of the
355 papers presented. Thus, the interest of adult
educators in evaluation theory seems to be limited.
Impact evaluation as a theoretical topic in
adult education seems to have developed more as a
pragmatic response than a theoretical one.
Examples of some of the recent work include
Copeland's (1985) study of impact of adult literacy
education and Darkenwald and Valentine's (1984)
study of adult basic education. The work of
Darkenwald and Valentine (1984) moves toward a
theoretical treatment by providing a model for
statewide student follow-up. Even though the
education of adults proceeds through the agency of
diverse institutions and organizations which employ
a range of procedures and methods, much of the
evaluation literature seems to be based on
procedures normally associated with traditional
educational institutions. The literature is
perceived to inadequately reflect the strategies
and methods of evaluation employed by other service
oriented social institutions.
A theory of evaluation in adult education,
however, must be broader than raw accountability.

Evaluation serves a number of purposes such as policy and political goal, that are often excluded in discussions of the process. More often the reader is advised of the uses to which evaluation may be put, i.e., impact, or the process is highlighted. Only infrequently are the two combined to become comprehensive. Process evaluation is an insufficient indicator of impact. In turn, impact evaluation without process evaluation is incomplete. Thus, when the policy and political question implications of evaluation are adequately considered, comprehensive evaluation that employes both process and impact evaluation is strongly recommended.

Increasing emphasis on accountability is likely to stimulate additional concerns about the process of evaluating education programs for adults. These evaluations are likely to address several levels of activities: programmatic and institutional activities, individual development, change, achievement, etc., and social impacts. Issues related to both evaluation and program efficacy are particularly salient in the occupational and professional education areas. Concerns about the meaning or value of the containing Education Unit contributed to the development of a set of guidelines (Council on the Continuing Education Unit, 1984) that more easily lend themselves to measurement, and hence evaluation. Emphasis on mandatory continuing education (MCE) for professional and occupational areas raised a number of issues that are related to evaluation. For example, one assumption underlying MCE is that participation in continuing education improves practice and protects the public interest. More stringent evaluation may be needed to confirm the effectiveness of continuing MCE. In the absence of such hard data the issue remains loaded with opinion and personal bias. Empirical verification of the effectiveness and impact of MCE is needed before the issue can be resolved, at least at the level of effectiveness.

Cervero (1984) has turned his attention to the issue of impact in another fashion. His interest is in what he terms " effectiveness" in continuing professional education (CPE).(More is said about CPE in general later in this chapter.) Cervero has formulated a framework that explains behavioral change in CPE as the consequence of four major elements as illustrated in figure 7:1.

Theoretical Perspectives

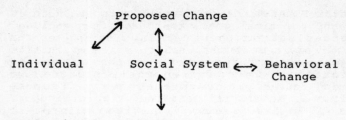

Figure 7-1.   Framework Linking CPE and Behavioral
Change (Cervero,p.2)

Nine variables have been identified in the major elements in Cervero's model: demographic data, individual attitudes to professional practice, intention to implement educational goals, program relevance, clarity of program objectives, faculty effectiveness, match of educational strategies to learning preferences, supervisor's performance score, participant's performance score (Cervero, 1984). None of the variables proposed by Cervero are particularly surprising. They all have face validity and reflect a common sense realization that job performance after a training or educational activity is not completely determined by the effectiveness of education or training.

The model does appear to contain some identifiable weaknesses, however. Inclusion of variable seven, "match of educational strategies to learning preferences" as an important element requires further study. Long (1985) notes that some research indicates that learning achievement may be inhibited by matching educational strategies to learning preferences. However, learning preference may be defined differently by Cervero than in the studies reviewed by Long..

Including only one variable in the social system element is questionable. It is possible that the supervisor is one of the dominant sources of influence, but other studies of the work environment indicate that peers exert strong influence on behavior (Long, 1968). Ways to include peers, organizational structure and policy into the social system element should be explored.

CONTINUING PROFESSIONAL EDUCATION

Theoretical attention is increasingly focusing on continuing professional education (CPE). Accountability, mandatory continuing education and documentation of continuing education using continuing education units (CEUs) have combined to stimulate theoretical interest in this topic. Houle's (1980) recent work on the topic may also be credited with contributing to recent theoretical and empirical works in the area. An additional source of stimulation is the provided by a publication of the Council on the Continuing Education Unit(1984). This document places a strong emphasis on learning outcomes and assessment of those outcomes.

The increasing importance attributed to CPE has encouraged study of several aspects of the topic. Interest in effectiveness or impact of CPE and program development has been particularly keen. As a result, a variety of models of impact evaluation are available in the growing body of CPE and Continuing Medical Education (CME), (Fox, 1983; LeBreton, et al, 1979). Recently published works illustrate the increasing dynamism of CPE and two worthy developments are discussed in the following paragraphs.

Practice Audit Model

A number of CPE models for program planning and development have been reported in the literature (LeBreton, et al, 1979, Mazmanian, 1980, and Pennington and Green, 1976). While each of the above is interesting, space does not permit detailed description. In contrast, an approach currently in use in the Penn State University program should be discussed.

Pennsylvania State University received funding from the W. K. Kellogg Foundation to develop and apply the Practice Audit Model in CPE. According to information released by the Continuing Professional Education Project (1981) at Penn State, the Practice model emerged from previous experiences in CPE. It is also based on the recognition that program planning procedures in CPE often have been subjected to criticism. Criticisms have focused on problems of delivering relevant quality CPE programs and of assuming professional competence.

As a result, the procedure employed in the Practice Audit Model is based on the following assumptions: (a) the two problems noted above can be addressed simultaneously; (b) the task is a long-term systematic one that focuses on professionals' practice oriented needs. Key elements in the process include closely relating learning and assessment processes to the practice setting and to factors that contribute to adequate performance. Consequently, determination of practice-related educational needs is the ultimate objective of the Practice Audit Model (PAM).

Identification of practice-related educational needs is not as simple as it sounds. Educators of adults have long lauded efforts to relate educational programs to needs as determined by needs assessment procedures. Pennington (1980) and Dubin (1972) among others have reported procedures to identify needs through a variety of procedures. Criticism of approaches of this kind is also available (Bryson, 1936; Long, 1983b, Pottinger, 1980). To overcome the criticism of other methods of needs assessment the Practice Audit Model is based on systematic procedures that are broader than many of the other efforts. The PAM may be summarized as follows:

Phase I   Establish a profession team including factulty members, professional association representatives, continuing education professionals and other relevant parties such as consultants and practitioners

Phase II   Identify practice standards or professional competence

Phase III   Construct assessment materials

Phase IV   Conduct assessment workshops

Phase V   Analyze assessment results

Phase VI   Plan and develop CPE programs

Phase VII   Implement and evaluate CPE programs

According to material published by the CPE Development Project (Smutz et al, 1981) the Practice Audit Model is believed to be unique for the following reasons:

1. The impetus for its development grew out of a consortium of continuing professional education providers.

2. It brings together the resources of professional school administrators, academic content experts, practitioners and professional association leaders, maintaining this operating team from the earliest planning stages through the

development and execution of educational programs.
3. The model provides a systematic method of addressing the needs assessment/program development process.
4. The process involves faculty and practitioners in structured, face-to-face situations that provide for critical analyses of practitioners' performance.
5. The program provides for the repetition of the process in a three-to-four year cycle, thus giving continuity to lifelong learning (Smutz, et al, 1981, p. 48).

Smutz, et al (1981) candidly recognize that while the Practice Audit Model overcomes some of the criticisms of other CPE program planning models, it is not immune to criticism. It is a lengthy, time-consuming process that requires careful attention to each of the seven phases. Interpersonal, interorganizational and political problems may occur at any time in the process. Questions of validity and reliability of assessment procedures are important. It is also difficult to translate the assessment results into educational programs. Nevertheless, the experience with the first Practice Audit Model with pharmacists encouraged the W. K. Kellogg Foundation to support the application of the model in six professional areas between 1980 and 1985. As a result, the model has been used in the development of CPE programs for the following professions: accounting, architecture, clinical dietetics, clinical psychology, nursing and pharmacy.

Toombs (1984) has shared some provocative observations concerning the Practice Audit Model based on three and one-half years experience with the project. Briefly stated, findings reported emerged from three areas of interest: (a) the practice situation, (b) attributes of the profession and (c) components of the project. Major conclusions are reported below in outline form:

A. The Practice Situation
1. Almost no one practices a profession in isolation.
2. The single definition of "client" for many professions has become complex.
3. Interaction in several aspects has particular importance in professional practice.

       4.   The essential paradigm of professional practice is one of problem-solving.

       5.   It is difficult for practitioners to achieve a 'global' or holistic view of their activities.

B.   Attributes of the Profession

       1.   Just about all of the professions are beset by anxieties about their state of status.

       2.   Performance is viewed in two quite different ways by well socialized professionals.

C.   Components of the Project

       1.   The profession team design, with its emphasis on the consensual process of decision-making and collegial relationship, is an effective vehicle for collaboration.

       2.   Professions have demonstrated a "readiness" to explore continuing Professional Education but still have many questions about the forms it may take.

       3.   New directions and strategies are emerging for the definition, format, and pricing of continuing professional education programs.

       4.   The project work to date has captured much of the practice situation. (Toombs, 1984, pp. 2-7)

Experience with the Practice Audit Model is contributing additional questions of theory and application in CPE that may also have important implications for program planning processes in general.

OTHER THEORETICAL IDEAS

Theoretical models of education agency development have been of interest to educators of adults in the United States for more than twenty years. Knowles (1952) has provided a generalized model of programmatic development, Carey (1961) and Griffith (1963) contributed thoughts concerning stages of development. More recently, Beder (1972; 1978) and Beder and Smith (1977) suggested a quantitatively based theoretical model of agency development.

A variety of disciplines have recently begun to take a new look at the problem of illiteracy. As noted in Chapter five, illiteracy has been a persistent problem in American culture for over two centuries. As high tech reaches into the furtherest recesses of the culture, the effects and causes of illiteracy will receive greater attention. Some educators of adults have suggested new and radical approaches such as "oracracy" that seem to be designed to by-pass the problem completely while others tend to take more conservative and traditional approaches.

Despite the high interest in group dynamics and small group theory during the 1950s and 1960s, theory concerning group instruction or the learning-teaching transaction is relatively impoverished. It is interesting to observe that since the early 1970s adult educators have devoted high levels of energy to self-directed learning issues and theory as discussed earlier in this chapter while neglecting group learning or group instruction. Here and there one discovers bits and pieces such as the various studies of the effects of learner participation in planning educational activities (Arnold, 1955; Long, 1983b). An emerging interest, based on conference presentations at the 1985 National Adult Education conference, is learning styles. However, much of the work in that area seems to be limited spin-offs from the discipline of psychology with inadequate theoretical underpinnings in adult education. Darkenwald (1982) has attempted to develop a sequential line of inquiry into issues associated with teaching adults, but a particular theory of teaching adults has yet to emerge from his work.

A useful summary of the historical development of five major "theories" of adult learning is provided by Stubblefield (1983). The theories he identified include the laboratory education method, identified above as the group dynamics, Indiana University's Participation Training method, andragogy, Tough's self-directed learning and intentional change theory, and Mezirow's theory of perspective transformation. The reader will recognize that the above share some central themes or common ground: the learner, rather than the teacher is emphasized; learning is dominant rather than education; and process prevails over content. Stubblefield says, "each of the theories posit the learner as a growing, evolving person capable of directing his/her life. Learning is a central

195

process in the life of the mature adult" (1983, p. 148).

Stubblefield believes the five theories have been useful in pointing the way to what he calls "the new adult learning" (1983, p. 148). This new adult learning identified by Stubblefield rests on five assumptions:

1. Adulthood is a period of development and change in which learning is a normal occurrence to be integrated into life tasks.
2. How adult learning is facilitated is a function of the characteristics of the adult learner.
3. The basic competency of the adult learner is the competency of learning.
4. The unique domain of adult learning is perspective transformation.
5. The basic task of the adult learning expert is to assist adults in a process of growth and change toward increased self-direction and self-awareness."

Stubblefield's positive views of the above "theories" notwithstanding, it appears that additional work is required in each of the topical areas he identified. Indeed, three of the above, andragogy, self-directed learning and Mezirow's perspective transformation ideas are discussed in an earlier section of this chapter. The Participation Training method developed at Indiana University was a specific application of a process that requires additional theoretical development. It was rooted in the idea that adults are motivated to learn when they become aware of some need or interest and that adults normally experience conflict when they obtain information that is inconsistent with beliefs or opinions they already hold. At this stage, it qualifies for the label of method rather than theory, however.

OBSERVATIONS

The education of adults in the United States is an extremely pluralistic enterprise. It is an activity served by many disciplines and fields of practice; it proceeds through a variety of modes including therapy, self-help procedures, as well as independent group processes and instruction. Adult education is the major field of graduate study to address the broadest concerns associated with the practice and theory of education for adults.

As a traditionally practice-oriented activity, graduate study has tended to be long on application and short on theory. Questions of what, when and how have dominated questions of why. Efforts to introduce a stronger theoretical foundation into both practice and study have been of two kinds: borrowing from other disciplines and more original explanations from within the field of adult education. Neither approach has been overly successful.

The theoretical base in adult education is in disarray. There are numerous incomplete and competing minitheories. Two of the foremost examples are in the areas of participation and self-directed learning. Theoretical work in participation at one time was heavily based on sociological concepts, later it shifted to a more psychological framework with limited efforts to develop a comprehensive theory that encompassed important elements of both disciplines. Current efforts to explain participation have eventually evolved models that provide for an interaction between sociological and psychological properties. These models, yet, remain to be adequately tested.

Advances in the area of self-direction in learning have also been slow. For a number of years too little effort was made to expand and enlarge on Tough's original work. Currently, the trend can be described as a mini-explosion with research proceeding on a broader range of topics. Despite these advances, the nomological nets developed for many of the investigators are incomplete. Two apparently opposing views concerning self-directed learning are now emerging. One view suggests that self-directed learning is a special kind of process in which learners engage according to certain conditions or circumstances. Another perspective implies that self-directed learning is a personality trait and as such it should be enduring and persistent across circumstances and conditions.

Another cleavage point also may be developing among students of self-direction in learning. Heretofore, for purposes of research and practice, unintentional and random learning was excluded from study by definition. This operational decision did not deny the existence of unintentional learning; it merely excluded it from the research activity and explanation. Recent work has recognized unintentional cumulative learning as a major type of self-directed learning.

As yet, this writer is not familiar with any over-arching theory that would justify either of the competing positions or one that would demonstrate the complementary nature (if there is one) of the two positions.

Elsewhere, this writer has raised the question concerning the possibility of a theoretical paradigm that encompasses several of the microtheoretical topics in the education of adults. For example, participation in group learning activity is the source of some kind of circumstance, condition and personal motive. Continuing enrolment in the learning activity, or dropping out may also be closely associated with the original factors in enrolment. Participation in education implies a motivation to learn, hence, what is the association between motivation to engage in group learning and self-directed learning (variously defined)? Cross (1981) is one of the few writers who has suggested such a broad theoretical framework. Generally, educators of adults have failed to raise questions concerning the linkages among the microtheories.

Mezirow's perspective transformation theory (1981) and Long's (1984c) historically based concept of purposes of education for adults complement the above paradigm. Education of adults has multiple purposes, is stimulated by a variety of circumstances and has taken many forms. Unfortunately, the complexity of the enterprise has complicated efforts to develop parisimonous explanations. Nevertheless, encouraging progress is being made in the development of microtheories which subsequently may be enlarged.

Adult educators, generally, seem to reflect a Newtonian orientation to science rather than a perception based on quantum mechanics. Briefly stated, the difference is as follows: Newtonian theory is based on a view of the universe that is equated with clockwork; quantum mechanics theory is based on the premise that chance is a part of all events that occur at dimensions of atoms and their components (Judson, 1985). Stated another way, Newtonian theory leads to the belief that if one could know the status of a phenomenon at a given instant, given the computational power one could accurately predict the state to which the phenomenon would move. Quantum theory takes a different view that does not place the burden on prediction completely upon the instruments or

experimental strategies employed by the scientist.
Adapting Heisenberg's uncertainty principle to
adult education, we could say that we may not
precisely know both the state of a variable and the
speed at which it is changing . If quantum theory
recognizes the difficulties imposed on prediction
by chance and uncertainty where physical phenomenon
are concerned, how much more likely are social and
psychological variables subject to these elements?

Adult educators are challenged to reconsider
their views of science as the natural scientists
have. Our models of society and the human organism
are too simplistic to allow the kind of prediction
and theoretical developments that are needed to
adequately understand and explain the significant
processes involved in the education of adults.

SUMMARY

This chapter has provided a description of, and
comments upon, several different theoretical issues
in the education of adults. Specific detailed
attention focused on Boyd and Apps' (1980)
conceptual model of adult education; participation
theory; andragogy; education versus learning and
the related interest in self-direction in learning;
perspective transformation as a learning theory;
program planning and development; general models ;
evaluation; continuing professional education; and
other miscellaneous theoretical ideas . Topics
included in the last category includes observations
concerning adult education agency development,
illiteracy, instruction and a viewpoint on theories
of adult learning. Observations concerning these
theories and the general trend in theory
development were also made.

The status of theory in adult education is
illustrated by the andragogy. A great deal of
confusion exists concerning this topic. First,
there is the question, is andragogy a theory? If
so, of what? Is it a theory of learning as
suggested by Stubblefield (1983)? Or is it a
curriculum theory? Or is it a philosophical
position (Hartree, 1984)? If confusion exists
concerning what is one of the more prominent
concepts in adult education literature in the
United States about such basic issues then it is
easy to speculate that other less popular concepts

also suffer from lack of clarity , precision and coherence.

As implied by the above observation, theory in adult education generally is limited in its development. There are diverse numerous partial explanations for a variety of relationships and conditions of interest to educators of adults. These explanations, however, are lacking in comprehensiveness and rigor. As a result, they have been referred to here as mini or microtheories. As noted in chapter six, both the research and theory in adult education suffer the consequences of weak, inadequate or incomplete conceptualization.

PART FOUR

THE FUTURE

Offering a perspective on the education of adults
in the United States is within itself a challenging
task. The size of the nation, differences among
sections of the country and social-racial-ethnic-
cultural groups add to the already complex task.
Education of adults as a variegated diverse
pluralistic ill-defined activity further compounds
the task. So, to attempt to present a futuristic
perspective is tantamount to hallucinating.
Nevertheless, this volume would be incomplete, the
writer would be unfulfilled and the reader could
correctly be frustrated if an attempt were not
made.
    Without abandoning all caution or constraints,
the following chapter discusses a few selected
topics, how they point to the future and their
interrelationships. To meet criteria for inclusion
in chapter eight, each topic had to be closely
associated with the others. Beginning from the
philosophical positions concerning governmental
authority and responsibility for education,
historical contrasts between adult and childhood
education are drawn. The scenario emphasizes
governmental authority, governmental responsibility
and personal responsibility. Authority for
education has not been accompanied by
responsibility in every instance. It could also be
argued, especially in education for adults, that
governmental authority has often exceeded
responsibility. Evidence from the MCE or
re-licensure area is supportive of this premise.
    Other topics emerging from the above include
lifelong learning as an organizational concept and
the interaction of certification and technology
with lifelong learning and concepts of authority

and responsibility. Other topics included in chapter eight discuss such diverse areas issues and predictions. Four major issues that are apparent from the Preface to the conclusion include providers, access, quality assurance and economic revitalization. These issues are played out time and again in various parts of the book including chapters two, three, four and five. It is appropriate that the final chapter summarizes them in a new way based on the authoritative position of Cross's (1984) work. This "new" perspective on the education of adults completes a journey begun with a discussion of participation to some of the concerns of participation in the future. Eight predictions concerning the education of adults in the United States completes the chapter.

Chapter Eight

PERSPECTIVES ON THE FUTURE

The first seven chapters have analyzed, described and interpreted a variety of topics of interest to educators of adults. The first chapter discussed participation of adults in educational activities in the United States while attention was directed in the second chapter to philosophies, purposes and concepts that characterize adult education. Corporate education and the education of adults in the corporate image was discussed in the third chapter. Education of the elderly and literacy education completed the second major divison while research and theory constitute the third major section of the book.

It is suggested time and again there is little unaninmity among adult educators in the United States except on the importance of adult education. Diverse opinions concerning the purposes, concepts and forms of education for adults appear to be closely associated with the historical character of education in the nation. All education , particularly institutionalized provisions , in the United States has tended until recent years to be spontaneous (Educational Review, 1900, p.481). An unidentified writer described education in the United States as follows:

> Spontaneity is the keynote of education in the United States. Its varied form, its uneven progress, its lack of symmetry, its practical effectiveness, are all due to the fact that it has sprung, unbidden and unenforced, from the and aspirations of the people. Local prefer- ences and individual initiative have been

> ruling forces. What men have wished for they
> have done. They have not waited for State
> control. As a result, there is, in the
> European sense, no American system of
> education.

While the above description does not totally agree
with the current reality of public education in the
United States, it remains a fair description of
adult education. It reflects those characteristics
of adult education noted by Long (1980d): dynamic,
creative, pluralistic,, pragmatic and voluntary.
As noted in chapter two, however, the voluntary
nature of adult education may be changing.

It should, therefore, be no surprise that a
range of opinions concerning the philosophy,
purposes, concepts, programs, research needs and
theoretical bases of adult education exists. In a
way, the education of adults remains an anachronism
in contemporary America. It has resisted efforts to
be tied to one philosophy, one purpose or agency
despite the pleas for centralized planning and
provision. But what about the future? What are some
of the important developments that may have
implications for education of adults?

This chapter provides some comments on six
general topics that may pose implications for the
education of adults in the United States. The first
of these topics continues the discussion of
governmental roles in adult education followed
closely by a report on a new initiative. Other
topics include major changes such as education of
women, aging, expanding information, workplace
education and lifelong learning concepts.
Certification developments including credit for
prior experience and the continuing education unit
(CEU) are mentioned as are developments in
technology. Four important issues in the education
of adults such as providers, access, quality
assurance and economic revitalization are noted.
Finally, seven general predictions concerning
education of adults in the future are provided. A
summary concludes the chapter.

GOVERNMENTAL ROLES

As can be inferred from information presented in
the preceding seven chapters, there is no national
policy concerning the education of adults. If
there is one, it is a policy to not have a policy.
As a consequence, the purposes, structure and

financing of education of adults in the United States is even more confusing than childhood education.

Conceptually, adult education generally has followed childhood education. The Puritans' recognition of the social implications of education at both the basic and advanced levels led to the creation of Harvard and the first school laws in the same decade. From the 1640's onward social authority for childhood education has been an accepted ingredient of American life. Social authority as set forth in the Massachusett's laws of 1642 later evolved into social responsibility with the adoption of the Northwest Ordinance of 1783. Social responsibility was further emphasized in the use of property taxes to support education in the nineteenth century and widespread adoption of compulsory school laws in the twentieth century. Shifts in local, state and federal roles in education in the last half of the current century represent additional modifications in concepts of social responsibility.

Students of the history of education for adults see some contrasts between the scenario for childhood education and adult education. Adult education has tended to remain a personal responsibility. Some exceptions are noteworthy, however, as occasionally philanthropic organizations and governmental bodies have devised and offered narrow special purpose education for adults. These include the Mechanics Institutes, and the Chatauqua of the nineteenth century. Literacy education has been a recipient of irregular socially mandated aid since the Society for the Propagation of the Gospel in Foreign Parts encouraged religious and literacy education in the eighteenth century to the state provisions of the early twentieth century to current programs. Mandatory continuing education (MCE) emerged in the 1970's as an indication of social authority for certain kinds of education for adults. The social authority, which resulted in the adoption of minimum continuing education requirements for relicensure in selected professional and occupational areas was limited, however. Social responsibility for the provision of education for MCE purposes was diffused among professional associations and other agencies rather than government. Responsibility for costs associated with MCE largely remain with the individual even though the requirements are justified in terms of social benefits.

As a general rule, Americans have taken the position government has the primary authority and responsibility for childhood education. As a consequence, attendance, calendars, curricula, financing and other practice dimensions are addressed by governmental policy at three levels, local, state and federal. Simultaneously, education for adults has been perceived as a personal responsibility. Only in a few areas, as previously noted, has governmental authority and responsibility applied in adult education.

The absence of active governmental involvement in education of adults is cited as both a strength and weakness of adult education in the United States. It is a source of strength as no one or two curricula concepts (and content) or purposes of education dominate the field. There is less bureaucracy, governmental controls, and other restrictions on education for adults. Simultaneously, lack of governmental responsibility is a source of weakness to the degree that practice and study in adult education occurs within very broad parameters with little quality control. In addition, financing and general social/governmental support is limited, in-direct and/or often non-existent.

There can be little doubt the status of theory and research in adult education would be at a higher level of development if adult education had the same legitimacy as childhood education. There is reason to suspect some changes may soon provide additional legitimacy to education of adults. For example, changes in five areas are productive topics of discussion. Two of the areas of change include special populations : (a) women and (b) aging. One kind of change is of a social/technological nature: the expansion of information. Finally, the remaining area of change concerns attitudes about the nature of education , i.e., purposes and concepts as they relate to education for the work place and lifelong education or lifelong learning.

A NEW INITIATIVE

As indicated at the beginning of this chapter adult education in the United States has generally operated with little or very limited governmental interference, except as noted in the discussion of licensure or relicensure activites and in literacy education. A few other exceptions include provision for military personnel and the indirect assistance provided through tax incentives to business and industry and to professionals. Yet since the 1960s there has been a persistent and increasing interest in additional assistance to institutions and individuals, particularly adult students whose age classifies them as " non-traditional " students. One of the recent efforts to obtain additional recognition and support for the non-traditonal aged adult student was mounted by the Commission on Higher Education and the Adult Learner. Some of the proposals and positions of the Commission are provided here.

The Commission duly recognized the importance of adult learners by refering to them as " key to the nation's future" (Commission on Higher Education and the Adult Learner, 1984). While the Commission's proposals may appear to be mired in the same economic/human resource development syndrome discussed in chapter three, the five challenges identified in the report are informative. They are as follows:

1. developing or renewing employability of the unemployed;
2. maintaining and enhancing occupational skills in the face of technological change;
3. eliminating adult illiteracy;
4. providing equal access to education for all adults; and
5. developing knowledgeable citizens in an information -technological society .(p.9)

Four major impediments to meeting the above challenges are identified by the Commission. They include institutional barriers erected by higher education institutions that do not see adult learners as their clientele, or included in a central way in their mission. Inadequate funding for both institutions and individual learners and lack of awareness of learning opportunities among adults complete the list of identified barriers.

While one might quarrel with the above lists recognition of lifelong learning and the importance of learning in adulthood is welcome. Perhaps one of the most forceful calls for support of adult learners yet seen by this writer appears in the Commission's report:

For reasons of national interest embedded in the economic, political and social determinants of the quality of life, the fostering of learn-

ing by adults is an immediate and compelling
national need, requiring a lucid and forthright
statement of national policy and immediate
attention by the nation's colleges and universities (p.1).

Educators of adults also should be encouraged by
the Commission's call for funds to develop in
higher education institutions new capabilities to
serve adult learners by creating models which will
bring about basic changes in institutional
procedures in higher education. The maturity and
distinctive qualities and life syles of adults are
emphasized in the recommendations.

It would be easy, after decades of hearing that
the golden age of adult education is on the horizon
to become blase about such reports as this one.
Especially when reviews of most utopian societies
indicate they too provided for the continuing
learning of adults. However, most utopian schemes
were flawed in some fundamental way such as the
need for extensive, time consuming and physically
demanding labor or limited resources for the
provision of the learning opportunities. In some
respects both of the barriers have been mitigated
in western high tech societies. Perhaps for the
first time in history the need, justification and
resources to provide extensive education for adults
is now available in a few countries such as the
United States.

SELECTED MAJOR CHANGES

Changes occuring in American society in recent
decades have been numerous and diverse. It would
be intemperate to suggest all events and change in
the immediate past contain implications for the
education of adults. It would also be fallacious to
imply that all of the important changes that have
implications for the future practice and study of
adult education could be identified and discussed
here. Therefore, only a few of the more significant
changes, as noted above, are briefly discussed in
the following pages.

Education of Women
Increasing rates of participation by women in adult
education is one of the major persistent
conclusions that can be obtained from the triennial
surveys of adult education. The rapid expansion of

female participation in adult and continuing education has implications at two levels: the practitioner level and the learner level. No data have been identified that support the following observation, but it appears that there has been a significant increase in the numbers of female practitioners at the higher education level of adult education, it also seems as if a similar increase might be noted in other related areas of practice.

The numbers and percentages of women in occupations formerly dominated by men continue to increase. Such changes in the occupational structure have a variety of implications for adult education. Some of these implications, such as the possible modifications in the motives of women's participation have already been noted. Therefore , let us turn our attention to supporting data. Hall and Wessell,1985 p.37N) report the following statistics concerning the involvement of women in selected fields of university study. In 1983, according to Hall and Wessell (1985 p.37N) women comprised 50 percent of all undergraduate students, 45 percent of all graduate students, more than 30 percent of masters of business administration students, 50 percent of law students and 55 percent of accounting students.

A related implication of these data is found in the family setting. Increasingly, families in the United States are dependent upon dual careers. Approximately 60 percent of all working families bring home dual incomes (incomes earned by both male and female adults). Hall and Wessell (1985) indicate the U. S. Department of Labor project the percentage will rise to 75 percent by 1990. In other words, the traditional patterns of husband= breadwinner and wife=homemaker will apply in only a small minority of families. This basic structural change in family relationships will be reflected in such diverse areas as how we plan our work lives, rear and educate our children, plan our financial futures, arrange leisure time and activities and maintain our educational levels.

More substantive data are available concerning women participants in adult education as noted in the NCES reports discussed in chapter two. The increase in female participation is not a simple thing to analyze, however, as suggested in chapter two the changes in women's participation in both the workforce and education are believed to have implications for programs of education for women. Whereas, Continuing Education for Women (CEW) was a

popular program area in the 1970s (Long,1983a) the
popularity of these kinds of programs may decline
without serious rethinking of the purposes and
formats of CEW.

Expanding Information

Yet another area of change that has implications
that have yet to be explicated is what is labelled
"expanding information". The implications of this
phenomenon are found in the workplace as well as
other areas of adult life. More is said about
workplace education in another section of this
chapter, but it is important that the connection be
established here also. Expanding information has
implications for at least two work related topics:
(a) information used in the workplace and (b)
changes in the workplace itself. It is not uncommon
to hear someone lament that after twenty years in a
given job with the same employer the job has
changed underneath their feet. Such changes have
encouraged a number of friends to plan early
retirements or changes in jobs.

Expanding information has implications for
other areas of life in addition to the workplace.
Complex social systems that are constantly changing
require greater attention. Health care, leisure
activity, home maintenance and a variety of
activites related to being a social organism and to
maintaining human qualities require constant
attention to an information system that is much
more complex and dynamic than previously known.

Aging

One of the great riddles of contemporary American
life is how to address the challenges and
opportunites of an aging society. The possible
connection between an aging society and adult
education is almost as obvious as is the
relationship between aging and health care. In a
way the problems are similar. The traditional model
of health care has been a preventive one and the
traditional model of American adult education has
strongly favored a remedial thrust. If the trends
in adult education favor workplace education as
strongly as they seem to do, will the older adult
increasingly have fewer options for education,
options that are restricted to workplace education?
Will changes in demographics and the economy
require longer work lives in the future? These and

additional questions related to aging and education demand an answer.

Workplace Education

Occupational and economic justification for education have deep roots in the American mind. While childhood education was slow to respond to these educational purposes, adults readily identified the association between specialized and skill training with economic advancement. The industrialization of the United States, usually dated about 1880, was followed by increasing efforts to conceptualize and justify childhood education in terms of occupational preparation. Following World War II economic considerations emerged as national defense factors as well. Science, engineering and all kinds of other areas of study were perceived as instruments of national policy in international relations.

The advancement of science and technology was accompanied by widespread changes in communications, occupational skills, medicine, health care and general life styles. Gradually educators, corporate executives and others are recognizing the sum total of education cannot be compressed into the first 18-24 years of life. Information presented in chapters two and three reveal the increasing emphasis corporations are placing on education and training.

Thus, education of adults increasingly amounts to education for and in the workplace. Despite the negative implications presented by this development, it is giving increasing legitimacy to the concept of lifelong education which in turn has some potential benefits for adult education.

Conditions are favorable for significant changes in education in the United States. Comprehensive modifications in the system of American education must of necessity include provisions of adult education. Yet, the scenario by which the change will occur and how extensive it might be is yet unclear. It can be assumed, however, that the field of practice and study now identified as adult education will also be changed. Theory and practice, in many areas, may become more integrated into the new pre-adult system. Changes must also be in the pre-adult system. Thus, what is envisioned is not just a simple adding-on process. Basic changes must occur in childhood education before childhood and adult education are more closely integrated.

211

Lifelong Education

Integration of childhood and adult education under the rubric of lifelong education does not require a total submersion of all educational provisions into the governmental system of education. Education of adults by labor unions, churches, synagogues and other religious organizations, some elements of higher education, professional associations, and so forth should continue free of governmental controls. Where education for adults may be conducted by some of the above organizations to facilitate national policy goals, they should be eligible for governmental support. For example, chapter five contains a recommendation that literacy education be more closely related to community organizations. If such a recommendation is ever accepted by the educational establishment it would be appropriate, if not necessary to provide governmental support for the literacy education conducted by community organizations. However, to emphasize the strength that resides in independence of adult education efforts to control, regulate and otherwise circumscribe the range, variety and extent of educational provisions for adults should be resisted. As a result, the concept of lifelong education should be finely balanced in terms of implementation. Governmental, work, and social organizations should be encouraged to employ lifelong learning/education philosophy and goals, but mandatory requirements should be resisted.

Pressures for lifelong education exists in considerable quantity. Long (1974) identifies three major sources of pressures to accept, facilitate and implement lifelong education in the United States. In the order in which he discussed the pressures for acceptance, they are (a) basic human growth needs; (b) social and technological factors; and (c) education institutional pressures. Other possible categories include combinations of the above in various ways. For example, education institutional pressures may interact with political/economic needs and thereby exert extremely strong forces on society to accept and assimilate lifelong education or lifelong learning as a social norm.

Development and acceptance of a philosophy and practice of lifelong education present numerous challenges to the education establishment in the United States. Educators of adults, however, are not immune to the implications of lifelong education. According to Farmer (1974) adult educators are in a favorable position both to promote lifelong education and to become a part of the new breed of professionals providing lifelong education. The potential for adult education is not without some danger, however. Farmer (1974) indicates involvement in lifelong education may interfere with the professionalization process of adult education. An identity crisis is one possible consequence of increased popularity of lifelong education. Accordingly, three factors may determine how successfully adult educators handle their identity crisis:

1. society's need for and acceptance of lifelong learning and lifelong education;
2. the stance taken by adult educators themselves for professionalization of adult education;
3. adult educators' reactions to lifelong learning and lifelong education. (Farmer, 1974, p. 63)

Four alternative reactions to lifelong education that may be considered by adult educators are defined by Farmer (1974) as reactionary, conservative, liberal and radical. The reactionary stance favors a regression to some past position or concept of adult education. The reactionary attitude may emerge from negative views of social change, a longing for a return to a less complicated time, fear for the status of field of adult education, and a desire to realize a sense of spontaneity and personal service in adult education. The conservative stance is predicted upon the belief that adult education and adult educators have little of nothing to gain by becoming involved in lifelong education.

A liberal stance is based on a philosophical view of lifelong education as normal, necessary and logical next step for adult education (Farmer, 1974). Reasons for accepting lifelong education may be based on a desire to contribute to the growing edge of education, or may emerge from a conviction that lifelong education is an emerging social reality, or a belief that lifelong education is an idea whose time has come, or as a hope that adult education may escape marginality by becoming an important part of the lifelong education concept.

A radical stance emerges from the belief that nothing short of rapid and extensive changes in education will suffice. Three reasons for adopting a radical position include a commitment to holistic approaches in understanding and coping with social problems, rejection of gradual strategies for implementing lifelong education, and belief that there is a need to break with the past by developing new theories, concepts and techniques for education.

Unless lifelong education turns to be a fad or rapidly loses popularity, adult educators along with other educators will be forced to take a reactionary, conservative, liberal or radical stance on the matter, according to Farmer (1974). For most adult educators, it would seem that there are advantages in at least becoming knowledgeable about lifelong learning and lifelong education and in seeking to bring about movement in that direction. Farmer (1974) discusses the possibilities if lifelong education is not needed or is not accepted by society in general, those who become involved in trying to promote it may nevertheless make some gains by having strengthened communication and working relationships between the various segments of education and between education and its environments. On the other hand, if societal needs mandate some form of lifelong learning and lifelong education, adult educators who choose to respond in a reactionary or conservative manner may well become increasingly marginal or even obsolete; those who accept the challenge to respond positively to and promote lifelong learning and lifelong education may well be taking a necessary step in helping adult education becoming increasingly relevant and effective.

The attractiveness of lifelong education is further enhanced by two additional phenomena: certification and technology. It is also probable that advances in technology are stimulating certification of learning. Most certificate or alternative credit procedures employ either complex or extensive record keeping procedures which are facilitated by computer technology and related electronic media. The certification and technology phenomena are briefly discussed in the following paragraphs.

CERTIFICATION

Sometime around 1900 Americans seem to have become increasingly conscious of "certified" learning. College degrees and certification of certain professional learning activities were sometimes perceived as goals in themselves. The attraction of certified learning was enhanced in the 1970's as many states expanded the list of occupations requiring relicensure. Yet, there is an important segment of adult learners who are not interested in degrees or learning for credit. Thus, two important groups are identifiable among adult learners: those whose learning objectives do not include credit goals and those who are motivated by credit, certificates and degrees.

An extensive variety of programs, schemes and organizations arose in the previous twenty years in response to the demand for credit for learning. As a consequence, a new term entered educational jargon to represent the variety of programmatic curricula and credit systems devised to address the desire for degrees and certificates. The term is "non-traditional education."

Credit for prior learning is one of the more important concepts adopted in response to the drive for degrees. Three national systems designed to evaluate prior learning for purposes of awarding college credit include the American Council on Education (ACE), The College Entrance Examination Board (CEEB) and Educational Testing Service (ETS). In addition to national systems, state systems such as the one developed in New York known as the New York Regents' Program on Noncollegiate Sponsored Instruction, were developed.

The systems vary in emphasis. The ACE program is based on an evaluation of coursework completed by military personnel and others in noncollegiate settings. About one-half of the noncollegiate organizations and courses evaluated by the ACE Program on Institutions using the ACE guides award college credit for those experiences according to recommended guidelines. In contrast, the CEEB and ETS use batteries of tests to determine credit for experience and knowledge gained outside of the educational institutions.

Other organizations such as Empire State College in New York uses a portfolio method that provides a detailed description of the proposed educational plan, past records of current proposals concerning prior learning to be considered for advanced standing, and outlines of additional work planned to meet remaining requirements.

In the 1970's a paradoxical credit system was also developed in the United States. It is known as the Continuing Education Unit (CEU). The CEU was fashioned to meet a variety of needs including accountability in continuing education

organizations. But its greatest attraction seems
to have been a form of recognition for non-credit
educational activity. As noted in the previous
paragraphs, a variety of methods were used to award
college credit for a variety of life experiences.
Within such an environment it is not too surprising
that the CEU was devised to give a form of credit
for non-credit continuing education. The CEU has
been the topic of considerable discussion in
continuing education literature, but basically the
value of the CEU as a form of recognition resides
with the various agencies, organizations and
enterprises that use it. It's value is completely
determined by those organizations rather than by
traditional education institutions. Some
professional areas such as nursing have accepted
the CEU and have built educational schemes for
re-licensure on it.

Issues surrounding the CEU are numerous (Long
and Lord, 1978), nevertheless, it has been widely
used as a device to address numerous needs in
continuing education for both learners and
providers. In an effort to strengthen the
acceptance and validity of the CEU the Council on
the Continuing Education Unit published guidelines
of good practice in continuing education (1984).
The document addressed two main objectives:

1. To promote the strengthening of standards
   in the field of continuing education and
   training.
2. To work cooperatively with educational
   organizations; proprietary organizations;
   professional societies; units of government; and other organizations engaged in
   noncredit continuing education and
   training (p. ii).

Contributors to the document identified 18
general principles and 70 elements of good practice
under five general headings: learning needs,
learning outcomes, learning experiences, assessment
of learning outcomes and administration. Many of
the principles and elements identified are straight
forward and within themselves are not particularly
controversial. For example, principle 1.1 is
stated as follows:

Sponsors or providers of continuing education
programs/activities utilize appropriate processes to define and analyze the issue(s) or
problem(s) of individuals, groups, and
organizations for the purpose of determining

learning needs (p. 9).

Three amplifications and interpretations are also given. They are noted below:

1.1.1   The procedure(s) utilized in assessing learner needs is systematic and identifiable.

1.1.2   The procedure(s) utilized in assessing learner needs minimize assumptions and maximize the use of objective data.

1.1.3   The documentation produced during needs assessment becomes the basis for developing learning outcomes (p. 9).

Part two of the guidelines, which emphasizes learning outcomes and Part four, which focuses on learning assessment are more controversial as they communicate a behavioral and applied concept of education akin to the corporate image of education discussed in chapter three. This view stimulated Mezirow's (1984) critical review. He says:

They reduce all significant personal learning needs to expressed personal needs; they reduce all significant learning interests to those fostering individual performance and organizational efficiency; they reduce the learning process to content mastery and problem solving; they reduce learning gains to measurable outcomes; they reduce continuing education to a training ground for production and consumption . . . (p. 28).

He also challenges the ideology of adult and continuing education as collectively reflected in the 18 principles :   limiting learning to individual performance and organizational efficiency.   Let Mezirow speak for himself here, he says:

Since when was organizational efficiency a goal of education? Adults are not 'human resources' for organizational efficiency. Organizations are resources for human development (p. 28).

Despite the well deserved criticism that Mezirow has levelled at the principles of good practice document, it should not be overlooked that the developers of the principles of good practice struggling with what might be an impossible task as suggested by the purposes discussed in chapter two. The very need for the CEU itself reflects an ideology that pervades contemporary American attitudes concerning education. Emphasis on credentials as opposed to focusing on learning recalls an observation of William James; speaking to a friend concerning the, then, new American interest in degrees, he said "mediocrity in America is rushing to get a fictitious label; watch it leap into the saddle and ride!" (quoted by Mearns, 1941).

TECHNOLOGY

As noted in chapter three, corporations and others are required to develop complex information systems to maintain employee training and educational records. Computers provide the technology for storage and retrieval of detailed information on Continuing Education Units (CEUs) college coursework, corporate training and other information that might be useful in awarding credit for past education and work experience.

It is not surprising that the above technology has been joined with other electronic media to create the National Technological University (NTU). NTU was formed by 15 prestigious universities from the Association for Media-Based Continuing Education for Engineers and 12 leading corporations. NTU operates via satellite to provide coursework for engineers in corporate classrooms who are enrolled in advanced professional work leading to NTU's master of science degree. Eurich (1985) describes NTU as a "bold and potentially very large venture, NTU's delivery system takes higher quality instruction from major universities to the workplace" (p. 17).

NTU is one answer to the major recommendations in MIT's comprehensive report on Lifelong Cooperative Education (Bruce, Siebert, Snullin and Fano, 1982) for engineers. Specifically, the report recommended opening engineering schools to employed engineers for part-time study and to follow an example set by Stanford University to take classes to engineers via instructional television into the industries around MIT.

Other examples of electronic media based degrees and courses are available in the literature. General Motors Institute offers videotaped courses for their master's degree in

218

manufacturing management. American College offers coursework prepared and distributed from its central campus at Bryn Mawr, Pennsylvania. Examinations on demand are available through the PLATO computerized system at Control Data Learning Centers in metropolitan areas throughout the United States (Eurich, 1985).

SOME ISSUES

Four issues in the education of adults as identified by Cross (1984) are mentioned in the Preface of this work. The are issues of providers, access, quality assurance and economic revitalization. Each of these issues is brifely discussed in the following paragraphs.

Providers
Historically the providers of education services for adults has been diverse. Cross (1984) believes the number and variety of providers are increasing. Casual awareness of the American scene and the educational community would seem to confirm and support her proposition. In fact, it could be argued that the number and diversity of educational providers catering to adults are directly related to the size of the population and the complexity of society. This truth can be discovered in the 1965 work of Johnstone and Rivera and Long's (1969) study of adult education in Brevard County, Florida during the apex of the American manned space program. More recent supporting data are derived by Cross. In 1981, 46 percent of all courses taken by adults were provided by nonschools: business and industry, labor and professional associations, government agencies and community organizations. Yet, most states have only partial information concerning the educational opportunities available in their borders. Cross argues for more information lt the state level to determine what is distinctive about the missions of various providers, the extent of overlap, the effects of competition, and which sements of the population are being served.

States have become involved in issues concerning the relationships between providers within the formal education system. They have taken precautions to avoid duplication and competition. Yet states have been less involved in the relationships between higher education and business and industry. This is somewhat amazing considering

219

the trends in education for adults as noted and discussed in chapters two and three of this book. The distinction between training offered by employees and education offfered by colleges is becoming less clear. In fact, for a variety of reasons both colleges and business firms are known to use the terms interchangeably to meet different requirements and expectations of the two organizations.

Access

State officials have a longterm interest in access to postsecondary education for young people, but the gap between adults with little education and those who have more and want yet more continues to grow. Differences in participation between college graduates and high school dropouts are ssignificant and complex. Cross suggests four options for state officials concerned with the implications of lowering barriers to adult education. Summarized these options include offering education services to targeted groups, develop statewide linkage mechanisms, keep costs low for special courses and develop distance education.

Quality Assurance

New forms of quality assurance for adult programs are being requested. This development is discussed in part in other sections of this chapter and in chapter seven. Yet, Cross is of the opinion that almost all of the attention has gone to programs or procedures that are degree related. The discussion of the CEU in chapter seven indicates that while Cross may be correct, there are efforts being made in non-degree areas of education. Yet, there can be little doubt that quality assurance will require greater attention in the future as concepts of accountability gain stronger footholds in adult and continuing education.

Economic Revitalization

As discussed in chapters one, two and three, Cross identifies the the relationship between education of adults and economic revitalization as one of the more important issues in the education of adults. She notes, " Although it is generally acknowledges that the naure and structure of the nation's economy is changing, no consensus has been reached as to just what these changes mean for educating

and training America's workforce" (Cross,
1984,p.2).

SOME PREDICTIONS

When all of the above and other contemporary events
are taken into consideration what kind of
predictions concerning the education of adults in
the United States can be made? At least seven
predictions are suggested by the materials reviewed
for this book. They are briefly identified in the
following paragraphs.

First, increased competition for the adult
learner will be noted in the next decade. At least
five different kinds of agencies, organizations and
institutions will be involved in the battle for
adult learners. They include the vast array of
private providers such as dance schools,
occupational and training schools, and so forth.
Another large group of providers that will possibly
sharpen their competitive edge includes the public
schools; that part of the educational system that
has largely ignored the adult learner for the past
30 years. A bevy of public agencies will add
educational activities to their program procedures
as they attempt to resolve problems through
educational approaches. Postsecondary institutions
will be challenged at an intense level by the above
competitors. Finally, the information and mass
media will discover new and innovative ways to sell
their services and products as educational ones.

Second, we will see a new organization similar
to the Health Maintenance Organizations (HMOs)
which will focus on education or learning. They
may be known as Learning Maintenance Organizations
(LMOs). Actually, the HMOs may be the first to
organize and provide educational services similar
to the way they provide health care. It is likely
they will see the relationships between certain
physical and psychological conditions that might be
alleviated through exercise, mental health and so
forth. Postsecondary education institutions also
have the infrastructure to organize in a similar
fashion providing they can overcome the problems
posed by bureaucratic and other environmental
realities that characterize much of higher
education today.

Third, electronic media and hardware will be
improved and adults will develop a greater array of
skills in using the rich resources available
through these media.

221

Fourth, electronic media will not contribute to the extinction of group learning (Naisbitt, 1984). Yes, there will be three kinds of learners: the learning hermit who will prefer to learn in isolation, the plugged in learner who will use personal learning procedures but who will be "plugged-in" to others via modems and other devices with occasional face-to-face interaction, and the learning groupie who prefers the warmth and social support of other human beings. Each of the above kinds of learners will exist in the future.

Fifth, greater attention will be focused on the thirty and above age segment. Educators and administrators will recognize that educational institutions, agencies and organizations included in the first paragraph above, cannot be sustained by the population historically identified with schools and colleges in the United States.

Sixth, the traditional purpose of education for adults as noted by Long (1984c) and discussed earlier will persist.

Seventh, the above purposes may be identified according to two general classes: occupational and liberating. Adults will pursue both kinds of educational experiences. Different agencies and organizations and institutions may tend to specialize in one or the other while some may attempt to provide a range of activities.

Eighth, increasing emphasis upon education of adults and experience with adult learning may develop a feedback mechanism that will influence childhood education. Historically knowledge about education and learning was derived from experience with children and education for children. Much of this book has indicated a radical change in education services is possible by 1999. By then we should have greater knowledge of and experience with adult education as a significant element of American education.

SUMMARY

Perspectives on the future of education for and of adults in the United States could include a large number of topics. Subjects chosen for discussion in this chapter include:

First, a historical overview of the philosophical position concerning education for adults in the United States was presented. Accordingly, it was noted from the very early days of settlement, authority for childhood education

has been acccorded to the state. By 1800 state
responsibility for childhood was gaining
recognition and by the twentieth century the
state's authority and responsibility for childhood
education were almost beyond question. In
contrast, adulthood with few exceptions, has been
perceived as a personal responsibility with very
little governmental authority exerted in the area.

Second, there are some discernible signals
that education of adults may be the topic of
increasing governmental attention. The concept of
lifelong education is growing in popularity.
Increasingly, education of adults as well as
children is being defined in broader economic,
social and political goals rather than personal
ones. The concept of lifelong education, thus,
poses significant implications for the entire
education establishment in the United States
including adult education. There are dangers and
opportunities to be found in extensive and
intensive governmental involvement in education for
adults.

Third, a section on major changes that have
implications for the education of adults develops
information on such diverse topics as education of
women, expanding information, aging, workplace
education and the acceptance of the lifelong
education concept. These five areas of change are
merely illustrative, other wide and deep changes
have been selected easily by others.

Fourth, the American penchant for certified
learning was discussed. It is suggested that this
phenomenon interacts with the philosophical drift
toward lifelong education.

Fifth, technology and how it is currently
affecting education of adults in selected areas was
briefly discussed. Technological developments are
increasingly applied to education of adults and the
implications of these developments interact with
the three previously discussed topics.

Sixth, four important issues that underlie much
of what has been said in the first seven chapters
and Preface are specifically identified. They are
issues of providers, access, quality and economic
relationships with education of adults.

Seventh, some predictions, based on the content
of the first seven chapters and this final chapter
are shared.

The above topics that concern the future of
education of and for adults are associated with
much of what has been said in the first seven
chapters of this book. Complexity, creativity,

223

dynamism, pluralism , pragmatism and volunteerism are terms frequently used in written and oral discourse concerning the education of adults in the United States. For about 100 years the two major streams in the education of adults were widely separated. These two streams appear to be coming closer together as sponsored education for adults become more pervasive in society. Adults engage in education for multiple objectives and for a multiplicity of purposes and more providers are seeking to meet a wider range of the objectives and purposes. Social changes are revealed in patterns of educational provisions for adults. For example, adult participation in college credit degree oriented education has changed in a number of ways since 1940. From little participation to substantial enrolment. From the urban night college to state universities and private colleges and universities. From the option of full-time work or full-time education to either full-time work and part-time education or part-time work and part-time education, or part-time work and full-time education.

The topic of education of and for adults in the United States is much broader than either of the historical streams that included (a) the adult learner who was served by higher education but because of definition was not included in adult education participation data, theory, research and literature or (b) the part-time adult student who met the criteria imposed by the more commonly used definitions of adult education.

Trying to capture and present a perspective of education of adults in the United States would be difficult given years and pages to do so. It is even more difficult when one elects to present a timebound perspective in a few short pages. Even in a few months the ground can shift under the feet of the surveyor and frustration at not being able to chronicle every important event and topic mocks the writer. Nevertheless, within recognized boundaries and in accordance with realistic limitations the preceding pages contain one view of education of adults in the United States based on consideration of the past, present and future.

BIBLIOGRAPHY

Adams, J. (1944). The Frontiers of American
    Culture, C. Scribner's Sons, New York

Adler, M. (1982). .The Paideia Proposal, Macmillan
    Publishing Co., New York

Adult and Continuing Education Today (1984).
    Washington, D.C., xiv, 13 June 25, p. 1

Anania, P. (1969). Adult Age and the Education of
    Adults in Colonial America. Doctoral
    dissertation, University of California,
    Berkeley, California

Anderson, J. E. (1955).'Teaching and Learning' in
    W. Donahue (ed.) Education for Later Maturity,
    Whiteside, Inc., and William Morrow and
    Company, Inc., New York,

Anderson, R. and Darkenwald, G. (1979).
    Participation and Persistence in American Adult
    Education, Future Directions for a Learning
    Society, College Board, New York

Apps, J. (1972). 'Toward a Broader Definition of
    Research ', Adult Education, 23, 59-64

Apps, J. (1973). Toward a Working Philosophy of
    Adult Education, Occasional Paper No. 36,
    Publications in Continuing Education,
    Syracuse, New York

Apps, J. (1979). Problems in Continuing Education,
    McGraw-Hill, New York

225

Bibliography

Arnold, G. (1985). Variables Which May Effect
    Participant Input in Program Planning as
    Measured by Achievement or Satisfaction.
    Doctoral dissertation, University of Georgia,
    Athens, Georgia

Ash, R. (1972). Social Movements in America,
    Markham , Chicago

Aslanian, C. (1985). Personal correspondence

Aslanian, C. and Brickell, H. (1980). Americans in
    Transition. College Entrance Examination
    Board, New York

Bachus, G. (1981). Personal communication
    concerning his doctoral dissertation Trends in
    Doctoral Studies in Adult Education 1970-1977

Baltes, P. and Schaie, K. (1973). ' On Life-Span
    Developmental Research Paradigms: Retrospects
    and Prospects' in P. Baltes and K. Schaie (eds)
    Life-Span Developmental Psychology,
    Personality and Socialization, Academic Press,
    New York

Barrow, R. (1975) . Plato, Utilitarianism and
    Education, Routledge Kegan Paul, London

Beder, H. (1972). Community Linkages in Urban
    Public School Adult Basic Education Programs.
    Doctoral dissertation, Columbia University, New
    York

Beder, H. (1978). ' An Environmental Interaction
    Model for Agency Development in Adult
    Education', Adult Education, 28, 176-90

Beder, H. and Darkenwald, G. (1982). ' Differences
    Between Teaching Adults and Pre-Adults: Some
    Propositions and Findings', Adult Education
    Quarterly, 32 , 142-55

Beder, H. and Smith F. (1977). Developing an Adult
    Education Program Through Community Linkages.
    Adult Education Association of the U.S.A.,
    Washington, D.C.

Bergevin, P. (1967). A Philosophy for Adult
    Education, Seabury Press, New York

Berry, D. (1971). ' A Multiphasic Motivational
    Paradigm for Adult Education', Adult Education,
    22, 48-56

Birren, J. and Cunningham, W. (1985). 'Research on
    the Psychology of Aging: Principles, Concepts
    and Theory' in J. Birren and W. Schaie (eds)
    Handbook of the Psychology of Aging 2nd.
    edition. New York, Van Nostrand, Reinhold,
    pp. 3-34

Birren, J., Cunningham, W. and Yamamoto, K. (1983).
    ' Psychology of Adult Development and Aging',
    Annual Review of Psychology, 34, 543-75

Bittner, W. S. (1950). ' Adult Education' in W. S.
    Monroe (ed.) Encyclopedia of Educational
    Research (Rev. edition),   Macmillan, New York

Boshier, R. (1973). ' Educational Participation and
    Dropout: A Theoretical Model', Adult
    Education, 23, 255-82

Boshier, R. and Collins, J. (1982). ' Education
    Participation Scale Factor Structure and
    Correlates for Twelve Thousand
    Learners ', .Proceedings of the Twenty-Third
    Annual Adult Education Research Conference,
    April 1-3, Lincoln, Neb.

Botsman, P. (1975). The Learning Needs and
    Interests of Adult Blue Collar Workers, New
    York State College of Human Ecology
    Ithica, New York

Boyd, R. and Apps, J. (1980). 'A Conceptual Model
    for Adult Education' in R. Boyd, J. Apps and
    Associates Redefining the Discipline of Adult
    Education, Jossey-Bass, San Francisco, pp.1-15

Boyle, P. (1965). ' Planning with Principles' in C.
    Verner and T. White (eds) Administration of
    Adult Education, Adult Education Association of
    the U.S.A., Washington, D.C.

Boyle, P. (1981). Planning Better Programs,
    McGraw-Hill, New York

Brady, H. (1982) . Research Needs in Adult
    Education, University of South Florida, Tampa

Bibliography

Brickell, H. and Aslanian, C. (1981). 'The
     Colleges and Business Competition' New York
     Times Survey of Continuing Education
     Section, August 30, p. 37

Brockett, R. (1985). ' A Response to Brookfield's
     Critical Paradigm of Self-Directed Adult
     Learning', Adult Education Quarterly, 36,
     55-59

Brookfield, S. (1982). 'Adult Education Research:
     A Comparative Analysis of Perceptions and
     Practice' Proceedings of the Twenty-Third
     Annual Adult Education Research Conference.
     Department of Adult and Continuing Education,
     University of Nebraska, Lincoln, 42-47

Bruce, J., Siebert, W., Smullin, L., and Fano, R.
     (1982). Lifelong Cooperative Education, Report
     of the Centennial Study Committee.
     Massachusetts Institute of Technology,
     Department of Electrical Engineering and
     Computer Science, MIT, Cambridge,
     Massachusetts

Brunner, E. ; Wilder D. ; Kirchner , C. ; and
     Newberry, J. , Jr. (1959). An Overview of
     Adult Education Research, Adult Education
     Association of the U.S.A., Washington, D.C.

Bryson, L. (1936). Adult Education, American Book
     Co., New York

Burgess, P. (1971). ' Reasons for Adult
     Participation in Group Educational Activities',
     Adult Education, 22, 3-29

Caffarella, R. and O'Donnell, J. (1985). '
     Self-Directed Adult Learning: A Critical
     Paradigm Revisited'. Unpublished paper
     presented at Commission of Professors of Adult
     Education Conference, Milwaukee, Wisconsin

Carey, J. (1961). Forms and Forces in University
     Adult Education, Center for the Study of
     Liberal Education for Adults, Chicago

Carlson, R. (1979). ' The Time of Andragogy', Adult
     Education, 30, 55-56

Carlson, R. (1980). 'The Foundation of Adult Education: Analyzing the Boyd-Apps Model' in R. Boyd, J. Apps and Associates, Redefining the Discipline of Adult Education, Jossey-Bass, San Francisco, pp. 174-184

Carp, A., Peterson, R., and Roelfs, P. (1974). ' Adult Learning Interests and Experiences' in K. Cross and J. Valley (eds), Planning Non-Traditional Programs, Jossey-Bass, San Francisco

Cartwright, M. (1935). Ten Years of Adult Education MacMillan, New York

Cervero, R. (1984). ' Analyzing the Effectiveness of Continuing Professional Education', Council on the Continuing Education Unit, Silver Springs, Maryland

Cetrone, M., Soriano, B. and Gayle, B.(1985). Schools of the Future, McGraw-Hill Book Company, New York

Chin, K. (1984, May 7) 'The Elderly Learn to Compute', Info World, 6, pp.24-25, 27,

Christian Science Monitor (1985). April, 29, p. 23

Chronicle of Higher Education (1984a). June 27, p. 10

Chronicle of Higher Education (1984b). August 1, pp. 41 and 43

Clark, B. (1958). Adult Education in Transition: A Study of Institutional Insecurity. University of California Press, Berkeley, California

Coleman, G. (1928). ' Statement', in Digest of the Proceedings of the Annual Meeting of the American Association for Adult Education, American Association for Adult Education, New York

Columns (1985). 12, pp. 1 & 3 (University of Georgia)

Commission on Higher Education and the Adult Learner (1984). Adult Learners Key to the Nation's Future, The Commission, Columbia, Maryland

Bibliography

Conti, G. (1985). ' The Relationship Between
     Teaching Style and Adult Student Learning',
     Adult Education Quarterly, 35, 220-28

Copeland, H. Ploetz, G. and Winterbauer, M. (1985).
     ' Assessing the Impact of Adult Literacy: A
     Pilot Study', Adult Education Research
     Conference Proceedings, 116-21

Copperman, P. (1978). The Literacy Hoax. William
     Morrow and Company, Inc., New York

Cotton, W. (1968). On Behalf of Adult Education,
     Center for the Study of Liberal Education for
     Adults, Boston

Council on the Continuing Education Unit
     (1984).Principles of Good Practice in
     Continuing Education, Silver Springs, Maryland

Courtenay , B. and Moore A. (1985). '
     Educational Tests and Measures: Data Collection
     from Older Adults, ' in D. B. Lumsden (ed.)
     The Older Adult as Learner: Aspects of
     Educational Gerontology, Hemisphere Publishing
     Corporation, Washington, D.C., 119-37

Courtenay , B. , Suhart , M. , McConatha, D. &
     Stevenson, R. (1983) 'Assessing the Educational
     Needs of Undereducated Older Adults: A Case
     for the Service Provider', Educational
     Gerontology, 9, 205-16

Courtenay , B. , Stevenson , R. and Suhart , M.
     (1982). 'Functional Literacy Among the Elderly:
     Where We Are(n't), Educational Gerontology,
     8, 339-52

Covey, H.(1980). 'An Exploratory Study of the
     Acquisition of a College Student Role by Older
     People', The Gerontologist, 20, 173-81

Covey, H.(1981).'American Higher Education and
     Older People', Educational Gerontology, 6,
     373-83

Covey, H.(1982).' Preliminary Findings on Designing
     Higher Education Programs for Older People',
     Educational Gerontology, 8, 463-71

Cross, K. (1981). Adults as Learners:
    Increasing Participation and Facilitating
    Learning, Jossey-Bass, San Francisco

Cross, K. (1984).' Adult Learning: State Policies
    and Institutional Practices'. Higher Education
    Research Reports: Executive Summary, Report
    No.1, Association for the Study of Higher
    Education and ERIC Clearinghouse on Higher
    Education

Dannenmmaier, W. D. (1962). 'A Brief Review of
    Published Research in Adult Education' in P.
    H. Dubois and K. M. Wientge (eds.)
    Objectives and Methods of Research in Adult
    Education, Department of Psychology,
    Washington University, St. Louis, pp.9-11,

Darkenwald, G. (1981). Retaining Adult Students,
    ERIC Clearinghouse on Adult, Career and
    Vocational Education and the National Center
    for Research in Vocational Education, Ohio
    State University, Columbus, Ohio

Darkenwald, G. (1982). ' Factorial Structure of
    Differences in Teaching Behavior Related to
    Adult/PreAdult Student Age Status', Adult
    Education, 32, 197-204

Darkenwald, G. and Merriam, S. (1982). Adult
    Education: Foundations of Practice, Harper
    and Row, New York

Darkenwald, G. and Valentine J. (1985). Outcomes
    and Impact of Adult Basic Education, Center
    for Adult Development, Rutgers University,
    New Brunswick, New Jersey

Davenport, J. and Davenport, J. (1985). ' A
    Chronology and Analysis of the Andragogy
    Debate', Adult Education Quarterly ,
    35, 152-59

Davison, F. (1982). 'Remarks' Speech presented at
    National Association of State Universities
    and Land Grant Colleges, November 9, St.
    Louis

DeCrow, R. and Loague, N. (1970). Adult Education
    Dissertation Abstracts, 1963-1967. Adult
    Education Association of the U.S.A.,
    Washington, D.C.

Bibliography

Deitch, K. (1981). 'A Price War for Higher
    Education', Change, pp. 24-26

Dewey, J. (1916). Democracy and Education,
    Macmillan Company, New York

Dickinson, G. (1971). 'Educational Variables and
    Participation in Adult Education: An
    Exploratory Study', Adult Education,
    22, 36-47

Dickinson, G. (1979). Contributions to a
    Discipline of Adult Education: A Review and
    Analysis of the Publications of Coolie Verner,
    Center for Continuing Education, University of
    British Columbia, Vancouver

Dickinson, G. and Blunt, A. (1980). 'Survey
    Research' in H. B. Long, R. Hiemstra and Assoc
    -iates Changing Approaches to Studying Adult
    Education. Jossey-Bass, San Francisco

Dickinson, G. and Rusnell, D. (1971). 'A Content
    Analysis of Adult Education', Adult Education,
    21, 177-85

Donahue, W. (1956) 'Learning, Motivation, and
    Education of the Aging' in J. E. Anderson (ed.)
    Psychological Aspects of Aging, American
    Psychological Association, Washington, D.C.,
    pp. 200-06

Drotter, M. W. (1981) 'Education for the Elderly:
    Trends and Problems in the 1980's', Educational
    Gerontology, 7, 105-10

Dubin, S. (1972). 'Obsolesence or Lifelong
    Education: A Choice for the Professional',
    American Psychologist, 27, 486-98

Duggar, R. (1974). ' The Counting House of
    Academe', Harpers 248,70-81

Easterlin, R. (1980). Birth and Fortune: The
    Impact of Numbers on Personal Welfare, Basic
    Books, New York

Easting, G. (1975). 'Programme Research and its
    Application to Adult Education' Studies in
    Adult Education, 11, 62-66

232

Education Commission of the States (1983). Action
for Excellence: A Comprehensive Plan to Improve
Our Nation's Schools, The Commission, Denver,
Colorado

Educational Review (1900). 'Introduction', 19,
p.481

Elias, J. (1979). ' Andragogy Revisited', Adult
Education, 29, 252-56

Elias, J. and Merriam, S. (1980). Philosophical
Foundations of Adult Education, Robert Kreiger
Publishing Co., Huntington, New York

Eurich, N. (1985). Corporate Classrooms: The
Learning Business, College Entrance Examination
Board, Princeton University Press

Faure, E., et al (1972). Learning to Be, UNESCO,
Paris

First Professor (1982). Personal Communication

Fishstein, O. & Feier, C. (1982). ' Education for
Older Adults: Out of the College and Into the
Community', Educational Gerontology, 8, 243-49

Fisk, E. (1985). ' Booming Corporate Education
Efforts Rival College Programs, Study Says'.
New York Times, Jan.28

Flavell, J. (1970). 'Cognitive Changes in
Adulthood' in P. Baltes and L. Goulet (eds.)
Lifespan Developmental Psychology: Theory and
Research, Academic Press, New York

Flesch, R. (1955). Why Johnny Can't Read, Harper,
New York

Flesch, R. (1981). Why Johnny Still Can't Read,
Harper & Row, New York

Fox, R. and West, R. (1985). ' Personality Traits
and Perceived Benefits Associated with
Different Approaches of Medical Students to
Self-Directed Learning Projects', Proceedings
of Twenty- Fourth Annual Adult Education
Research Conference, 99-104

Friere, P. (1968). The Pedagogy of the Oppressed.
Seabury Press, New York

Bibliography

Freire, P. (1973). Education for Critical
    Consciousness, Seabury Press, New York

Fromm, E. (1955). The Sane Society. Rinehart, New
    York

Gainesville Sun (1984). Monday, August 20, p. 10A

Galbraith, J. (1967). The Industrial State.
    Houghton Mifflin Company, Boston

Gibson, Q. (1960). The Logic of Social Inquiry,
    Routledge and Kegan Paul, London

Glynn, S. and Muth, K. (1979). 'Text-Learning
    Capabilities of Older Adults', Educational
    Gerontology, 4, 253-69

Goodlad, J. (1984). A Place Called School.
    McGraw-Hill Book Co., Princeton, New Jersey

Goodrow, B. A. (1975). 'Limiting Factors in
    Reducing Participation in Older Adult Learning
    Opportunities', The Gerontologist, 15, 418-22

Gorham, J. (1985). ' Differences Between Teaching
    Adults and Pre-Adults: A Closer Look', Adult
    Education Quarterly, 35, 194-209

Gove, P. (1961) (ed). Webster's Third New
    International Dictionary of the English
    Language, Unabridged, G. & C. Merriam
    Company, Springfield, Mass. p.1172

Grabowski, S. (1973). Adult Education Dissertation
    Abstracts,1935-1962, Adult Education
    Association of the U.S.A., Washington, D.C.

Grabowski, S. (1980). 'Trends in Graduate Research'
    in H. Long, R. Hiemstra and Associates
    Changing Approaches to Studying Adult
    Education, Jossey-Bass, San Francisco

Grabowski, S. and Loague, N. (1970) (eds.). Adult
    Education Dissertation Abstracts, 1968-1969.
    Adult Education Association of the U.S.A.,
    Washington, D.C.

Graney, M. and Hays, W. (1976).' Seminar Students:
    Higher Education After Age 62', Educational
    Gerontology, 1, 343-59

234

Grattan, C. (1955). In Quest of Knowledge: A
    Historical Perspective on Adult Education,
    Association Press, New York

Griffith, W. (1963). A Growth Model of
    Institutions of Adult Education. Doctoral
    dissertation, University of Chicago, Chicago

Griffith , W.   (1979). 'Adult Education Research
    - Emerging Developments', Studies in Adult
    Education, 11, 125-44

Guglielmino, L. (1977). Development of the Self-
    Directed Learning Readiness Scale. Doctoral
    dissertation, University of Georgia, Athens,Ga.

Habermas, J. (1971). Knowledge and Human Interest,
    Beacon Press,Boston

Hall, V. and Wessell, J. (1985). Atlanta   Journal
    -Constitution, Sunday, Oct. 13, 37N

Hart,J. (1927). Adult Education, Thomas Y. Crowell
    Co., New York

Hartree, A. (1984). ' Malcolm Knowles' Theory of
    Andragogy: A Critique', International Journal
    of Lifelong Education, 3, 203-10

Hassan, A. (1981). An Investigation of the Learning
    Projects Among Adults of High and Low
    Readiness for Self-Direction in Learning.
    Doctoral dissertation, Iowa State University,
    Dissertation Abstracts International (1981),
    42, 3838A

Havighurst, R.(1976). 'Education Through the Adult
    Life Span', Educational Gerontology, 1, 41-51

Hayslip, B., Jr., & Kennelly, K. J. (1985).' Cog-
    nitive and Noncognitive Factors Affecting
    Learning Among Older Adults' in D. B. Lumsden
    (ed.) The Older Adult as Learner: Aspects
    of Educational Gerontology, Hemisphere
    Publishing Corporation, Washington, D.C., pp.
    73-98

Heisel, M.(1980).' Adult Education and the
    Disadvantaged Older Adult: An Analytical
    Review of the Research Literature', Educational
    Gerontology, 5, 125-37

Bibliography

Heisel, M., Darkenwald, G. and Anderson, R.(1981).
    ' Participation in Organized Educational
    Activities Among Adults Age 60 and Over',
    Educational Gerontology, 61, 227-40

Hiemstra, R. (1975). The Older Adult and Learning,
    Department of Adult and Continuing Education,
    University of Nebraska, Lincoln, Nebraska, ERIC
    Document Service, ED 117371

Hiemstra, R. (1976). 'The Older Adult's Learning
    Projects', Educational Gerontology, 1, 331-41

Higher Education Daily (1985). 'Colleges Beware:
    Corporations are Storming the Academic World',
    January 28, pp.3-4

Hirsch, H. (1978). 'The Educated Senior Citizen:
    Continuing Education After Retirement', Liberal
    Education, 64, 163-70

Holden, J. (1958). ' A Survey of Participation in
    Adult Education Classes', Adult Leadership, 6,
    258-60,70

Houle, C. (1960). ' The Education of Adult
    Education Leaders' in M. Knowles (ed) Handbook
    of Adult Education in the United States, Adult
    Education Association of the U. S. A.,Chicago

Houle, C. (1961). The Inquiring Mind, University
    of Wisconsin Press, Madison, Wisconsin

Houle, C. (1984)   Patterns of Learning ,
    Jossey-Bass, San Francisco

Hunter C. and Harman, D. (1979). Adult Illiteracy
    in the United States, McGraw-Hill, New York

Irish, G. (1978). Persistence and Dropout in Adult
    Education:Their Relation to Differential
    Reinforcement of Attendance. Doctoral
    dissertation, Columbia University, New York

Jarvis, P. (1983). Adult and Continuing Education:
    Theory and Practice, Croom-Helm, London

Jarvis, P. (1985). The Sociology of Adult and
    Continuing Education, Croom-Helm, Dover, New
    Hampshire

Jensen, G. (1964). 'Social Psychology and Adult
    Education Practice' in G. Jensen, A. Liveright
    and W. Hallenbeck (eds.) Adult Education:
    Outlines of an Emerging Field of University
    Study, Adult Education Association of the
    U.S.A., Washington, D.C.

Jensen, G., Liveright, A. and Hallenbeck, W.
    (1964). Adult Education: Outlines of an
    Emerging Field of University Study, Adult
    Education Association of the U.S.A.,
    Washington, D.C.

Johns, W. (1973). Selected Characteristics of the
    Learning Projects Pursued by Practicing
    Pharmicists. Doctoral dissertation, University
    of Georgia, Athens, Georgia, Dissertation
    Abstracts International,(1974), 34,4577A

Johnson, A. (1930). 'Repairmen or Artisans? A
    Statement of Adult Education Objectives',
    Journal of Adult Education, 2, 237

Johnstone, W. and Rivera, R. (1965). Volunteers for
    Learning, Aldine Publishing Company, Chicago

Judson, H. (1985). ' Paradoxes of Prediction: The
    Shape of Things to Come', Science 85, Nov.
    pp.32-36

Kallen, H. (1962). Philosophical Issues in Adult
    Education, Charles C. Thomas, Springfield

Kasl, S.(1974).' Work and Mental Health" in J.
    O'Toole (ed.) Work and Quality of Life,
    MIT Press, Cambridge

Kasworm, C. (1982). 'An Exploratory Study of the
    Development of Self-Directed Learning as an
    Instructional/Curriculum Strategy' in G.
    Whaples and W. Rivera (eds.) Lifelong
    Learning Research Conference Proceedings,
    Department of Agricultural and Extension
    Education, University of Maryland, College
    Park, Maryland, 125-29

Katchadourian, H. (1967). A Critical Study in
    Method, Martinus Nyhoff, The Hague, Netherlands

Kearsley, G. & Furlong, M. (1984). Computers for
    Kids Over Sixty: Keeping Up With the Computer

Generation, Reading, MA., Addison-Wesley
Publishing Co., Inc.

Keppel, F. (1926). Education for Adults: And Other
    Essays, Columbia University Press, New York

Kidd, J. (1973) . How Adults Learn. (Revised
    edition), Association Press, New York

Kilpatrick, W. H. (1933) (ed). The Educational
    Frontier, D. Appleton-Century Company, New York

Kilpatrick, W. H. (1951) . Philosophy of Education,
    Macmillan Co., New York

Kingston, A.(1982). 'Attitudes and Problems of
    Elderly Students in the University System of
    Georgia', Educational Gerontology, 8, 87-92

Kingston, A. and Drotter, M. (1983). 'A Comparison
    of Elderly College Students in Two Geographic-
    ally Different Areas', Educational Gerontology,
    9, 399-403

Klapper, J. (1965) ' What We Know About the Effects
    of Mass Communication: The Brink of Hope ' in
    O. Lerbinger and A. Sullivan (eds) Information,
    Influence & Communication: A Reader in Public
    Relations, Basic Books, New York, 314-34

Knowles, M. (1955). ' Adult Education in the United
    States', Adult Education, 5, 67-77

Knowles, M.(1960)(ed.). Handbook of Adult Educat-
    ion in the United States, Adult Education Assoc
    iation of the U.S.A., Chicago, Illinois

Knowles, M. (1962). The Adult Education Movement in
    the United States.Holt,Rinehart & Winston,N.Y.

Knowles, M. (1970). The Modern Practice of Adult
    Education: Andragogy Versus Pedagogy.
    Association Press, New York

Knowles, M. (1973).' Sequential Research in
    Evolving Disciplines of Social Practice',
    Adult Education, 23, 298-303

Knowles, M. (1977). The Adult Education Movement
    in the United States, (Revised edition),
    Robert Kreiger, Malabar, Florida

Knowles, M. (1979). ' Andragogy Revisited', Adult Education, 30, 52-53

Knowles, M.(1980). The Modern Practice of Adult Education(rev.ed.), Cambridge Book, New York

Knox, A. (1985). Personal Comments, University of Georgia, Athens, GA

Knox, A. (1977). Current Research Needs Related to Systematic Learning by Adults. Office of

Knudson, R. (1979). ' Humanagoy Anyone?' , Adult Education, 29,261-64

Kornhauser, A. (1965). Mental Health of the Industrial Worker, Wiley, New York

Kozol, J. (1985). Illiterate America , Anchor/ Doubleday, New York

Krech, D. (1968). 'The Chemistry of Learning', Saturday Review, 51, January 20, 48

Kreitlow, B. (1960). ' Research in Adult Education in M. Knowles (ed.) Handbook of Adult Education in the United States. Adult Education Association of the United States, Chicago, pp.106-16

Krietlow, B. (1964). Research Priorities in Adult Education, University of Wisconsin, Madison

Krietlow, B. (1965). ' Needed Research', Review of Educational Research, 35, 240-45

Krietlow, B. (1970). ' Research and Theory' in R. Smith, G. Aker and J. Kidd (eds.) Handbook of Adult Education, Macmillan, New York

Krietlow, B. and Associates (1981). Examining Controversies in Adult Education , Jossey-Bass, San Francisco

Langer, J. (1969). Theories of Development, Holt, Rhinehart and Winston, New York

LeBreton, P. , Bryant, V., Zweizig, D., Middaugh, D D., Bryant, A. and Corbe, H. (eds) (1979). The Evaluation of Continuing Education for

Professionals: A Systems View, University of
Washington, Seattle

Lerbinger O. (1965). ' Influence: The Generalized
Medium of Public Communication in O. Lerbinger
and A. Sullivan (eds.) Information, Influence
and Communication: A Reader in Public
Affairs. Basic Books, New York 253-72

Liebow, E. (1967). Talley's Corner, Little, Brown,
Boston

Lindeman. E. (1961). The Meaning of Adult Education. Reprint. Harvest House , Montreal
(Original work published in 1926)

Liveright, A. (1964). 'The Nature and Aims of
Adult Education as a Field of Graduate
Education in G. Jensen, A. Liveright and
W. Hallenbeck (eds.) Adult Education: Outlines
of an Emerging Field of University Study.
Adult Education Association of the U.S.A.,
Washington, D.C., 85-111

Liveright, A. (1968). A Study of Adult Education
in the United States, Center for the Study of
Liberal Education for Adults, Boston

Livingstone, R. (1949). On Education, Cambridge
University Press, New York

London, J. (1963). 'Attitudes Toward Adult
Education by Social Class', Adult Education,
13, 226-33

London, J. (1964). 'The Relevance of the Study of
Sociology to Adult Education Practice' in G.
Jensen, A. Liveright and W. Hallenbeck, (eds.)
Adult Education: Outlines of an Emerging Field
of University Study, Adult Education
Association of the U.S.A., Washington, D.C.

London, J. (1970). 'The Influence of Social Class
Behavior Upon Adult Education Participation',
Adult Education, 20, 140-53

Long, H. (1967). ' A Summary Report: Adult
Education Participation in Brevard County,
Florida', Adult Education, 19(17), 34-42

Long, H. (1968). 'Factors Influencing the
Relationship Between Dogmatism and Conformity

in an Employee Group', Journal of Social
Psychology, 74, 209-13

Long, H. (1972). Psychology of Aging: How it
Affects Learning, Prentice-Hall, Englewood
Cliffs, New Jersey

Long, H. (1974). 'Lifelong Learning: Pressures for
Acceptance', Journal of Research and
Development in Education, 7, 4, 2-12

Long, H. (1976). Continuing Education of Adults in
Colonial America, Syracuse Publications in
Continuing Education, Syracuse, New York

Long, H. (1977). 'Publication Activity of Selected
Professors of Adult Education', Adult
Education, 27, 173-86

Long, H. (1980a). 'A Perspective on Adult
Education Research' in H. B. Long, R. Hiemstra
and Associates Changing Approaches to Studying
Adult Education, Jossey-Bass, San Francisco

Long, H. (1980b). ' Characteristics of Senior
Citizens' Educational Tuition Waivers in
Twenty-one States: A Follow-up Study',
Educational Gerontology, 5, 139-49

Long, H. (1980c). ' Experimental Research' in H. B.
Long, R. Hiemstra and Associates, Changing
Approaches to Studying Adult Education,
Jossey-Bass, San Francisco, 78-99

Long, H. (1980d). ' Historical Characteristics of
Adult Education United States of America.
Unpublished paper presented to visiting
delegation of educators from the Peoples
Republic of China, Belmont, Maryland, October

Long, H. (1981). ' Survey of AEA, USA Editorial
Board Members'. Unpublished data, Adult
Education Dept., University of Georgia

Long, H. (1982). 'Meta-Research and Research Needs
in Lifelong Learning' Lifelong Learning
Research Conference Proceedings, University of
Maryland, Silver Springs, 252-61

Long, H. (1983a). Adult and Continuing Education:
Responding to Change, Teachers College Press,
New York

Bibliography

Long, H. (1983b). Adult Learning: Research and Practice, Cambridge Book, New York

Long, H. (1983c). ' Characteristics of Adult Education Research Reported at the Adult Education Research Conference, 1971-80' Adult Education, 33, 79-96

Long, H. (1983d). 'Descriptive Research in Adult Education in the United States,' International Journal of Lifelong Education, 1, 385-94

Long, H. (1983e). ' Evolving Sequential Research Methods in Adult Education'. Paper presented at National Adult Education Conference, Philadelphia, Dec.

Long, H. (1983f). Recent Trends in Adult Education in the United States of America, Department of Educational Studies, University of Surrey, Guildford, Surrey, U.K.

Long, H. (1984a) ' Adult Education: A Content Analysis, 1974-1982'. Unpublished paper, Adult Education Dept., University of Georgia, Athens, Georgia

Long, H. (1984b) . ' Literacy Education for Adults in Colonial America as Revealed by Selected Newspapers' in W. Rivera and S. Walker (compilers) Lifelong Learning Research Conference Proceedings, Dept. of Agricultural and Extension Education and Cooperative Extension Service, University of Maryland, College Park, Maryland, 61-66

Long, H. (1984c). 'Purposes of Adult Education in the United States: An Historical Analysis'.Unpublished paper, Department of Adult Education, University of Georgia, Athens, Georgia

Long, H. (1984d) . Responses to Circular Letter to Commission of Professors of Adult Education. Unpublished data, Adult Education Department, University of Georgia, Athens, Ga.

Long, H. (1985a).' Contradictory Expectations? Achievement and Satisfaction in Adult Learning,' The Journal of Continuing Higher Education, 33, (3), 10-12

Long, H. (1985b) ' Independence in Self-Directed Learning: A Conceptual Analysis (A Preliminary Report),' Paper presented at Region III National University Continuing Education Association Conference, Knoxville, Tennessee, Oct.17

Long, H. (In Press a). ' A Brief Hisory of Education in the United States with Some Implications for Public Education of Older Adults'(tentative title) in J. Birren, D. Peterson and J. Thorton (eds) Education and Aging (tentative title), Prentice-Hall, Englewood Cliffs , N. J.)

Long, H. (In Press b).' Post-Compulsory Education and Training in the United States' in D. Cosgrove (ed) Post Compulsory Education and Training: An International Survey,

Long, H. and Agyekum, S. (1974). 'Adult Education 1964-1973: Reflections of a Changing Discipline', Adult Education, 24, 99-120

Long, H. and Agyekum, S. (1983). 'Guglielmino's Self-Directed Learning Readiness Scale: A Validation Study', Higher Education, 12, 77-87

Long, H. and Agyekum, S. (1984). 'Teacher Ratings in the Validation of Guglielmino's Self-Directed Learning Readiness Scale',Higher Education, 13, 709-15

Long, H., Anderson, R. and Blubaugh,J.(1973)(eds.). Approaches to Community Development. NUEA and ACT, Iowa City

Long, H. and Ashford, M.(1976).' Self-Directed Inquiry as a Method of Continuing Education in Colonial America,' The Journal of General Education, 28, 245-55

Long, H. and Fisher, R. (1979). 'Adult Education: A Content Analysis, 1974-1979'.Unpublished paper, Adult Education Department, University of Georgia, Athens, GA

Long, H. and Lord, C. (1978). The Continuing Education Unit: Concept,Issues and Use, Georgia Center for Continuing Education, University of Georgia, Athens, Georgia

Bibliography

Long, H., Lester, N. and Flowers, W. Jr. (1979).
AEA's National Learning Center: A Timely
Opportunity', Lifelong Learning: The Adult
Years, 2, 12-15

Long, H. and Ross, J. (1984). 'Forces for
Self-Direction in Learning: A Tentative
Model'. Unpublished paper. Adult Education
Department, University of Georgia, Athens,
Georgia

Long, H. and Rossing, B. (1979). 'Tuition
Waiver Plans for Older Americans in
Postsecondary Public Education Institutions',
Educational Gerontology, 4, 161-74

Lorge, I. (1956). 'Learning, Motivation and
Education' in J. E. Anderson (ed.)
Psychological Aspects of Aging,
American Psychological Association,
Washington, D.C.,pp. 207-10

Lorimer, F. (1931). The Making of Adult Minds in a
Metropolitan Area, Macmillan, New York

Love, R. (1953). ' The Use of Motivational
Research to Determine Interest in Adult
College-Level Training', Educational Record
34, 212-13

Lumsden, D. (1985) (ed) . The Older Adult as
Learner: Aspects of Educational Gerontology,
Hemisphere Publishing Corporation, Washington,
D.C.

Lyle, B. (1977). Adult Functional Competence: A
Summary of the Research , Adult Performance
Level Project, Reprint, Division of
Extension, The University of Texas, Austin,
Texas

McCluskey, H. Y. 'Education for Aging: The Scope
of the Field and Perspectives for the Future'
in S. Grabowski & W. D. Mason (eds.) Learning
For Aging, Adult Education Association/USA,
Washington, pp. 324-55

McDougald, D. (1983). An Analysis of the Concept
'Satisfaction'as Employed in Ordinary Language
and Adult Education Discourse, Doctoral
dissertation, University of Georgia, Athens,
Georgia, Dissertation Abstracts

International(1984) <u>44,</u> 11, 3247A, Order number
DA 8405062

McKeachie, W. (1954). ' Individual Conformity to
Attitudes of Classroom Groups', <u>J. of Abnormal</u>
<u>& Social Psychology,</u> <u>49,</u> 282-89

McKenzie, L. (1977). ' The Issue of Andragogy',
<u>Adult Education,</u> <u>27,</u> 225-29

McKenzie, L. (1979). ' A Response to Elias', <u>Adult</u>
<u>Education,</u> <u>29,</u> 256-61

McKinley, J. (1973). 'Perspectives on Diagnostics
in Adult Education' <u>Viewpoints,</u> (Indiana
University) <u>49,</u> 69-83

March, G. , Hooper, J. and Baum, J. (1977).
'Life Span Education and the Older Adult:
Living is Learning', <u>Educational Gerontology,</u>
<u>2,</u> 163-72

Marcus, E. (1977). <u>Effect of Age on Perception of</u>
<u>the Utility of Participation in Education,</u>
ERIC, ED 141,691

Marcus, E. (1978). ' Effects of Age, Sex, and
Status on Perception of the Utility of
Educational Participation', <u>Educational</u>
<u>Gerontology,</u> <u>3,</u> 295-319

Marienau, C. and Klinger, K. (1977). <u>An</u>
<u>Anthropological Approach to the Study of</u>
<u>Educational Barriers of Adults at the Post-</u>
<u>Secondary Level,</u> ERIC, ED 141 511

Maritain, J. (1970). ' Education at the Crossroads'
in E. Cahn (ed) <u>The Philosophical Foundations</u>
<u>of Education,</u> Harper and Row, New York
(Original work published in 1943)

Matkin, G. W. (1980). 'Theory, Method and
Appropriateness in Adult Education Research'
<u>Proceedings of the Twenty-first</u>
<u>Adult Education Research Conference,</u> Vancouver,
138-143

Mazmanian, P. (1980). ' A Decision Making Approach
to Needs Assessment and Objectives Setting in
Continuing Medical Education Program Development', <u>Adult Education,</u> <u>31,</u> 3-17

Bibliography

Mearns, Hughes (1941). The Creative Adult:
    Self-Education in the Art of Living, Doubleday,
    Doran & Co., Inc. New York

Merriam, S. and Mullins,, L. (1980). ' Havighurst's
    Adult Developmental Tasks: 'A Factor Analysis',
    in G. Whaples and G. Ewart (eds), Proceedings:
    Lifelong Learning Research Conference,
    Department of Agricultural and Extension
    Education, University of Maryland, College
    Park, Maryland, 65-66

Mezirow, J. (1971). 'Toward a Theory of Practice',
    Adult Education, 21, 135-47

Mezirow, J. (1978a). Education for Perspective
    Transformation: Women's Re-entry Programs in
    Community Colleges, Center for Adult Education,
    Teachers College, Columbia University, New York

Mezirow, J. (1978b). 'Perspective Transformation',
    Adult Education, 28, 100-10

Mezirow, J. (1981). 'A Critical Theory of Adult
    Learning and Evaluation', Adult Education, 32,
    3-24

Mezirow, J. (1984). ' Review of Principles of Good
    Practice in Continuing Education', Adult
    Learning: An Omnibus of Research and Practice,
    8, (3), pp.27-28,30

Mezirow, J., Darkenwald, G. and Knox, A. (1975).
    Last Gamble on Education, Adult Education
    Association of the U.S.A., Washington, D.C.

Miller, H. (1967). Participation of Adults in
    Education: A Force Field Analysis, Occasional
    Paper No.14, Center for the Study of Liberal
    Education for Adults, Brookline, Mass.

Miller H.B. and Williams, W. (1982).The Limits of
    Utilitarianism, University of Minnesota Press,
    Minneapolis, Minn.

Mocker, D. and Spear, G. (1982). Lifelong
    Learning: Formal, Nonformal and Self-Directed,
    The ERIC Clearinghouse on Adult, Career and
    Vocational Education and the National Center
    for Research in Vocational Education, Columbus,
    Ohio

Monette, M. (1977). 'The Concept of Educational Need: An Analysis of Selected Literature', Adult Education, 27, 116-27

Morris, W. (1969) (ed). The American Heritage Dictionary of the English Language, American Heritage Publishing Company & Houghton Mifflin Company, Boston

Moses, S. (1971). The Learning Force, Syracuse University Publications in Continuing Education, Syracuse, New York

Murgatroyd, S. (1977). ' Observing Adult Learning Groups,' Studies in Adult Education, 9, 177-96

Murphy, E. (1958). Human Potentialities, Basic Books, New York

Naisbitt, J. (1982). Megatrends, Warner, New York

New York Times (1984), December 27

Noble, K. (1981). 'The Corporate Halls of Ivy Grow', New York Times Continuing Education Survey Section, August 30, p. 21

Nussbaum , L. (1984,). 'Teaching and Aging' in C. M. N. Mehrotra (ed.) New Directions for Teaching and Learning, 19, 75-82, Jossey-Bass Publishers, Washington, D.C.

Oddi, L. (1984). Development of an Instrument to Measure Self-Directed Continuing Learning, Doctoral dissertation, Northern Illinois University, Dissertation Abstracts International, (1984), 46, 49A

Patterson, R. (1979). Values, Education and the Adult, Routledge and Kegan Paul, Boston

Pennington, F. (1980).' Needs Assessment: Concepts, Models and Characteristics' in F. Pennington (ed.) New Directions for Continuing Education: Assessing Educational Needs of Adults, Jossey-Bass, San Francisco

Pennington, F. and Green J. (1976). 'Comparative Analysis of Program Devlopment Processes in Six Professions', Adult Education, 27, 13-23

Bibliography

Peters, R. (1967a). Ethics and Education, Scott, Foresman, Atlanta, Georgia

Peters, R.(1967b). ' What is an Educational Process?' in R. Peters (ed) The Concept of Education, Routledge & Kegan Paul, London

Peterson, D. (1975). 'Life Span Education and Gerontology' The Gerontologist, 15, 436-41

Peterson, D. (1980). 'Who Are the Educational Gerontologists?' Educational Gerontology, 5, 65-77

Peterson, D. (1981). 'Participation in Education by Older People', Educational Gerontology, 7, 245-56

Peterson, D. (1983). Facilitating Education for Older Learners, Jossey-Bass Publishers, Washington, D.C.

Peterson, R. (1979). ' Present Sources of Education and Learning' in R. Peterson, et al (eds) Lifelong Learning in America, Jossey-Bass, San Francisco

Peterson, R. et al(1979). Lifelong Learning in America, Jossey-Bass, San Francisco

Pottinger, P. (1979).' Competence Assessment: Comments on Current Practice'in P. Pottinger and J. Goldsmith (eds.) New Directions for Experimental Learning Defining and Measuring Competencies, Jossey-Bass, San Francisco

Price, W. and Lyon, L.(1982). 'Educational Orientation of the Aged: An Attitudinal Inquiry', Educational Gerontology, 8, 473-84

Rauch, D. (1972) (ed). Priorities in Adult Education. Macmillan Company, New York

Rigg, P. & Kazemek, F. (1983). 'Literacy and Elders: What We Know and What We Need to Know', Educational Gerontology, 9, 417-24

Rockhill, K. (1982) ' Researching Participation in Adult Education : The Potential of the

Qualitative Perspective', Adult Education Quarterly, 33, 3-19

Romaniuk , J.   (1982a).   The Older Adult Learner in Higher Education: An Analysis of State Public Policy. National Council on the Aging, Inc., Washington, D.C.

Romaniuk , J.   (1982b).   Tuition-waiver Policies for Older Adults: Impact on States and Institutions of Higher Education, National Council on the Aging, Inc., Washington, D.C.

Romaniuk , J.   (1983).   'Educational Tuition-waiver Policies: A Secondary Analysis of Institutional Impact in Virginia', Educational Gerontology, 9, 279-92

Romaniuk , J. (1984).   'Tuition-waiver Policies for Older Adults: What are the Assumptions?', Educational Gerontology, 10, 119-33

Rosenblum, S. and Darkenwald, G. (1983). ' Effects of Adult Learner Participation in Course Planing and Achievement and Satisfaction', Adult Education Quarterly, 33, 147-53

Rubenson, J. (1979). Recruitment to Adult Education in the Nordic Countries: Research and Outreaching Activities, Stockholm Institute of Education, Stockholm. Paper presented at ICAE and Swedish National Federation of Adult Educational Association Conference on Research in Adult Education, June 25-27, 1979, Kungalv, Sweden

Rubenson, K.(1982). ' Adult Education Research: In Quest of a Map of the Territory', Adult Education, 32, 57-74

Rubenson, K. and Hoghielm, R. (1978). The Teaching Process and Study Dropouts in Adult Education, Stockholm Institute of Education, Stockholm, Sweden

Sabbaghian, Z. (1979). Adult Self-Directedness and Self-Concept: An Exploration of Relationship. Doctoral dissertation, Iowa State University, Ames, Iowa

Saindon, J. (1982). Participation of Industrial Workers in Continuing Education. Doctoral dissertation, University of Georgia, Athens, Georgia

Saindon, J. and Long, H. (1983). Occupation and Participation in Continuing Education. International Journal of Lifelong Education, 2, 371-82

Schlesinger, A. ,Jr.(1957). The Crises of the Old Order:1919-33, Riverside Press, Cambridge, Mass.

Schroeder, W. (1980). 'Typology of Adult Learning Systems'in J. Peters and Associates Building an Effective Adult Education Enterprise, Jossey-Bass, New York

Sheffield, S. (1964). 'The Orientations of Adult Continuing Learners' in D. Solomon (ed.) The Continuing Learner, Center for the Study of Liberal Education for Adults, Chicago

Sheppard, N. A. (1983). 'Vocational Education Needs Assessment of Older Americans: Methodology and Some Findings',Educational Gerontology, 9, 359-76

Shils, E. (1970). Selected Essays, Center for Social Organization Studies, University of Chicago, Chicago, Illinois

Sirkin, J. (1985). 'The Challenge of Corporate Classrooms' New York Times, January 30

Skager, B. (1981). The Relationship Between Involvement of Professional Nurses in Self-Directed Learning Activity, Loci of Control and Readiness for Self-Directed Learning Activities. Doctoral dissertation, Austin Texas

Smith, R. , Aker, G. and Kidd, J. (1970) (eds). Handbook of Adult Education, Macmillan, New York

Smutz, W., Kalman, S., Lindsay, C., Pietrusko, R. and Seaman, J. (1981). A Process for Continuing Professional Education Needs Assessment and Program Development (edited by Donna S. Queeny). Penn State University, Continuing Professional Education Development Project, State College, Pennsylvania

Soldo, B. (1980). ' America's Elderly in the 1980s' Population Bulletin, 35, (4)

Sork, T. (1980). ' Meta-Research in Adult Education: An Historical Analysis and Critical Appraisal ', A paper presented at the Adult Education Research Conference, Vancouver, B. C.

Spear, G. and Mocker, D. (1984). ' The Organizing Circumstance: Environmental Determinants in Self-Directed Learning', Adult Education Quarterly, 35, 1-10

Spring, J. (1976). The Sorting Machine: National Educational Policy Since 1945, David McKay Company, New York

Stern, M. (1983). ' A Disorderly Market' in M. Stern (ed.), Power and Conflict in Continuing Professional Education, Wadsworth Publishing Company, Belmont, California

Stewart, C. (1922). Moonlight Schools, E.P. Dutton & Co., New York

Stewart, C. (1930). Mother's First Book. Johnson Publishing Co., Atlanta, Georgia

Stokes, K. (1970). 'Religious Institutions' in Smith, R., Aker, G. and Kidd, J. (eds) Handbook of Adult Education, Adult Education Association of the U.S.A. and the Macmillan Company, New York, 353-70

Stubblefield, H. (1983). 'Contemporary Adult Learning Theories: A Historical and Comparative Analysis', Lifelong Learning Research Conference Proceedings, Department of Agricultural and Extension Education, University of Maryland, College Park, Maryland, 145-49

Taub, H. A. (1984). 'Underlining of Prose Material for Elderly Adults', Educational Gerontology, 10, 401-05

Tennenbaum, S. (1951). William Heard Kilpatrick: Trail Blazer in Education, Harper and Brothers, New York

Thomas, A. (1964). 'The Concept of Program in Adult Education'in G. Jensen, A. Liveright and

Bibliography

W. Hallenbeck (eds.) <u>Adult Education: Outlines of an Emerging Field of University Study</u>, Adult Education Association of the U.S.A.,Washington, D.C.

Thomas, K. (1985). ' Video Rentals Transform Viewer Habits', <u>Atlanta Journal</u>, September 27, p.6B6B

Tinto, V. (1975). 'Dropout from Higher Education: A Theoretical Synthesis of Recent Research', <u>Review of Educational Research</u>, <u>45</u>, 89-124

Toffler, A.(1970). <u>Future Shock</u>, Random House, New York

Toffler, A. (1980). <u>The Third Wave</u>, William Morrow, New York

Toombs, W. (1984). Continuing Professional Education Development Project, Reflections in Mid-Stream, A report to the National Adv. Committee

Torrance, E.and Mourad, S.(1977).'Some Creativity and Styles of Learning and Thinking Correlates of Guglielmino's Self-Directed Learning Readiness Scale',<u>Psychological Reports</u>, <u>43</u>, 1167-71

Tough, A. (1965). <u>The Teaching Tasks Performed by Adult Self-Teachers</u>. Doctoral dissertation, University of Chicago, Chicago, Illinois

Tough, A. (1966). ' The Assistance Obtained by Adult Self- Teachers', <u>Adult Education</u>, <u>17</u>, 30-37

Tough, A.(1971). <u>The Adult's Learning Projects: A Fresh Approach to Theory and Practice in Adult Learning</u>, OISE, Toronto

Tough, A. (1978). ' Major Learning Efforts: Recent Research and Future Directions', <u>Adult Education</u>, <u>28</u>, 250-63

Tough, A. (1979). <u>The Adult's Learning Project</u> (2nd edn.), Learning Concepts, Austin, Texas

Tuckman, J. (1955). 'Educational Programming' in W. Donahue (ed.) <u>Education for Later Maturity</u>, Whiteside, Inc., and William Morrow and Company, Inc., New York, pp. 95-288.

Ulmer, C. (1968). Teaching the Disadvantaged Adult.
    The University of Georgia and the Georgia State
    Department of Education, Athens, Georgia

Ulmer, C. (1974). Teaching the Disadvantaged,
    NAPCEA, Washington, D. C.

Ulmer, C. and Dorland, J. (1981). ' Modern Adult
    Basic Education: An Overview', in L. Mercier
    (ed) Outlook for the 80's: Adult Literacy,
    Basic Skills Improvement Program, U.S.
    Department of Education, Washington, D. C.

United State Department of Education (1983). The
    Condition of Education 1983 Edition, U. S.
    Government Printing Office, Washington, D. C.

United States Dept.of Education (1985). The
    Condition of Education:1985 Edition, U. S.
    Government Printing Office, Washington, D. C.

United States Office of Education (1978). The Adult
    Education Act, U. S. Government Printing
    Office, Washington, D. C.

United States Senate Special Committee on Aging
    (1984), Developments in Aging: 1983, (volume
    I),' A Report of the Special Committee on
    Aging', U. S. Government Printing Office,
    Washington, D. C.

United States Senate Special Committee on Aging
    (1983).Aging America: Funds and Projections,
    U.S. Government Printing Office, Washington,

U.S. News and World Report, (1982a) May 17, p.53

U.S. News and World Report, (1982b), Aug.16, p.69

Ventura, C. (1982). Education for Older Adults: A
    Catalogue of Program Profiles, The National
    Council on the Aging, Inc., Washington

Ventura, C. and Worthy, E. , Jr. (1982).
    Education for Older Adults: A Synthesis of
    Significant Data, The National Council on the
    Aging, Inc., Washington

Verner, C. (1978). ' Organizing Graduate
    Professional Education for Adult Education' in
    J. Kidd and G. Selman (eds.) Coming of Age:

Bibliography

Canadian Adult Education in the 1960s, Canadian
Adult Education Association, Toronto

Verner, C. (1964). ' Definition of Terms' in G.
Jensen, A. Liveright and W. Hallenbeck (eds.)
Adult Education: Outlines of an Emerging Field
of University Study, Adult Education
Association of the U.S.A., Washington, D.C.

Wasserman, F. M. (1976). ' The Educational
Interests of the Elderly: A Case Study',
Educational Gerontology, 1, 323-30

White, T. (1962). ' A Consumer's Perspective of
Research in Adult Education' in P.Dubois and
K.Wientage(eds.) Objectives and Methods of
Research in Adult Education. Dept. of Psy-
chology, Washington University, St.Louis, 28-35

Wilson, J. (1966). Thinking with Concepts,
Cambridge University Press, Cambridge

Wilson, R. (1985) .' States That Shy Away From
Adult Education Services are Urged to do More',
Chronicles of Higher Education, Nov. 27, 15

Yonge, G. (1985). ' Andragogy and Pedagogy: Two
Ways of Accompaniment', Adult Education
Quarterly , 35, 160-67

Young, J. (1984). 'Innovation and the Education
Process' T. H. E. Journal, March, pp. 72-74

Academy of Senior Pro-
fessionals 96
accountability 56, 57,
80
Adams, J. 28
Adler, M. 57
adult basic education 113
program 117; see also
adult literacy educa-
tion
Adult Basic Education
Act 108, 111-12
adult education 5, 14,
37, 57, 88, 121-22,
127, 130, 166
access 220; and eco-
nomic revitalization
220; agencies 1, 3-15;
characteristics 204;
concepts 1, 2, 204,
213; conceptualiza-
tions 1, 15, 18, 37-
47, 49; defined 177;
discipline 27; field
of practice 163, 166;
goals 41; golden age
208; graduate study
196-7; justification
58; literature 70, 74,
160-1; mission 28;
movement 38; partici-
pants 5, 6, 7, 10, 14;
participation 1; philo-
sophical issues 28;
philosophies 1, 14;
professors of 164,
167, see also Commis-

sion of Professors of
Adult Education; pro-
gramming 51; programs
51; providers 13,
219; purposes 1, 2,
15, 18, 30, 33, 48,
49; quality 220; re-
search 131, 165; the-
oretical base 197;
theory 200
Adult Education Associa-
tion of the U.S.A.
(AEA,USA) 158
Adult Education Research
Conference (AERC)
142, 147
adult educators 2, 26,
45, 137, 163, 167,
198
adult learners 59, 142,
207
adult learning theories
of 195-6
adult literacy education
124; see also adult
basic education
adult literacy programs
122; see also adult
basic education; see
also adult literacy
education
adults
study of 129
adult students 26
agencies 221
agency 204
development 194-5

aging 210
    psychology of 165
agricultural education 3
Agyekum, S. 143, 146-7,
    182
Aker, G. 14
American Association for
    Adult Education 40,
    41, 42
American College 219
Americanization 3, 34,
    36, 185
American Idea 28, 48, 59
American Lyceum 3
analytical philosophy 23
Anderson, R. 11, 89,
    154, 160, 167
Anderson, R.C. 25
Anderson, J. 100
andragogy 22, 136, 173,
    175-7, 199
    assumptions 173, 175,
    176; criticism 173,
    175-6; definition 173
Apps, J. 2, 19, 20, 21,
    22, 23, 27, 47, 48,
    152, 166, 199
Arnold, G. 177, 195
Ash, R. 39-41
Ashford, M. 182
Aslanian, C. 5, 67, 68,
    170
assessment 193, 216
autonomy 175
Bachus, G. 153
Baltes, P. 139
Barrow, R. 29
basic education 11
    see also adult basic
    education; see also
    adult literacy educa-
    tion
Baum, J. 91
Beard, C. 22
Beder, H. 177, 194
behaviorism 24; see also
    philosophies
behavioristic education
    23, 24; see also
        philosophies
Bergevin, P. 139, 175
Bergsten, U. 167, 169

Berry, D. 171
Birren, J. 136-7, 165
Bittner, W. 141
Blakely, R. 27
Blaubaugh, J. 25
Blunt, A. 160
Boshier, R. 155, 170-2
Botsman, P. 10, 14, 167
Boyd, R. 166, 199
Boyle, P. 186-7
Brady, H. 149
Brickell H. 5, 67-8, 170
Brockett, R. 181-2
Bruce, J. 218
Brunner, E. 141-2, 145
Bryson, L. 32-4, 37, 42,
    48, 192
Burgess, P. 169-70
business 65-6, 74, 76-7,
    79
    and industry 43, 64,
    67, 75, 207
    see also occupational
    education
Caffarella, R. 181-2
Carey, J. 194
Carlson, R. 136, 166
Carp, A. 5
Cartwright, M. 5
certificate 56, 77, 80-1
certification 29, 122,
    201, 204, 214-17
    of learning 214
Cervero, R. 189-90
Cetrone, M. 57
Chatuaqua 3, 205
Chin K. 104
Clark, B. 44-5
cognitive style 174
Coleman, G. 41
Collins, J. 170
Commission of Professors
    of Adult Education
    43, 133, 143;
    see also adult educa-
    tion, professors
Commission on Higher Ed-
    ucation and the Adult
    Learner 207
competence 57
conceptualizations 58;
    see also adult educa-

tion
continuing education 67,
68, 96, 209, 216;
see also adult educa-
tion
Continuing Education for
Women (CEW) 209-10
Continuing Education
Unit 189, 191, 204,
216 guidelines 216
Continuing Medical Edu-
cation 191
Continuing Professional
Education (CPE) 51,
190-1, 194
Cooperative Extension
Service 3
Cooptation 59, 75-77
Copeland, H. 188
Copperman, P. 57
corporate 29, 46, 49, 53,
59, 64, 69, 75, 78-9
approach 59
education 51, 76;
systems 54, 55-6;
training 218
corporation college 58,
76-7
corrections education
51, 57
Cotton, W. 2, 19, 26-8,
47-8
Council on the Continu-
ing Education Unit
189, 216
see also Continuing
Education Unit
Courtenay, B. 90-1, 100,
102
Covey, H. 89, 103
Criser, M. 63
Cross, K. 5, 154, 169,
202, 219, 221
Cunningham, W. 136-7, 165
Dannenmaier, W. 140-1
Darkenwald, G. 11, 89,
116, 149, 154, 160,
167, 169, 171-3, 177,
188
Davenport Joe, 176
Davenport, J. 176
Davison, F. 65-6

DeCrow, R. 143
demography theory 168
Deitch, K. 67
descriptive research
143-4, 146-7, 161
Dewey, J. 25
dialogic learning 183
Dickinson, G. 135, 140,
143, 146-7, 156, 160,
169
diffusion theory 167
District Council 37
Retirees Educational
Program 98
doctoral degrees 127
Donahue, W. 84, 94, 99
Dorland, J. 113, 122
dropout 171
Drotter, M. 87-8, 91
Dubin, S. 192
Duggar, R. 60
Easterlin, R. 168
Easting, G. 155
Economic Opportunity Act
108
education
authority 201, 205-6;
goals 37, 58, 217;
for adults 19, 34;
for application 34,
185; for elderly 83;
for enlightenment 34,
for literacy 34, 185,
see also adult basic
education, basic edu-
cation and literacy
education; for occu-
pational purposes 35-
6; for older adults
103; for personal
liberation 35, 185;
for social improve-
ment 34; for social
liberation 34, 36,
185; justification
61, 81, 211; of
adults 17, 29, 32,
43, 58, 163, 201-2,
205-6; see also
adult education;
philosophies 17, 19,
51,

see also philoso-
phies;
providers 77, 80
purposes 51, 54, 58;
responsibility 201,
205-6
educational institutions
72
educational opportuni-
ties 35, 103
Educational Review 203
Education Commission of
the States 57
educators
of adults 2, 59, 78,
204, 208-210;
see also adult educa-
tors
Elderhostel 96
elderly 84, 95-6, 102
elementary schools 56
Elias, J. 2, 19, 22,
26-8; 47-8, 136, 176
Eurich, N. 43, 76, 218-9
evaluation 188-9,
theory 188
expectancy - valence
model 171-2
experimental designs 143
Fano, F. 218
Farmer, J. 212-14
Faure Commission 118
Faure E. 120, 122
Feier, C. 91
Fisher, A. 143, 146, 147
Fisher, D. 27
Fishtein, O. 91
Flavell, J. 184
Flesch, R. 56
Flowers, W., Jr. 47
Fox, R. 182, 191
Friere, P. 26, 120, 121,
183
Fromm, E. 71
Functional literacy 111
See also adult basic
education, basic edu-
cation and literacy
education
Furlong, M. 90, 104
Galbraith, J. 72
General Motors Institute

218
gerontological education
51
gerontologists 84, 137
Gibson, Q. 171
Gibson, R. 66
Glynn, S. 100
Goodlad, J. 57
Goodrow, B. 91-2, 100
Gorham, J. 177
Gove, P. 29
Grabowski, S. 140, 143,
147
Graney, M. 91, 103
Graltan, C. 0
Green, J. 191
Griffith, W. 141, 194
grounded theory 147
group dynamics 132, 195
Guglielmino, L. 178-9,
181-2
Habermas, J. 182
Hall, V. 209
Hallenbeck, W. 141, 174
Harman, C. 116, 118,
120, 122
Hart, J. 26, 41
Hartree, A. 176, 199
Harris Poll 86, 88, 93
Harvard 205
Hassan, A. 182
Havighurst, R. 103
Hays, W. 91, 103
Hayslip, B. 99
Health Maintenance Orga-
nizations (HMOs) 221
Heisel, M. 89
Hiemstra, R. 101, 130,
141, 164, 177-8
higher education 62-8,
73, 76, 88;
see also postsecond-
ary education
Hirsch, H. 97
Hoghielm, R. 171-2
Holden, J. 5
Hooper, J. 91
Houle, C. 5, 43-4, 169-
70, 178, 180, 187
human potential 51
humanistic 30
see also philosophy

humanistic education
   see also philosophy
Hunter, C. 116, 118,
   120, 122
idealism 21; see also
   philosophies
illiteracy 107-8, 112-
   13, 116, 195
   problems of 114
   public policy 114,
   119 see also adult
   basic education,
   basic education and
   literacy education
illiterate adults 118,
   121
illiterates 109
   characteristics of 109
independent learning 29
individual differences
   137-8
industry 65, 67, 75
   see also business
Institute for Retired
   Professionals 97
instructional learning
   182
instrumentalism 29
   see also philosophies
instructional television
   218
Irish, G. 154, 172-3
James, W. 22, 29, 218
Jarvis, P. 176, 178
Jensen, G. 141, 164
Johns, W. 177-8
Johnson, A. 27, 45
Johnson, L. 61
Johnstone, J. 5, 167, 219
Judson, H. 198
Kallen, H. 2, 17, 19, 22,
   28-9, 42, 47-8, 59
Kasl, S. 167
Kasworm, C. 178
Katchadournan, H. 23
Kazemek, F. 102
Kearsley, G. 90, 104
Kennedy, J. 61
Kennelly, K. 99
Kepple, F. 41
Kidd, J. 14, 17, 26, 174
Kilpatrick, W. 22, 26,

   184
Kingston, A. 89, 91
Klinger, C. 149, 169
Knowles, M. 13, 22, 25,
   28, 39, 40-1, 69, 70
   73, 99-101, 131, 136,
   139, 152, 174, 194
Knox, A. 116, 141, 149,
   150, 156, 161, 178
Knudson, R. 136, 176
Kornhauser, A. 167
Kozol, J. 108, 113
Krech, D. 152
Kreitlow, B. 17, 25, 140
Langer, J. 23
Laski, H. 26
Lauback, F. 115
   Literacy Program 115
leadership pyramid 43
learners
   self-directed 177
learning
   ability 62, 63, 129;
   associated 185;
   aldendit 185; autono-
   mous 29, 177; free
   181; force 46;
   independent 177;
   intentional 178;
   of adults 164; see
   also adult education;
   outcomes 216; primary
   185; processes 164;
   self-directed 177-81;
   styles 130, 195;
   types of 180; unin-
   tentional 178
Learning Maintenance Or-
   ganizations (LMOs)
   221
LeBreton, P. 191
leisure education 51
Lester, N. 47
Lewin, K. 183
liberal arts 89
liberal education 23-4,
   33, 49, 51
Liebow, E. 108
Life Enrichment Center
   96
lifelong education 104,
   206, 213, 214; see

also lifelong learning; acceptance 212; national policy 212; goals 212
lifelong learning 56, 58, 71, 103-4, 129-30, 201, 204, 206 goals 212 philosophies of 72; see also lifelong education
Lifelong Learning Research Conference 142
literacy 14, 90, 102, 107-8, 110, 114, 125 education 3, 51, 115, 123; programs 117, 120 see also adult basic education, basic education and illiteracy
Lindeman, E. 17, 22, 26, 28, 41
Literacy Volunteers of America (LVA) 115, 116
Liveright, A. 75, 141, 174
Livingstone, R. 57
Loague, N. 143, 147
London, J. 135, 167, 169
Long, H. 5, 11, 19, 22, 25, 35, 42-3, 47, 71, 74-5, 88, 95, 114, 130-31, 135, 139, 140-3, 145-7, 149, 150, 152, 156, 160-61, 164, 168-71, 173, 179-82, 185-90, 192, 195, 198, 204, 210, 212, 216, 219, 222
Lord, C. 216
Lorge, I. 101
Lorimer, F. 41
Love, R. 4
Lumsden, D. 94
Lyle, B. 111
Lyon, L. 91, 94
McClosky, H. 90, 171
McConatha, D. 90-1
McDougald, D. 26
McKenzie, L. 136, 176
McNamara, R. 61
Mandatory Continuing Education (MCE) 189, 201, 205
March, G. 91
marginal 44-5
Marieneau, C. 149, 169
Maritain, J. 20
marketing 67, 94
Marston, R. 63
Maslow, A. 172
Matkin, G. 147, 161
Mazmanian, 191
Mearns, H. 218
measurement 57
Mechanics Institutes 3
Merriam, S. 2, 19, 23, 26, 27-8, 47-8, 169, 171
meta-research 144-5, 161
Mezirow, J. 29, 116, 149, 164, 170, 182-5, 195, 198, 217
microtheories 165, 169, 200
Miller, Harlan 29
Miller, Harry 27, 28, 171
Mills' Canons 139
MIT 218
Mocker, D. 178, 180
Monnette, M. 151
Moonlight School 114
Moore, A. 100
Morrill Act 118
Morris, W. 0
Moses, S. 44-6, 54
motivation 173 see also interests
Murgatroyd, S. 139
Murphy, E. 71
Muth, K. 100
Naisbitt, J. 118
NASA 61
National Center for Educational Statistics (NCES) 1, 5, 6, 11, 86-8, 160, 209
National Technological University 218
needs 70-1, 73, 151 assessment 192
New School for Social Research 41, 45, 97

Newtonian theory 198
noncredit 78
Nussbaum, L. 96
obsolesence 58
occupational education
    32, 49, 57, 62; see
    also business and in-
    dustry; see also edu-
    cation
O'Donnell, J. 181, 182
Oddis, L. 178, 180, 182
Older adults 83-6, 89-
    91, 94, 100, 104-5
    barriers to partici-
    pation 91-2; hetero-
    genity of, 95, 99-103;
    middleclass 88;
    participant 87; parti-
    cipation of 95; parti-
    cipation variables;
    preferred topics 90
    see also elderly
Opportunities Industrial-
    ization Center (OIC)
    116
Overstreet, H. 27
Parker, T. 29
participant
    definitions of 5, 6;
    see also adult educa-
    tion and participa-
    tion
participation 1, 3, 4,
    86-7, 168-70, 197
    and age 6, 11; and
    education 8, 11, 12,
    129; and income 9;
    and marital status 11,
    and race 6, 8, 11; and
    sex 6, 8, 11, 14;
    models 170; motives 4;
    of elderly 87, 89;
    occupational status 9,
    11, 167; rates 7, 10,
    14; socioeconomic
    variables 11; research
    134, 154, 170; studies
    of 5; theory 169;
    trends 12, 14; vari-
    ables 11, 169; working
    conditions 167
Participation Training

195-6
Patterson, R. 0, 175
Pennington, F. 191-2
Pennsylvania State Uni-
    versity 191
peripheral 45
perspective transforma-
    tion 170, 182-4, 195,
    198, 199
Peters, R. 0
Peterson, D. 83, 94, 99,
    101, 104
Peterson, R. 5, 13, 75-6
philosophies 47, 58
    eclectic 48; eclecti-
    cism 26, 27; essen-
    tialism 21-2; exist-
    entialism 21-2;
    humanism 24; idealism
    21;
    instrumentalism 29
    of adult education
    26; of education 24,
    30, 48; perennialism
    21-2; pragmaticism
    29; progressivism
    21-2; realism 21
philosophy 54
Piaget, J. 183
Pierce, C. 22; see also
    philosophies
political education 33
postsecondary education
    54-5, 57, 64, 74-5,
    78-81, 97; see also
    higher education
postsecondary institu-
    tions 221
PoHinger, P. 192
Practice Audit Model
    191-194; see also
    Continuing Profes-
    sional Education
pragmaticism 29; see
    also James and
    philosophies
predictions 202, 221
Presidential Commission
    on National Aid to
    Education (1914) 35;
    recommendations of 35
Price, W. 91, 94

professional 26, 43, 48,
49; see also adult
educators and educa-
tors of adults
program planning 185;
components of 187;
see also adult educa-
tion
progressive education
22-5; see also phi-
losophies
progressivism 21-2; see
also philosophies
providers 13-4
of education 83
psychological barrier 91
psychological studies
134-5
Public Access Cable Tele-
vision 97
qualitative research
139, 148-9
qualitative studies 149,
see also qualitative
research and research
Quality of American Life
Survey (1978) 160
quantum theory 198
Rauch, D. 17
radical education 23-5;
see also philosophies
realism 21; see also
philosophies
reconstructionism 21-2;
see also philosophies
reinforcement theory 173
relational education 33
relicensure 201, 205-6
remedial education 32
research 128; agendas
145; analogy 133;
approaches 130, 143,
161; atheoretical 128;
bibliographies 142;
characteristics 135-9;
concepts 151-2; con-
ceptualization 159;
criticism 145; design
132; focus 133; influ-
ence 139; interests
161; inventories 144;
methodology 159; needs

130, 149-50, 161;
problems 133; produc-
tive areas 134; pro-
grams 155; quality
159; reviews 145;
spiral 140; status of
130, 140, 161;
strengths 158; struc-
tures 127; topics
150; tradition 132;
weakness 158
retention 171, 173
Rigg, P. 102
Rivera, R. 5, 167, 219
Robenson, K. 134-5;
169, 1970-72
Rockhill, K. 170
Roelfs, A. 5
Romaniuk, J. 95
Rosenblum, S. 177
Ross, J. 179-80
Rossing, B. 95
Rusnell, D. 140, 143,
146, 148
Saindon, J. 160, 167-8,
171
Schaie, W. 139
Schlesinger, A. 40
Scholastic Achievement
Test (SAT) 56
Schroeder, W. 186
science 129
Self-directed learning
29, 101, 197
history 182; research
134, 181-2; see also
autonomy and learning
self-improvement 30, 31;
see also adult educa-
tion
self-reflective learning
183
senior citizens
education program 98;
see also elderly
Sheffield, S. 169
Sheppard, N. 90-1
Shils, E. 46
Siebert, N. 218
Silverman, D. 139
Skager, B., 178
Smith, F. 194

Smith, R. 14
Smutz, W. 192-3
Snullin, L. 218
social change 31-2; 49
social movement 39-42;
    see also adult educa-
    tion
social reform 26; see
    also adult education
    purposes and philos-
    ophies
social reformist 48;
    see also adult educa-
    tion and philosophies
Society for the Propaga-
    tion of the Gospel in
    Foreign Parts 205
sociological studies
    134-5
Soldo, B. 85
Sork, T. 144
Spear, G. 178, 180
Spring, J. 37, 73-4
Stanford University 218
Stern, M. 67, 74
Stevenson, R. 90-1, 102
Stewart, C. 114, 116
Stokes, K. 20
Stubblefield, H. 195-6,
    199
Suhart, M. 90-1, 102
Sullivan, L. 116
Taub, H. 100
technocrats 73
Tenenbaum, S. 184
theory 200
    status of 197
Thomas, A. 185
Thomism, 20; see also
    philosophies
Tinto, V. 171, 173
theory 127, 128
    adult education 200,
    status of 199, 206
Toffler, A. 72, 118
Toombs, W. 193
Tough, A. 177-8, 180-1,
    195, 197
Trachtenberg, S. 66
Tuckman, J. 94
tuition waivers 95
Ulmer, C. 109, 113,

119-22
University Extension 3
University of Florida 66
University of Georgia 65
University of Michigan
    160
unlearning 29
Urich, N. 77
U.S. Office of Education
    46
utilitarianism 29; see
    also philosophies
utopian 25
Valentine, T. 188
Ventura, C. 87-9, 91,
    93-4, 97-8
Verner, C. 135, 154-5,
    164, 169, 177
vocational education 90
voluntary 42
Wasserman, F. 91
Webb, J. 61
Weinberger, C. 60
Wessell, J. 209
West, R. 182
White, T. 136, 140-1
Williams, W. 29
Wilson, J. 23-4
W.K. Kellogg Founda-
    tion 191, 193
workplace 210
workplace education 204,
    211; see also adult
    education and occupa-
    tional education
Worthy, E., Jr. 87-9,
    91, 93
Yamamoto, K. 137
Yonge, G. 176
Young, J. 58